THE ROYALIST WAR EFFORT
1642–1646

D1078703

The Royalist war effort 1642–1646

Ronald Hutton

Longman
London and New York

Longman Group Limited
Longman House, Burnt Mill, Harlow
Essex CM20 2JE, England
Associated Companies throughout the world

Published in the United States of America
by Longman Inc., New York

© Ronald Hutton 1982

First published 1982
First paperback edition 1984

British Library Cataloguing in Publication Data

Hutton, Ronald
   The Royalist war effort 1642–1646.
   1.   Great Britain — History — Civil War, 1642–1649 —
Campaigns
   I.   Title
   942.06'2   DA415

ISBN 0–582–49411–7

Library of Congress Cataloging in Publication Data

Hutton, Ronald.
   The Royalist war effort, 1642–1646.

   Reprint. Originally published: 1982.
   Bibliography: p.
   Includes index.
   1. Great Britain — History — Civil War, 1642–1649.
   2. Royalists — Great Britain — History — 17th
century.
   I. Title.
   DA415. H88   1984   941.06'2   84–5709
   ISBN 0–582–49411–7 (pbk.)

Printed by MCD Pte. Ltd.

To my Mother, in memoriam

Contents

Contents

List of maps

Acknowledgements

This book began its life as an Oxford D.Phil. thesis commenced in the autumn of 1976. In the years since then several people have contributed considerably not merely to the progress of the research involved but to my pleasure in it. Most deserving of gratitude is Hugh Trevor-Roper, now Lord Dacre of Glanton, who supervised the work on the thesis and devoted so much of his permanently overstrained time to the heroic struggle to turn me into a scholar and a writer. An only slightly smaller debt is owed to Doctor John Morrill, who gave me his friendship, knowledge and advice at each stage of the research. Likewise Brigadier Peter Young supplied hospitality and information with a gusto beyond the call of duty. A different sort of gratitude is owed to the President and Fellows of St John's College and to the Department of Education and Science for affording me a home and a means of sustenance during my work on the thesis and to the President and Fellows of Magdalen College for allowing me the leisure to turn it into a book. Mr D.H. Pennington and Professor Austin Woolrych, who examined the thesis, made many valuable suggestions towards this process. I would also like to thank the Earl of Dartmouth for his permission to read his family papers, and the staff of the various libraries and record offices I have used, of whom those of Duke Humphrey's Library in the Bodleian complex are exemplars. Last, I must thank Irene Ray-Crosby for supplying the intangible quality of constant encouragement throughout this work. The Republic of Letters is a reality.

Abbreviations

Add.	Additional
Bod. L.	Bodleian Library
Brit. L.	British Library
CJ	Journals of the House of Commons
CL	Cathedral Library
CSPD	Calendar of State Papers Domestic
DNB	Dictionary of National Biography
DWB	Dictionary of Welsh Biography
E.	British Library Thomason Tracts
Harl.	Harleian
HMC	Historical Manuscripts Commission
LJ	Journals of the House of Lords
NLW	National Library of Wales
PRO	Public Record Office
RL	Reference Library
RO	Record Office
THSC	Transactions of the Honourable Society of Cymmrodorion
TRHS	Transactions of the Royal Historical Society
TSANHS	Transactions of the Shropshire Archaeological and Natural History Society
UCNW	University College of North Wales
VCH	Victoria County History
WSL	William Salt Library

Introduction: 'Wrong but Wromantic'?

No event in English history has inspired as much lasting acrimony as the Civil War. Other occurrences, such as the battles of Hastings or Trafalgar, or the signing of Magna Carta, live on as vividly in the national imagination, but have lacked the same capacity to inspire successive generations of historians with something approaching the pitch of emotion of the original combatants. Indeed, for nearly two hundred years the writing of histories of the Civil War consisted really of attempts to marshall evidence to prove the virtues of the principles for which Royalists or Parliamentarians claimed to have fought. Those principles had become the respective foundations of the rival Whig and Tory political philosophies of the late seventeenth and the eighteenth centuries, and the historiography of the Great Rebellion was an effective means of asserting or questioning the fundamental validity of either. At first this propaganda war was carried on by editing key documents, such as those in the rival collections of Rushworth and Nalson, then by publishing apologies and memoirs of leading participants, such as Ludlow and Clarendon, and finally by combining both forms of record into formal histories, such as those of Oldmixon and Hume. This process, as often noted, precluded the attainment of historical truth, but it also precluded any close consideration of the nature and methods of the rival parties, and of the warfare itself. The propaganda of the war period certainly invited such a study, the Royalists denouncing their opponents' supporters as religious schismatics, proletarians or parvenus, the Parliamentarians labelling the Royalist soldiers Catholics, foreigners or debauchees. Each side accused the other of exacting military supplies by force, and claimed the willing compliance of the populace to its own demands. Yet the preoccupation of the following generations with the validity of the ideas fought for distracted attention from the men who fought.

As the eighteenth century gave way to the nineteenth the great changes occurring in English political, social and economic life made the Civil War period seem less immediate, if no less relevant, to historians. Men began to identify with Royalists and Parliamentarians as heroic spiritual ancestors rather than colleagues in a struggle to some degree still continuing. The Parliamentarian cause found a champion of this new variety in 1845, when Thomas Carlyle's edition of Cromwell's letters and speeches was published, erecting Cromwell into the ideal of the sober, patriotic, pious, hard-fighting Englishman. A Royalist reply was needed, and provided. The greatest surviving collection of unpublished Royalist source material at that stage was the correspondence of Prince Rupert, preserved by the Benett family in Wiltshire. In the late 1840s the family sold most of this collection to a publisher, Richard Bentley, who set about preparing a selection for print. He hired as editor a man distinguished not for Civil War studies but for a popular book on the Crusades, Eliot Warburton. Warburton set to work with gusto, and the result was published as *Memoirs Of Prince Rupert And The Cavaliers* in 1849. It proved a best-seller, excellent publicity for Bentley's subsequent auction of the Rupert papers, and the foundation of the modern Cavalier cult. Warburton's purple prose portrayed the Royalists as physically glamorous, personally heroic and impeccably loyal to King and Country. Against the figure of Cromwell he set up Prince Rupert, younger, more flamboyant and better-looking, foiled only in his efforts to bring victory to the King by the slow wits of the Royalist peers and the dastardly intrigues of the Borgia-like Lord Digby. The dashing and doomed Cavaliers of Victorian painters and Captain Marryat novels had arrived.

Warburton's view of the Civil War, and his literary style, received a massive implied rebuke when Samuel Rawson Gardiner published his series of weighty volumes upon the early Stuarts, beginning in 1863. Gardiner rejoiced in the political, personal and religious freedom which he felt to be the finest achievement of English civilisation, and believed that the critical stage of that achievement lay in the early seventeenth century. His books were dedicated to charting its progress in the work of the parliamentary opposition to the early Stuarts, culminating in the victory of the Parliamentarian cause in the Civil War. To these books Gardiner brought not only a high purpose and serious tone, but a new standard of meticulous scholarship, upon which his great reputation became based. It was, none the less, pressed into the service of his ulterior purpose, and despite the complexity and sophistication of his narrative the Royalists inevitably emerge from it as at best misguided, being opponents of the process which the author was attempting to portray. Furthermore, they barely emerge from it at all: as compared with the care with which Gardiner analyses the development of the wartime Parliamentarian party he shows only a glancing interest in their opponents.

The public interest in the Civil War generated by Carlyle, Warburton and Gardiner coincided with a new enthusiasm for local history and archaeology, a mixture of scientific curiosity and sentimental interest in a vanishing world. The two fused in the series of books upon the Civil War in individual counties which appeared from the 1860s. All were the work of local amateurs, often clergymen, but they retain a value that greater works have lost, partly for the charm of their style and partly for their use of sources now vanished. The work of the Rev. John and the Rev. T.W. Webb, on Herefordshire, published in 1879, remains an exemplar of both these qualities. However, although such studies contributed details to the general picture of Royalist activity, they did little to explain the activity itself. Their view of the war was narrowly military, and set firmly in the accepted framework laid down by historians of the national events. The only local study to consider an area larger than a county, J.R. Phillips's book on Wales and the Marches, now seems the least satisfying, lacking both the local colour and lost documents of the county studies and the grand perspective of Gardiner.

Thus the Royalists emerged into the present century as a compound of Warburton's and Gardiner's views, glamorous in their persons but suspect in their cause, and apart from the omnipresent Rupert, generally rather shadowy and stylised figures. In the succeeding eighty years, much has been done to build directly upon the foundations of the Victorians' achievements, and re-evaluate their conclusions. The succession of old-style county histories was continued down to A.L. Leach's study of Pembrokeshire in 1937. In the 1950s Dame Veronica Wedgwood published a narrative history of the Civil War which equalled Gardiner in its use of source material and surpassed him in the verve of the writing and the intuitive sympathy accorded to both sides. Its interests, however, remained those of Gardiner, concentrating upon the main military events and the central politics of both parties, and paying little attention to the machinery or methods of war or its impact upon the provinces. Gardiner's analysis of the Parliamentarian party was decisively challenged in 1941 by J.H. Hexter, since when Valerie Pearl, David

Underdown, George Yule, Lotte Glow, A.B. Worden and Mark Kishlansky have continued the re-evaluation of Parliamentarian politics to the present day. No such work, however, has been attempted for the Royalists.

The major recent developments in the study of the Civil War itself have come about, indeed, not as a result of building upon the nineteenth-century histories, but of questioning their perspective completely. This work took the form of the celebrated 'Gentry Controversy', commencing with two articles by R.H. Tawney in 1941 and turned into a full-scale debate by H.R. Trevor-Roper ten years later. However deeply the historians concerned disagreed with each other, they were united in agreement that the Civil War was the product of basic changes in the structure and behaviour of the English gentry, of which the political issues were only a reflection. Although on examination none of the theories provided proved sound, the whole debate had the salutary effect of redirecting attention, for the first time since the actual war, from the political leaders to their followers and from the centre to the provinces.

Two important and very different tendencies in works upon the war arose as a result of this redirection. The first consisted of the belief that the natural sympathies of the common people lay with Parliament, as the Royalists represented political tyranny and a paternalist, aristocratic form of society, both of which the Parliamentarians contested. This theme was first stressed by Christopher Hill, in a series of books and articles from the 1950s onward, and in the 1970s became the major preoccupation of the work of Brian Manning, and, with more subtlety, of Joyce Malcolm. All these writers, not surprisingly, depended heavily for their case upon the Parliamentarian propaganda against their opponents, of which their works were virtually a restatement. Despite this obvious weakness, and the fact that the majority of historians held aloof from the theory, it has never suffered a direct attack, and thereby with time acquired a spurious respectability. Its popularity among students was assured by the great radicalisation of educated youth in the years 1965–75, which made Levellers, Diggers and the New Model Army represent the same heroic forebears to young intellectuals that Cromwell had been for Carlyle. Its reception by the general public was assured when it infected the film industry, becoming a message of such different productions as *Cromwell* (1970) and *Winstanley* (1976).

Unfortunately, the counter-swing of sympathy for Royalism in recent years has taken a form unacceptable to intellectual circles. The same period which witnessed the radicalisation of youth also produced a desire to escape the mental constraints of modern industrial civilisation. This manifested itself in the formation of societies dedicated to the re-enactment of Civil War engagements in full costume, providing the mixed pleasures of a carnival and a rugby match. The Royalists, traditionally the more colourful and exciting party, have generally been more heavily represented on these occasions. The literary avatar of the movement is Brigadier Peter Young, whose meticulously-researched and much underrated monographs upon the major battles, commencing with Edgehill in 1967, have done much to improve knowledge of the equipment, organisation and tactics of the armies involved in each action. A general counterpart to this work, consisting of a full examination of the royal field army throughout the whole war, should soon be provided by Ian Roy, who has been working upon it since 1960. No substantial work of his, however, has yet been published.

The second great tendency in historical writing arising after the 'Gentry Controversy' was the appearance of county studies of a new sort. These were dedicated to using every surviving record, including many hitherto disregarded manuscripts, to analyse the impact of the Civil War upon individual county communities and the manner in which those communities came to divide and to remain divided. Such an interest had been presaged a generation before, with Mary Coate's study of Cornwall, published in 1933, and A.C. Wood's work on Nottinghamshire, in 1937, which represent a transition stage between the old and the new county studies. The full impact of the new, however, came only in 1966, with the simultaneous publication of Alan Everitt's *The Community Of Kent And The Great Rebellion* and an article by D.H. Pennington in the *North Staffordshire Journal Of Field Studies*. These works were swiftly followed by others by both authors, and by David Underdown, Eugene Andriette, J.S. Morrill and Anthony Fletcher. The greatest discovery of all these studies was the smallness of the numbers of committed partisans in each shire and the considerable reluctance of the community as a whole to engage in the conflict. They also built up a good picture of how the Parliamentarian war effort was carried on at a local level. Unfortunately, they were far less informative upon the Royalists. The most sophisticated of these works, or those most concerned with the nature of the war effort, were of counties where the Royalists either possessed no hold or very little. Furthermore, the very nature of the genre precluded the consideration of large-scale strategic and administrative perspectives needed to understand the relations between centre and localities upon which a war effort depends.

Introduction: 'Wrong but Wromantic'?

In the mid 1970s two books which did take such a wider perspective highlighted dramatically the continuing lack of information upon Royalism. The first was Clive Holmes's *The Eastern Association In The English Civil War*, published in 1975. This was the first careful study of a whole region, and portrayed how much difficulty the Parliamentarians had in obtaining men, money and supplies from this, supposedly their best-protected and most loyal area. It also explained how they came to overcome these difficulties, begging the question of whether the Royalists lost the war because they had somehow failed to do so. The second work, in 1976, was John Morrill's *The Revolt Of The Provinces*, which neatly synthesised all the local studies of the previous ten years. This explicitly suggested that the Royalists' failure lay in their relations with the local communities within their territory. At the same time the slenderness of the treatment of Royalism in the book, compared with the now considerable information upon Parliamentarian administration, indicated that the major research upon it was yet to be undertaken.

The present work is intended to provide the first step in this further research. It considers the Royalist war effort as a whole, and makes comparisons between the different Royalist regions. For detailed case-studies, it draws upon Wales, the Marches and the West Midlands, the twenty counties west of, and including, Staffordshire, Warwickshire and Gloucestershire. It was in this area that the King first gathered an army; on it he depended for men and materials for that army throughout the war, and in it his supporters staged their last stand. If the Royalist cause failed because its relations with the local community broke down, then the failure must lie there. So must also the story of how the King came to find supporters in the first place, and to maintain troops in the field for so long. That story is the matter of this book.

PART ONE

The achievement of civil war

As stated above, it has been the custom in recent studies of the English Civil War to stress the presence, in each locality, of a majority of neutral or vacillating men standing between the rival partisans and acting as a limiting factor upon the virulence of the war at a local level. The object of this first section is to turn this picture inside out and enquire how, amid such a general atmosphere of moderation and hostility to the war, rival partisans came to be formed at all, and how they dragged their local communities into a conflict which the majority in those communities did not desire.

CHAPTER ONE

The emergence of the Cavaliers

However far back into history one may postulate the origins of the English Civil War, the actual development of hostilities was extremely rapid. A civil war became physically possible only in March 1642, when Charles the First left a London dominated by his opponents to set up headquarters at York and attract supporters. In June he felt ready to call the country to arms and by August two rival armies were actually gathering and marching. The most serious of all divisions of the English people had occurred in a mere five months.

This picture becomes infinitely more striking when it is appreciated that, whatever was happening at York and London, in the future Royalist areas of England there is almost no sign of impending civil war for three of those five months, March to June. In particular, with one exception, there is no trace of an emerging Royalist party. No loyal petitions were sent to the King, though petititons from Lancashire,[1]* Cornwall,[2] Staffordshire[3] and Herefordshire[4] were sent to Parliament affirming support for it. Addresses sent to Charles from Cheshire[5] and Lancashire[6] in May merely urged him to make peace with Parliament. Nor, again with one exception, has any trace survived of the growth of local groups of men hostile to Parliament and favourable to the King. This is not the result of a paucity of records. In most of the future Royalist counties some family collections exist for the period, and they show a real awareness of national events. Even in western Caernarvonshire gentry had the latest news forwarded to them by post.[7] Men foresaw conflict between King and Parliament, but even those who were to become ardent Royalists

* Notes for this chapter are on p. 206.

showed no disposition to involve themselves. They waited upon events, with foreboding.

The exception noted above was Herefordshire, where the address sent to Parliament aroused a great deal of hostility among a set of gentry led by Sir William Croft of Croft Castle, who proceeded to sever ties with old friends who had promoted it. By June the common people were strongly partisan, shooting images 'in derision of Roundheads' at Croft and silencing a 'Roundhead sermon' in Hereford Cathedral. The gentry had despatched a letter to the King assuring him of support.[8]

This is not to give the impression that outside Herefordshire England was at peace; on the contrary, it was in a ferment of anxiety. From November 1641 onwards great cities like Gloucester,[9] large towns like Shrewsbury,[10] and small settlements like Stratford-upon-Avon[11] were alike repairing their defences, doubling the watch and buying weapons. This activity was not generated entirely by fear of the growing division between King and Parliament, for in these months Englishmen were at least as worried by the prospect of a Roman Catholic uprising as by the possibility of civil war. In October the Catholic natives of Ireland actually had risen in bloody rebellion, and it was feared that their co-religionists in England might make common cause with them. The Cheshire petition to Charles was specifically inspired by this anxiety. Throughout the future Royalist areas men talked of Catholic plots and in Lancashire,[12] Staffordshire,[13] Pembrokeshire[14] and Anglesey[15] believed that they had uncovered them. This situation does not seem an obvious prelude to civil war. Local communities do not appear to have been dividing. On the contrary they were closing ranks, against a traditional enemy.

As local Royalism does not seem to have existed before the actual declaration of war except in Herefordshire, which will be analysed below, the source of its generation must lie somewhere in the maelstrom at York. There, in these months, the King and his most ardent supporters were preparing the blueprints for war and the arguments which might persuade men to fight it. This process is almost entirely mysterious, no records having survived, if any were made, to indicate the men who attended the King at particular policy decisions at this time or to indicate how those decisions were reached. Only the resulting documents still exist, in considerable numbers, to testify to their industry.

The King's first task was to establish a case against Parliament which would either win it over or win him supporters against it.

From March till June he published a series of pamphlets[16] addressed to Parliament and justifying his complaints against it in great detail. A group of declarations in July and August[17] rounded out the Royalist case and thereafter it was repeated in simplified form in several subsequent speeches and in the preambles to most commissions and official letters signed by the King till the end of the war. The whole case had in fact the merit of simplicity. Charles's opponents stood for a reform of the Church and a limitation his constitutional powers. His riposte was to declare himself the defender of the accustomed laws, privileges and Church, defined as those of the revered Elizabeth the First, against a clique of incendiaries. It was a position calculated to appeal to the most powerful political instinct of the average Englishman of the day, entrenched conservatism. For years his opponents had enjoyed this position, claiming, with some justice, that Charles had attempted to subvert laws, privileges and Church himself. Ultimately their distrust of him had forced them into the role of reformers, to limit his powers in both Church and state, whereupon Charles had turned the tables on them. It remained to be seen whether men would be convinced by him, and would consider the issue worth fighting for.

At any rate, by June it had at least become obvious that his arguments had failed to impress the leaders of Parliament, who would neither retract their demands nor compromise. Hence Charles's task now was to raise the provinces on his behalf, to locate men in each county of sufficient standing to accomplish the task and with the will to do so. The chosen instrument to effect this work was the Commission of Array. This was an impressive-looking document written in Latin and in antique script upon a roll of parchment, signed by the King and impressed with the Great Seal. One was issued for each county and major city, and each contained the names of the leading men in that county or city whom the King believed might be expected to arm for him, and empowered them to take charge of it. Most of Charles's Commissions of Array have survived, in the original or in transcript.[18] The longest, for Glamorganshire, names thirty individuals; the shortest, for Radnorshire, names thirteen. How they were chosen is not known. Presumably in most cases one or two of the men from each county had actually made the pilgrimage to York to offer their services, and advised the King upon potential allies. Certainly the Warwickshire Commission was drawn up in the presence of the two men at the head of the list.[19] The names in some at least were public knowledge before they left York.[20] The men were on the whole accurately chosen. Up to a third of the gentry listed in each proved hostile or indifferent in the event, but the remainder always included the men who became the Royalist leaders of their counties. The English Commissions were apparently all issued in June, the earliest, for Warwickshire, dated the 6th, but the Welsh were drawn up in August. Each was reissued at least once in the following months, when the commissioners had gone into action, to replace those who had proved unresponsive with men who had volunteered their support.

In legal terms, the Commission of Array was a royal instrument resting upon an unrepealed statute of Henry the Fourth, obsolete since 1557 and revived by Charles's circle to provide some means of calling the country to arms without Parliament. Historians since Clarendon have criticised it as a dubious and antiquated legal trick unlikely to appeal to the English populace, but in fact, given the bizarre nature of the whole situation, with the two traditional halves of government attempting to fight each other, it seems unlikely that any device would have fared better. Certainly in the region studied it succeeded in producing Royalist activists, while none of those who abstained gave the Commission itself as their reason for so doing. The fact that it was written in Latin made no difference to the gentry, who clearly understood it, while for the common people, who did not, the King apparently enclosed with the Commission some specific message in English to their county, making clear his needs, to be proclaimed with it.[21]

The Commission was in fact only one of a set of papers with which the High Command equipped the men named in it. The activists who set off from York to raise Worcestershire carried at least three. Firstly they had the Commission itself.[22] Then they carried a set of detailed instructions to all commissioners, as to the manner of procedure.[23] Like the manifestos, they were calculated to appeal to public prejudice, in this case that for legalism. Those active for Parliament were to be imprisoned, but only by the JPs in the Commission. Money and armed men were to be received if offered voluntarily, only the county militia, which had a traditional duty to defend the locality, being called up. Similar instructions, with similar sentiments, seem to have been sent to most counties. Thus those to Cheshire warned commissioners to proceed tactfully with the disaffected,[24] those to Warwickshire warned them not to enlist Catholics.[25] The third document in the Worcestershire batch was a specific order to call up the militia, already signed and valid but with blank spaces left to write in the exact time and place of muster.[26] This took care not to offend the sentiment of localism, directing that any disaffected captains should be replaced only with local gentry. Possibly the Worcestershire packet contained some straightforward pro-•paganda tracts as well. At any rate one Staffordshire commissioner received a bundle through the post from the court, with instructions for dispersal.[27]

The task of the Commissioners of Array was twofold. Firstly they had to 'secure' their county, which effectively meant summoning the local militia and persuading it to declare for the King. Secondly, they had to collect local contributions of armed men and money and despatch them to the King to swell the army he was beginning to raise. It remains to be seen how each set of activities fared in each locality.

In Cheshire the King succeeded in winning the support of one of the two great factions dominating county politics, that led by Earl Rivers, Lords Kilmurrey, Cholmondeley and Brereton, Sir Thomas Aston and Sir Edward Fitton.[28] Of these the most obviously committed was Aston, who had been for a year an opponent of Parliament's ecclesiastical policy,[29] who was present at York in June[30] and whom Charles obviously regarded as his prime supporter in the county.[31] It seems safe to assume that he achieved the 'conversion', if any were necessary, of his faction. Against them the Parliamentarians could range only a few gentry around Sir William Brereton MP, a man isolated locally and suspect for his radical religious views. By the end of the summer these had given up the task of opposition and left the shire. From June to September the Royalist commissioners roved across it protected by bodies of horse, holding local musters and, despite the advice of the High Command, arbitrarily arresting ministers who refused to read Royalist propaganda in their churches and constables who failed to publicise Royalist musters.[32]

All this activity failed in its object, to secure Cheshire for the King. It was thwarted not by rival partisans but by a very different force, that of militant neutralism. It predated Royalist activity itself in the shire, for on 6th June, before the signing of the Commission of Array, a Cheshire petition was printed declaring obedience to both King and Parliament.[33] By 30th June the neutralists were in arms at Knutsford, to maintain that dual obedience.[34] On 11th August, when Brereton and the Royalists almost clashed at Nantwich, the local gentry produced a scheme for the demilitarisation of Nantwich hundred[35] and on the 25th a manifesto was produced proposing the same for the whole county.[36] A petition declaring neutrality was raised in the county in the same month and its signatures[37] have been analysed[38] to prove that the neutralist movement in

Map 1 Wales and the West Midlands

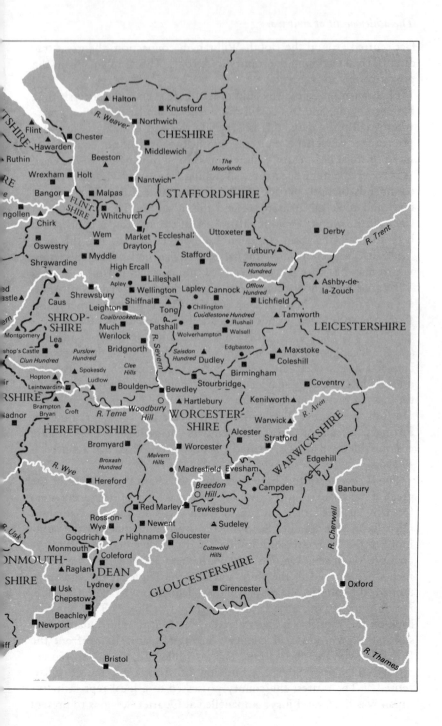

fact centred around the Booth-Wilbraham connection, the great traditional rival faction in the county to Aston's. This amply explains the
power of this movement.

Neutralism in Cheshire could indeed bear even more analysis than
has been made, and this is still more true of similar movements elsewhere. Unfortunately, this is precisely the sort of analysis that this
present study, which is concerned with Royalism, is not equipped to
make. It must be stressed that neutralism and moderation in the Civil
War covered a huge spectrum, stretching from men who obeyed the
commands of both parties to those who refused the commands of
both and took up arms to defend this position. To avoid at least
some of the worst semantic difficulties of the subject, it is proposed
here to omit the term 'moderate' altogether and to use the term
'neutralist' to denote only the latter, activist, end of the spectrum,
which may be more precisely termed 'militant neutralism'.

By mid September there were at least three such centres of militant neutralism in Cheshire. One was Knutsford, where another manifesto was subscribed, condemning the behaviour of the Royalists.[39]
Another was Nantwich, where the citizens had fortified themselves
and the local gentry taken an oath of neutrality.[40] The third was the
city of Chester itself. In July its citizens, summoned to a Royalist
muster, had declared against the war[41] and when Brereton entered
the city to recruit in August they ejected him as a troublemaker.[42]
On 6th September the corporation decreed[43] a programme of
fortification against 'imminent dangers' in general. The Cheshire
commissioners had not 'secured' their county. They had reduced it
to chaos.

For Worcestershire Charles was able to obtain the services of the
greatest magnate, Lord Coventry. He was one of ten peers who
formally declared their Royalism from York in June.[44] With him
must have been Samuel Sandys MP, who countersigned the summons to the Worcestershire militia[45] and was given command of the
county volunteers. On 7th July Parliament learned that the documents had arrived in the shire and that the High Sheriff had summoned the militia. It despatched a deputation to counter these
moves, armed with a declaration of their illegality.[46] This reported
back on the 13th that it had arrived at the Midsummer Quarter Sessions, the great seasonal county meeting, in time to confront the
Royalists with the declaration. The assembled gentry had thereupon
refused to support the Commission of Array and the Royalists
retired.[47] The nearest the county possessed to a local representative
organ was the Grand Jury, empanelled at Quarter Sessions to present

matters of concern to the community. This was now utilised to declare against the Commission in the name of that community.[48] The Sheriff apologised to Parliament, pleading ignorance.[49]

Within weeks this situation was reversed. Parliament's deputation returned to London, and a strong Royalist group was privately, and mysteriously, organised. By 1st August it included notable local gentry such as Sir William Russell of Strensham and Sir Thomas Lyttleton of Frankley and had called out the militia anew.[50] By the 3rd it had impanelled a new Grand Jury, at a Special Sessions, which issued a condemnation of the declaration against the Commission, declaring that as long as the King abided by the laws it would defend him.[51] Twenty-seven gentry underwrote it. They included Coventry, Sandys and Russell, but most of the names do not feature again as those of activists. By the time the Commission was reissued on 5th September,[52] however, the block of local Royalists had obviously filled out, because the commissioners represent accurately the men who would run the local war effort for the next three years. Lyttleton was obviously to the fore, because the King gave him command of the militia and summoned him to court as an adviser.[53] The militia had itself been mustered on 12th August,[54] and provision made to train volunteer companies.[55]

The effort, however, was already losing momentum. The Royalists suffered a fatal lack of arms and ammunition[56] and of cavalry.[57] As early as 23rd August they were forced to admit to the King that they had failed to arouse the local community and needed outside help.[58] On 5th September, the date of the new Commission, they suffered their cruellest blow. Having applied to the corporation of Worcester itself for permission to recruit and billet troops in the city, they received a polite but absolute negative. The citizens had decided it to be the nature of troops to plunder and cause trouble. Reports from elsewhere had confirmed this belief, and they were further alarmed by the appearance of strange Royalists in the city like Lord Lovelace, fleeing from Oxford before a Parliamentarian advance. All Royalists were to leave Worcester immediately. And so they had to.[59] Lovelace surrendered to Parliament in despair.[60] There was apparently a Parliamentarian group in the city[61] but the whole tone of the reply was one of a determined neutralism. The Worcestershire commissioners were already defeated, not by Parliament but by the indifference of their own neighbours.

Events in Worcestershire had some bearing on those in Shropshire. The Commission of Array arrived there on 24th July, delivered to the sympathetic High Sheriff, John Weld of Willey, who

11

immediately called the men named in it together.[62] They summoned a muster of the militia at Shrewsbury on 2nd August. However, as at Worcester, a Parliamentarian deputation arrived in time to forestall them, by calling out the militia themselves the day before. The muster took place but was disturbed by the Mayor, who threatened to arrest the Parliamentarians as rioters, and the Royalists Sir Paul Harris and Francis Ottley of Pichford, who brought a mob to disrupt proceedings and almost produced a riot. There was more disorder the following day, when the Parliamentarians began to drill a band of townsmen while Royalist bands trained under Sir Vincent Corbet of Moreton Corbet and the Denbighshire squire Richard Lloyd, the King's Attorney for North Wales. On the 3rd both sets of activists set out to obtain a more definite result elsewhere in the county.[63] The Royalists were encouraged by the example of their fellows in Worcestershire, and on the 8th impanelled a Grand Jury to produce a declaration modelled on that of Worcestershire on the 3rd, to uphold the King while he upheld the law.[64] It was underwritten by most of the future local Royalist leaders, including Harris, Corbet, Lloyd and Ottley. Of these Ottley rapidly emerged as the most active. He had been a man of no prominence before the war, and nothing is known of the motivation behind his fervent Royalism at its outbreak save that his family were devotees of Charles's Anglican Church.[65] Yet this is amply testified to by the energy with which he set about co-ordinating activities throughout the county in August.[66]

Again, however, the efforts of both sets of partisans foundered in a sea of local indifference. The individual Royalist activists tried to prevail upon their own neighbours, and the only resulting reports were of reluctance and hostility.[67] Even the studiously moderate declaration of the 8th found little support. On the 16th the commissioners issued another declaration,[68] from Much Wenlock, deploring this situation and beseeching the other gentry to join them, if only to obtain local peace. A great barrier to action must have been that the principal local dignitary, Sir Richard Newport of High Ercall, favoured the role of a conciliator of the local partisan groups.[69] Any hopes of obtaining Shrewsbury received a blow at the end of August when the corporation outlawed all partisan insignia within the town.[70]

In Staffordshire at the same period the rival activists achieved even less; in fact they themselves barely emerged. The county seemed to contain good potential for a Royalist mobilisation, as the leading magnate, Lord Paget, had joined the King in May,[71] and also for conflict, as it had within the past year produced both a loyal address to Parliament[72] and a petition against Parliament's Church policy.[73] Yet neither occurred. Paget was present in the shire in August and reported as raising men and money[74] but no general mobilisation took place. When on 2nd September the Cheshire and Shropshire Royalists wrote to the men named in the Staffordshire Commission of Array requesting co-operation they received the stony answer that these men declined without 'greater motives of more demonstrable dangers' to raise their county.[75] Nor did Parliament find any support there.

The first unequivocal Royalist success was in Herefordshire. The early Royalist groundswell there developed fast, and by 8th July this had produced the first militantly Royalist local declaration and dispersed it as far as London.[76] Although anonymous and undated, this broadsheet[77] encapsulated Charles's own self-justifications and promises and resolved to defend him on those terms. On 15th July it was formally attested by a Grand Jury and the militia and a volunteer band paraded at Hereford before the commissioners amid great popular rejoicing. The local JPs and the militia were purged of Parliamentarians, and by August soldiers and money had actually been despatched to the King[78] which on receipt were boasted as a hundred horse and £3,000.[79] The lead in this work was taken by Croft, in partnership with his old enemy Fitzwilliam Coningsby of Hampton Court, as the county's chief notable, Viscount Scudamore, remained in London uncommitted to either party. Coningsby acted as the county emissary to court, and was rewarded with the appointment of High Sheriff.[80]

Much of this success was due to lack of opposition. The local Parliamentarian leaders, the Harleys, who might have raised a considerable faction, were occupied at London leaving their castle of Brampton Bryan fortified but isolated. One must still, however, account for the considerable popular fervour for Royalism, on which the Parliamentarians themselves remarked. The answer seems to lie in the Church, the most efficient mass-media system of the age. In Herefordshire Charles's Church had produced a set of formidable ministers, committed to the ideals of that Church. Drs Rogers, Mason and Sherburn raised the county for the King by fiery preaching exactly as their enemies the Puritan ministers raised the London mob for Parliament. 'I fear for my life, wrote one Parliamentarian of the Herefordshire clergy. 'These men have wrought such hatred in the hearts of the people against me.' By August anybody in Herefordshire who was either Parliamentarian or Puritan was liable to be mobbed. A crowd threatened one JP, who had refused to contribute money for the King, in his very courtroom. Mason was in fact named as the author of the Royalist declaration. He certainly carried it to court, and was retained there as chaplain.[81]

This conclusion directs attention to an aspect of Royalist propaganda hitherto undiscussed. Like the most effective propaganda it provided not only ideals but a bogey. Whereas Parliament branded the Royalist party, with its commitment to the evolving Anglican tradition, as Catholics, the King labelled Parliamentarians, with their commitment to further reformation, separatists and sectaries, enemies of the religious and social order. Not merely was some clause against sectaries a feature of most of Charles's declarations, but specific orders were despatched in the summer to bishops and Royalist judges to extirpate them.[82] In practice Puritans could easily be labelled sectaries and, as was no doubt hoped, the terms sectary, Puritan and Parliamentarian become interchangeable in the public mind.

This certainly happened in Herefordshire that summer, and also in Worcestershire, where the Puritan minister Richard Baxter was twice nearly lynched and commented 'If a stranger passed in many places that had short hair and a civil habit the rabble presently cried "Down With The Roundheads", and some they knocked down in the open streets'.[83] The new Bishop of Worcester, Dr Prideaux, was certainly actively Royalist[84] but here the evidence for correlation between clerical, gentry and popular Royalism is missing. Nothing comparable can be produced for other counties at this period, although Royalist clergy were certainly active in Shropshire in August.[85]

In Gloucestershire the Parliamentarians closed the summer with what might be termed a potential success. The county's leading man, Lord Chandos, joined the King, but Gloucester itself followed the lead of its own MPs in standing by Parliament, although when volunteers actually began drilling in the city they created alarm.[86] Thus when Chandos came to execute the Commission of Array on 15th August he chose to do so at Cirencester. Unhappily for him, the citizens of that town misunderstood the Commission to signify instant military rule. Perhaps they had been deliberately misinformed. When Chandos entered they barricaded their streets against horsemen and forced him to disclaim the Commission and declare instead for local peace.[87] After this experience he left the shire. The initiative lay with Parliament, but in fact at the end of August neither side had yet mustered the militia.

Parliament had special reason to be afraid of Monmouthshire, because in its centre towered Raglan Castle, seat of the Earl of Worcester and his heir Edward, Lord Herbert. Both were immediately suspect as Catholics and Lord Herbert had been a favourite and supporter of Charles. Thus upon the King's move to York Parliament set about trying to transfer the county magazine from Monmouth, which like so much of the shire the Earl directly owned, to Newport, property of the rival local magnate, the Parliamentarian Earl of Pembroke.[88] In the process it encountered stiff opposition from the people of Monmouth, to whom the arms represented security, although some gentry, perhaps from Pembroke's faction, supported the move.

Herbert himself, however, proved amazingly amenable. Instead of joining the King he came to London in the summer and agreed to transfer the magazine to his rival's town of Caerleon. He went to court twice, but under a pass from Parliament, and when he returned to Raglan after the second visit, in early September, he wrote to Parliament for a pass to proceed again to London.[89] In fact Herbert was playing a double game, presumably intent on assisting Charles without associating himself openly with a risky venture for which he and his co-religionists might be made scapegoats. In July he had posted Charles £5,000, which paid for the King's first horse regiment, under Sir John Byron. On his journeys to court he smuggled further sums in cash and bills, and he secretly hired veteran soldiers and despatched them to the King. But of this Parliament and the public as yet knew nothing.[90]

Events in Wales in these months display a considerable contrast to those in the English counties studied. The divisive pattern of Royalist, Parliamentarian and neutralism or indifference does not appear; instead in most counties the entire community responded, howbeit sluggishly, to the appeals of the King and ignored those of Parliament. Some of the sluggishness may, ironically, have been the fault of Charles who does not seem to have realised the potential of Wales, for the first Welsh Commission of Array was only signed on 28th July, and the rest followed in August.[91] Significantly, most were signed following the arrival at York of a Royalist declaration in the name of all Wales on 1st August[92] and of individual county resolutions in the next few days.[93] Charles's slackness is the more surprising in view of the fact that individual Welshmen like Sir Thomas Salusbury MP, from Denbighshire, or Sir Edward Stradling, from Glamorganshire,[94] had been joining him in June and July. Perhaps they joined him later than the English activists, or perhaps he was deliberately attending to the more exposed and dubious counties first. Salusbury's decision to offer his services is noteworthy as it has

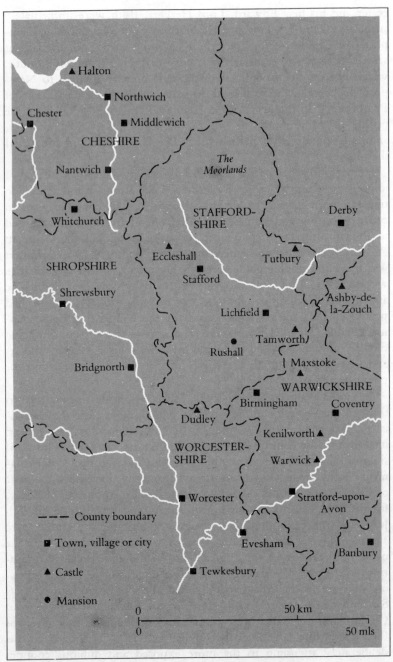

Map 2 *Military operations in the West Midlands in early 1643*

left one of the few portraits of a Royalist leader at the moment of his 'conversion'.[95] It literally was a conversion; he had read Charles's declarations, pondered the role of monarchy in the Bible and in modern history, and decided for the King. The county resolutions likewise cited the King's promises as the reason for their Royalism.

Not all Wales conformed to this pattern. The Sheriffs of Pembrokeshire, Carmarthenshire and Montgomeryshire maintained a civil correspondence with Parliament in August.[96] In Montgomeryshire Sir John Price MP withheld the county magazine from the Royalist leader, his fellow MP Richard Herbert, though as the Prices and Herberts were traditional enemies it is not clear whether he was acting consciously for Parliament.[97] But these were the most Anglicised parts of the Principality. In Caernarvonshire Thomas Glynne, John Bodwrda and William Lloyd, leaders of a county faction, were arrested in late summer as disaffected[98] and in Anglesey the dominant gentleman, Sir Thomas Cheadle, later received the same smear.[99] But smear it must have been, for Cheadle was actually the man who arrested the Caernarvonshire gentry while they, rapidly released, conformed throughout the war to the Royalism of their county. All appear to have been the victims of local enmities. Particularly impressive as an example of local Royalist solidarity is the case of the Caernarvonshire MP John Bodvel. He served at London from January till June 1642 as an active Parliamentarian[100] and went home in August to fortify his house.[101] Once home, however, he submerged into the community, only to reappear in time as an active Royalist.

The explanation given for Royalism in Herefordshire does not fit Wales. North Wales had petitioned against Parliament's Church policy in March[102] but there is no trace of intensive clerical activity there. The Welsh as a whole, like Salusbury, seem to have made an essentially political choice. Wales had certainly been shown particular favour by the Stuarts, who had been suspected of partiality to it. In addition they had inherited the reverence shown by the Welsh for their own Tudor dynasty.[103] This was however no blind loyalty as like the English they had reacted against the excesses of Charles's Personal Rule.[104] It has been suggested that the Welsh at this period were 'too firmly schooled in monarchial instincts ... not to rally round the Crown as soon as it seemed in danger of becoming the direct object to attack'.[105] This may be the key to the behaviour of Celtic Wales in 1642, but nothing positive can be advanced upon this question from the documents.

Events elsewhere in future Royalist areas bear out the pattern visible in those analysed in detail above. In Cumberland and Westmore-

land, an area as remote and poor as Celtic Wales, the situation mir-
rored that in the Celtic Welsh counties and the bulk of the gentry
declared their loyalty to the King. Having done so, however, they
did nothing to assist the wider war effort.[106] In Northumberland and
Durham the majority of the local leaders were equally loyal to the
King and equally inert. Here, however, Charles possessed a trump
card in the form of an exceptionally active, popular and powerful
magnate, the Earl of Newcastle, who persuaded some of the gentry
and urban oligarchs to secure the main strongpoints for the King.[107]
In Lancashire, another remote and backward county, the Earl of
Derby, another local notable of great power and prestige, performed
the same service. At Manchester, the most prosperous town in
the county and with the best communication with other regions,
he did, however, fail as dismally as Lord Coventry at Worcester.
The citizens showed no enthusiasm to declare for Parliament, but
refused to hand over their magazine to the Royalists or admit their
troops.[108]

In general, the more prosperous counties of England responded to
the appeals of King and Parliament in the same negative manner as
those of the Marches. The King had issued his Commissions of
Array from York, but as soon as he marched out of Yorkshire in
August to raise his standard at Nottingham his adherents in the
county began to negotiate a peace pact with the local Parliamentarians, and eventually signed one.[109] At Nottingham, as at Manchester, the townsmen refused to let the local Royalists take away
their magazine, only submitting when the King himself arrived.[110]
In Somerset a group of Royalists appeared in June and petitioned
Parliament to listen to the King's appeals.[111] When, however, they
raised troops in August and defeated a body of local Parliamentarians, a large section of the populace rose up, allied with the Parliamentarians and chased them out of the shire. The county community then declared, not for Parliament, but for neutrality.[112]
Likewise the citizens of Dorchester and Exeter were happy to use
Parliament's authority to fortify to protect themselves from the
armed Royalists fleeing Somerset, but not to do anything more
aggressive to assist Parliament.[113] In rural Devon the populace
ignored the appeals of the Royalist Earl of Bath, but their inertia
aroused the irritation of Parliamentarians.[114] At Marlborough in
Wiltshire, as at Manchester and Nottingham, the inhabitants refused
to let Royalists carry off the magazine which represented their protection in a time of insecurity.[115] The Cornish Commissioners of
Array became so demoralised by local indifference that they rapidly

signed a peace pact with the county Parliamentarians like that in Yorkshire.[116]

What had been achieved in all these counties by the end of the summer was not civil war. In most of them the King's appeals had won supporters, in some these dominated the county, but in each case where actual conflict seemed imminent between the rival partisans it had been stifled by a local community intent upon its own preservation. A new factor was needed to counter this force. In Warwickshire this factor came into play, and there was staged the dress rehearsal for the entire English Civil War.

The greatest magnate of the county was the Earl of Northampton, who had been one of the ten peers who had declared their Royalism in June.[117] He was also Recorder of Coventry, and on 25th June arrived in that city and asked support of its corporation for the King. The Mayor promised at least not to obey Parliament, and Northampton returned, satisfied, to court.[118] He was away for a month, on unknown business, and Parliament seized the initiative. Learning of the incident, it immediately ordered a deputation into the county to secure it.[119] At the head of this it placed Northampton's rival in the shire, Lord Brooke, a fervent Puritan and a person of national reputation.[120]

Accounts of the following events are bedevilled by partisan lies, but careful cross-comparison and the use of manuscripts can produce a coherent narrative. In early July Brooke successfully mustered the militia in each hundred, though none answered his warrants until he reissued them in the name of both King and Parliament.[121] At Coventry some aldermen had organised a Parliamentarian faction, though rival aldermen organised a Royalist group and the bulk of the city remained aloof from both. Brooke arrived to hearten his party and gradually built it up to considerable strength. In late July Northampton at last returned, and found his enemies now too strong in the city to dislodge, so he ordered his own adherents to secure the county magazine, kept at Coventry. Brooke forestalled them, seized the arms himself and transferred them to Warwick Castle, his home.[122] To safeguard them he rapidly recruited a strong private garrison by offering 4s. 8d. per week to each recruit.[123] Northampton proclaimed the Commission of Array at Coleshill and set about recruiting a private army to take the castle, which he swiftly raised from several Midland shires by offering 2s. per day.[124] In the process they brought about the appearance of a new animal upon the scene, the regular soldier, caring nothing for a local community in which he had no place, acting only at the will of his paymaster.

The county community as a whole held aloof from these proceedings[125] and both protagonists appealed for outside aid. Northampton failed to gain any from other local Royalists[126] but did receive a detachment from Charles's own embryo army under the experienced soldier Sir Nicholas Byron.[127] Brooke obtained some cannon for his castle from London,[128] but when he reached Banbury he found Northampton in his path. An agreement seems to have been made, in the name of local peace, to leave the cannon at Banbury. Local containment of the war appeared to have succeeded yet again. Northampton however waited until Brooke had departed, seized the guns and took them to bombard Warwick Castle.[129] In that instant he stepped over the line into civil war.

Ironically, the guns were too small to make much impact on the castle, and as its siege dragged on through August it became a *cause célèbre* for both parties. Parliament despatched to its relief part of its newly-raised field army, 3 000 foot and 400 horse.[130] Charles entered the county first, with most of his existing cavalry, 800, and 300 foot, and made straight for Coventry to secure the city.[131] Since July the Coventry Royalists had left to join Northampton,[132] and Parliamentarians had swarmed in from the county, mainly from Birmingham.[133] Yet when Charles appeared before it on 20th August, Coventry was still officially uncommitted to either party. The corporation had not yet declared for Parliament and had apologised to Northampton about the transfer of the magazine.[134] However, the King was informed that he would be admitted to the city, but not his army. Even to Parliament itself, the corporation insisted that it did not make this answer out of partisan loyalty, but out of fear of the plundering of the Royalist soldiers.[135] Indeed they might well have dealt roughly with a city filled with their enemies. Charles left his troops to besiege Coventry.

The case of Birmingham deserves further discussion. This small town is the exception to the rule developed in the previous pages, of urban indifference and hostility to the war. From the beginning to the end of hostilities it manifested a virulent and spontaneous Parliamentarianism.[136] It was a manufacturing centre, and its behaviour has provided a main prop of the theory equating artisans with Parliamentarians.[137] The main problem with this theory is that none of the other Black Country manufacturing towns manifested such an obvious political choice and some certainly at times helped the Royalists. The latter garrisoned Dudley Castle with the help of local 'colliers and nailers'.[138] Irregulars from Cannock and Walsall were to help them reduce Lichfield.[139] If it is argued in return that they may have done so under the influence of local notables, then one would like to know more about Birmingham figures such as the Mr Porter in whose blade-mill swords were made only for the Parliament, or the minister who preached against the Royalists.[140] There are no easy answers to this problem; it is one which only the most painstaking local research will solve.

To return to the events at Coventry, Charles's force had been attacking the city for three days when the Parliamentarian army arrived from London. The Royalist and Parliamentarian regular armies faced each other for the first time on Southam Heath and the Royalists, being outnumbered, retired and left the shire. Northampton's little army at Warwick, abandoned, raised the siege and followed them. Coventry, having committed itself against Charles, opened its gates to the Parliamentarians, part of whom settled there as its permanent garrison.[141]

Within a month, Warwickshire had become a county under military rule, its principal strongpoints occupied by regular soldiers responsive only to their partisan military leaders. The county community in general, for all its lack of co-operation, had been simply taken over. For the other counties in the region, the writing was upon the wall.

CHAPTER TWO
The King on the march

The instrument which created the Civil War was not, ultimately, the Commission of Array. It was a different sort of commission, issued to a single man to raise a number of regular soldiers for service under him in one of the partisan armies. Leading activists were commissioned as colonels, and then obtained commissions in turn for the senior officers of their regiments, who in turn commissioned their juniors, though it is by no means clear how much freedom each had in their choice. The normal paper strength of a foot regiment was 1 000 or 1 200 men, though rarely were units recruited to full strength.

The civilian Clarendon has left behind a persisting but misleading impression that the Royalist army was, like a feudal host, recruited from the tenants and dependents of Royalist magnates.[1*] It seems in fact to have been raised in a more 'modern' manner. A case-study may illustrate this point. In August 1642 Lord Paget was commissioned by Charles to raise a foot regiment. He put up the money for it and took a personal part in recruiting. His own lands lay in eastern Staffordshire, but he also went on a 'drive' in the south, where he seems to have had most success at Lichfield, whose powerful Dyott family co-operated with him.[2] He also wrote to gentry in the west of the shire asking for recruits.[3] The training and leadership of the regiment, however, were given to an experienced soldier,[4] Richard Bolle, who appointed another veteran from outside the county, D'Ewes, as his deputy. D'Ewes in turn commissioned lieutenants to beat drums in the villages and call for volunteers.[5] The captains were a mixture of younger sons of Staffordshire gentry[6] and of gentry of

* Notes for this chapter are on p. 209.

other counties.[7] Presumably they took a hand in raising their own companies. By this ramshackle process the regiment was completed within a month. It is not very different from the method by which men were recruited for the British army down to the last century. A later Lord Paget was to raise a regiment for the Napoleonic Wars by similar means.

Ten other Royalist activists were commissioned as colonels in Wales and the Marches in August and September. Their distribution bears no relationship at all to the success of the Commissioners of Array in the various counties. The only horse regiment was given to Aston, and mainly raised in his native Cheshire, though it included a Lancashire troop.[8] Aston's partners Earl Rivers and Fitton were both given foot regiments to raise, and both apparently raised them in Cheshire, their captains being local gentry with a leaven of 'foreign' veterans.[9] Salusbury was given another to raise in Flintshire and Denbighshire, and his captains were mostly local gentry, though one was an experienced outsider and the men came from as far as Anglesey.[10] In north-west Wales the veteran soldier John Owen of Clennenau was given a fourth,[11] and a fifth was granted to Richard Herbert in Montgomeryshire.[12] Herbert Price MP was given another in Breconshire, and in Glamorganshire Stradling raised a seventh, officered mainly by his relatives although one captain may have been from Carmarthenshire.[13] In south-west Wales the greatest dignitary, the Earl of Carbery, was commissioned for an eighth. Lastly, a single dragoon regiment was commissioned from Sir Thomas Hanmer, a Flintshire gentleman.[14] No Colonels seem to have been commissioned in Worcestershire, Shropshire and Herefordshire at this period, and the reasons for this are difficult to discover. It is possible that any record of the commissions there have failed to survive, but this is extremely unlikely as the records in these counties are better than elsewhere.

The execution of the Commissions of Array was essentially a public activity, demanding an official response from each county community. The execution of the colonels' commissions was by contrast virtually a private activity, working within the community but requiring no general response from it. Paget raised his regiment in a county which had officially disowned the war, while three were recruited in Cheshire where much of the county opposed the Royalist effort. Private money was being used to attract volunteers into the service of individuals. Yet this activity was to achieve what the Commissions of Array had failed to do, and draw most of the region into the war, by drawing the war itself into most of the region.

This process hinged upon the King himself. In mid September Charles was in danger of being out-manoeuvred. After two months' recruiting in Yorkshire and the East Midlands he had gathered round him at Nottingham five foot regiments and 500 horse.[15] These were greatly outnumbered by the Parliamentarian field army which had advanced to Northampton. Charles had however a potential greater strength if he could unite with the forces being raised for him to the west, the eleven regiments in Wales, Cheshire and Staffordshire, plus three in Lancashire and Sir John Byron's horse, which had been sent to occupy Oxford. He made the obvious move; on the 13th September he marched his little army westward, and on the 16th he entered Staffordshire.[16]

His mission there was twofold, to unite with Paget's regiment and to persuade the county community to enter the war. The first was accomplished,[17] and to achieve the second he had called the gentry to meet him at Uttoxeter.[18] The only record of that meeting is in a Parliamentarian newspaper,[19] which may be suspected of exaggeration. Its main import, however, is corroborated by subsequent events; the King failed to convince the gentry of the need to mobilise against Parliament. Staffordshire remained uncommitted and on 17th September the King continued to Stafford where he concerted plans for his entry into the Marches. His first concern was to send bodies of horse to extinguish by force the two centres of militant neutralism at opposite ends of the region, Nantwich and Worcester.[20] His second was to discover a base within it where he might settle to collect his forces. At the start of his march he seems to have considered Chester,[21] but by the time he had reached Stafford his hopes centred upon Shrewsbury, where Francis Ottley's long and careful work was at last achieving results.

A great strength of the Royalists in the northern Marches was their capacity for co-operation, which helped to compensate for their lack of numbers within each county. Brereton had commented sourly upon it in August[22] and by 2nd September the leading Royalists of Shropshire, Cheshire and Flintshire were meeting weekly at Whitchurch.[23] Soon they had united with Denbighshire in a formal Association.[24] Nobody benefited more from this process than the tireless Ottley, who built up personal links with fellow activists in neighbouring counties, especially Richard Herbert in Montgomeryshire and Richard Lloyd in Denbighshire, and also with the court, to which he went himself. His main contact there was Edward Hyde MP, the future historian Clarendon. From the King he obtained a commission to raise 200 men to secure Shrewsbury.[25] He was concerned however to achieve results by diplomacy, and extended his contacts in Shropshire society. A major victory must have been won on the day, its date lost, when he persuaded the respected Sir Richard Newport to appear before the Shrewsbury militia wearing Royalist emblems. He seems to have achieved this by using the fear of a Parliamentarian takeover.[26] He had used the same fear in August to secure good relations with the Mayor, and maintained these while Hyde, a man of notably mild political views and with his own Shrewsbury connections, worked upon the Mayor by letter.[27] It was presumably this pressure which secured the vital decision of the corporation on 15th September to admit the King to Shrewsbury if he came there.[28] Nine bundles of proclamations were prepared to convince the citizens.[29] It was a bloodless triumph, but in case it were reversed Ottley installed his soldiers in the town, together with 500 from Herbert.[30] If any Parliamentarians were still active in the shire, they fled now.

Coventry and Uttoxeter had taught Charles caution. From Stafford he sent Hyde to ascertain the situation in Shrewsbury.[31] Receiving Hyde's favourable report, he advanced to Wellington on 19th September. There he made a speech to his army laying down rules for its discipline and confirming his commitment to the traditional Church, laws and privileges. This he had published.[32] The next day Sheriff Weld formally escorted the King and his army to Shrewsbury, where a civic reception had been prepared.[33] It was the first unequivocal welcome Charles had received since leaving London. Weld and Ottley had earned the knighthoods they received.[34].

It would, however, be an empty success if Charles did not mobilise local resources swiftly. This task he undertook with determination. Upon arrival at Shrewsbury he ordered copies of his Wellington speech to be distributed to every parish in Shropshire,[35] to be read in church along with a summons to a meeting at Shrewsbury on the 28th.[36] On the 23rd he left his forces resting and hurried north to secure Chester. There were Royalists in the city and one of them, Orlando Bridgeman MP, the Bishop's son, had presented a Royalist declaration to the corporation in August.[37] However, Charles's haste in itself speaks for the likelihood that the city was still not officially committed to either party, and that when the King had written to the corporation from Stafford telling them to expect him[38] he had no idea of the reception he might encounter. As it happened, he met with an official welcome as warm as that at Shrewsbury.[39] It is possible that, as at Shrewsbury, the Royalists had taken over, but Charles's arrival, accompanied not by an army but only by an escort of local Royalist gentry, was not likely to provoke a city dominated by uncommitted men into excluding him. The King's behaviour was certainly tactful during his four-day stay. He thanked the corporation graciously and made another speech contrasting his own legalistic and moderate actions with Parliamentarian aggression.[40] He reviewed the local militia,[41] confirmed a Royalist, Thomas Leigh, as their commander,[42] knighted the High Sheriff[43] and left Chester garrisoned only by its own militiamen.[44]

Towards those who had actively opposed him, however, Charles was ruthless. He ordered the confiscation of the property of the absent local Parliamentarians, in both county and city.[45] The horse he had sent to Nantwich occupied the town and Charles fined the citizens £2,000 to be levied upon innocent and guilty alike.[46] The leaders of the Nantwich neutrality movement were carried off to Shrewsbury and their arms and money were seized.[47] With this example before it the other centre of militant neutralism at Knutsford seems to have submerged. Like Shropshire, Cheshire could now be said to have been 'secured' by the Royalists.

On his way back to Shrewsbury on the 27th, Charles stopped at Wrexham to dine with Richard Lloyd, review the local militia and address the assembled gentry of north-east Wales.[48] His speech dwelt in some detail upon the concept of himself as a refugee from rebels who threatened not only his legal rights but the whole traditional order. Such a personal appeal, made in circumstances of genuine flight and danger, must have had a powerful impact. Like all the King's previous speeches it was immediately published and dispersed.[49]

Even Charles's frantic energy was insufficient in the time available to make such a personal journey to countenance his supporters in south-east Wales. These were now fully active. On 13th September Parliament was reassured that Monmouthshire was perfectly quiet.[50] A few days later Lord Herbert seized the magazine at Caerleon and declared for the King.[51] A set of Protestant gentry, led by Sir William Morgan of Tredegar and his son-in-law Sir Trevor Williams, co-operated with him. Parliamentarians were disarmed and the county secured by local levies and 500 of Stradling's newly-raised foot from Glamorganshire.[52] In Radnorshire the High Sheriff, Hugh Lloyd, and Charles Price MP similarly became active for the King.[53] The King, unable to visit them, conceived the brilliant scheme of sending his heir, the twelve-year-old Prince of Wales, to Raglan to appeal to the Celtic nationalism of the south Welsh. The precocious boy played his part to perfection, addressing a meeting of gentry from the whole area with great charm and closing his speech with a toast to the 'ancient Britons'. His audience showered him with promises and donations.[54]

By the end of September, two weeks after the King had begun his march westward, the Royalist war effort had borne fruit in all the parts of the region where activists had appeared, save one. There, in Gloucestershire, Worcestershire and Herefordshire, disaster had occurred.

On 9th September the Gloucester MPs reported back to Parliament that they had arrived in the city, mustered the militia and raised volunteers.[55] In the county at large, however, they encountered the same reluctance to enter the war that had defeated Chandos.[56] When, some weeks later, two regiments of regular Parliamentarian soldiers arrived before Gloucester itself, the citizens took fright at the sight of them and slammed the gates in their faces as securely as the citizens of Coventry had on Charles. Some Parliamentarians let the troops in through a postern, and once inside they 'quashed the business'.[57] Gloucestershire became Parliamentarian territory, secured by a regular garrison at Gloucester.

The King did not truly 'lose' Gloucestershire, as he had not yet found supporters there, but in Worcestershire and Herefordshire were some of his most fervent devotees. Herefordshire being secure, he concentrated his attention upon Worcester. The horse he had ordered there from Stafford consisted of the best of his existing cavalry, under his Commander of Horse, his nephew Rupert. On about the 20th September this linked up in Worcestershire with Sir John Byron's regiment, which had evacuated Oxford, and, its walls being ruinous, they entered Worcester and took it over.[58] The result of this action was to draw down upon the city the entire Parliamentarian field army from Northampton. The motives of its commanders in marching on Worcester rather than Shrewsbury remain mysterious. Perhaps their intelligence was faulty. The result, for the local Royalists, was catastrophic. Rupert's horse retreated rapidly into Shropshire, abandoning Worcester to their enemies, who occupied the city on the 24th. On the 2nd October a detachment occupied Hereford.[59] From both counties the Royalist leaders fled, or defaced their working papers.[60] The most prominent, Lord Coventry, surrendered himself to Parliament.[61]

This success, striking as it was, nearly lost Parliament the war. Had its army marched on Shrewsbury instead of Worcester it could have destroyed the core of the King's army while he was absent' at Chester. Instead it went to Worcester, and compounded this blunder by remaining there two weeks, waiting for Charles to make a move. The motives for this immobility are even less intelligible than those for the original march. The Parliamentarian commanders seem to have had no conception of the numbers and intentions of the Royalists behind Rupert's cavalry screen, and to have lacked the will to probe them. Their strategic errors played directly into Charles's hands, for they granted him the precious time in which to build a full-scale army.

To construct any army required four ingredients: men, officers, weapons and money. Of these Charles certainly obtained the first, for by 13th October, when he called his forces together at Bridgnorth, they consisted of about 6 000 foot, 2 000 horse and 1 500 dragoons.[62] Earl Rivers's, Fitton's, Aston's and Salusbury's regiments had now joined, and other regiments had apparently arrived from outside the region. Much of the growth, however, must have been supplied by the recruitment of regiments commissioned elsewhere from Shropshire and its area. At times complete units were added; thus Lord Willoughby's Lincolnshire regiment acquired three Cheshire companies and Fielding's Foot two Herefordshire detachments.[63] Many recruits, however, must have signed up with the agent of whichever regiment found their village first. Thus the principal officers of Blagge's Foot were all Suffolk gentry, but the regiment first appears at Shrewsbury in October, and must have been recruited from that area as Suffolk was under Parliamentarian rule.[64] The same must be true of other 'foreign' regiments which materialised at this time and place. A splendid portrait of this process at work survives from Myddle, Shropshire.[65] The Commissioner of Array, Sir Paul Harris, called all local people to a meeting on Myddle Hill, where a recruiting agent 'with a paper in his hand and three or four soldiers' pikes stuck upright in the ground by him' offered 4s. 4d. a week to volunteers. Harris was not the local landlord, nor had he been comissioned to raise a regular unit himself, nor was he even popular with the common people. Yet twenty men from Myddle, Marton and Newton signed up, thirteen of whom were to die in action,[66] a casualty rate that exceeds these villages' losses in the First World War. To border farmers 4s. 4d. per week was a princely sum.

The King likewise obtained a sufficient supply of trained officers to drill the men. This procedure was absolutely vital, as the practice needed to operate the cumbersome musket of the 1640s or manoeuvre with an eighteen-foot pike rendered these weapons almost useless in the hands of raw recruits. The mere experience of an engagement to men who had never known battle was so traumatic that only instilled discipline would stop them breaking at once. The immense superiority of veterans over raw troops cannot be over-stressed, particularly in this war where veterans were often so scarce. In this respect the Welsh regiments had an advantage, in that the sheer poverty of Welsh agriculture had forced many gentry into the career of soldier of fortune. Owen, Herbert, Stradling and possibly Salusbury were themselves veterans, and so were many of their officers.[67] The other regiments nevertheless managed to obtain the services of experienced men, and, as indicated earlier, all whose composition is known included one or two.

The equipment of Charles's army was far less adequate. One pros-pective source of weapons was the local militia. Unfortunately this varied a great deal in quality, the Cheshire militia being apparently well equipped[68] while that of Anglesey and Caernarvonshire was not.[69] Furthermore, as the duty of the militiamen was to defend their homes they were understandably reluctant to give up their arms. Eventually it seems that only the bands of Denbighshire and Flint-shire were disarmed in the region studied.[70] The King apparently received a large convoy of weapons from the continent, which had been landed at Newcastle and carried across Lancashire to Chester.[71] To provide for the rest of his troops he relied upon the private armouries of the gentry, which in a hitherto peaceful country must have been meagre and antiquated. Some, those of Parliamentarians and neutralists, were confiscated outright. For the contents of the others Charles could only appeal, sometimes issuing a general request to be read in all churches,[72] sometimes writing pointedly to individual gentry whom he knew to be well equipped.[73] The appeals met with some response,[74] but by the time the King marched many foot soldiers, particularly in the Welsh regiments, were still armed only with pitch-forks and clubs.[75] Charles's army upon the march must have represented a curious living museum, some parts of it resembling an army of the 1640s, the rest bearing equipment associ-ated with the various centuries back to the Neolithic.

The final constituent was money, without which the best army would not hold together long. The sums needed to maintain the Royalist army were prodigious, especially at the attractive pay rates offered. To maintain a single foot company, minus officers, at the rate offered at Myddle required nearly £22 per week in an age when a rich man had £1,000 per year, and ready cash was notoriously scarce. Horse troops were about twice as expensive. The initial money to pay the new recruits and conduct them to the army was the respon-sibility of their colonels, although for Aston's horse and in the poor north Welsh counties it was raised by public subscription, not all of which was paid.[76] Once with the King, however, the soldiers' pay was the collective responsibility of Charles's High Command. Their task involved the gathering of money, its apportioning among the various regiments and the ordering of provisions upon which the soldiers might spend some of the money to feed themselves. This last was by itself an enormous task for a large force. The little army Charles had led to Stafford required £500 worth of bread alone to feed it for three days.[77] Apart from his food each soldier was expected to pay for his lodging, with some reluctant cottager. In practice lack of regular money meant that the soldier of this period often took 'free quarter', meaning that he paid for food and lodging with a certificate, which would be redeemed for cash by his paymaster if and when money came in. This system was universally detested among the civilian population, for the certificates were rarely redeemed, and actually illegal in England since the Petition of Right.

To meet these problems Charles at Shrewsbury, debarred from regular taxation which could be levied only in partnership with Parliament, depended entirely upon expediency and generosity. Both however worked surprisingly well. The sale of a peerage to Sir Richard Newport raised £6,000, the writing of letters to local Catholics asking for an advance upon their recusancy fines produced nearly £5,000 more.[78] Large sums were obtained by voluntary donation. Byron had brought back a considerable amount from Oxford University, the Prince had returned from Raglan with more, and many gifts were made by gentry from Shropshire and its region. Those who had cash sent it, in parcels of one or two hundred pounds each,[79] those who had not sent their family plate to be melted down.[80] Charles issued a moving appeal for such contributions to the county meeting at Shrewsbury on the 28th,[81] offering to melt his own plate first, and sent individual polite requests to wealthy gentry.[82] All donations were receipted, and repayment was promised. Doubtless some gentry gave out of loyalty, doubtless others were happy to purchase certificates of Royalism to be presented at court later when petitioning for favours. Thanks to these gifts, and the money confiscated from Parliamentarians and neutralists, the growth of the army continued and its morale seemed high. There seems no reason to doubt Clarendon's statement that the soldiers 'never went above a fortnight unpaid' at this time and that money was collected above this to cover the needs of the coming march.[83]

Clarendon's other statement that 'there was not a disorder of name', the soldiers being 'just and regardful to the country'[84] must be qualified. Individuals were plundered both by Charles's soldiers[85] and by their camp-followers.[86] Plundering is a phenomenon usually associated with times of pay failure, when troops loot from necessity, but even in times of full pay some will loot from greed, and the only answer to this problem is strict discipline. Charles faced the problem responsibly. He dispersed a circular throughout his army's quarters inviting any local people who suffered injury to report it to him, whereupon he promised justice and restitution.[87] Complaints were made, and when Charles marched he left six recruits to be tried like common thieves at the next Assizes.[88]

All told, Charles's achievement had been spectacular. In three weeks he had gathered together an army of volunteers, supported by voluntary donations, large enough to face his opponents. He had done this in one of the poorest regions of the country, which had already sent thousands of its best men overseas to quell the Irish rebellion,[89] and at harvest time when every hand was needed in the fields. It only remained for him to secure the area in his rear as he marched. He left Ottley with his men to hold Shrewsbury[90] and Richard Herbert, whose regiment was not ready, to garrison Bridgnorth.[91] He left Lloyd at Wrexham encouraged with a knighthood.[92] At Chester he was unable to persuade the reigning Mayor to accept re-election but was satisfied with the choice of a Royalist, William Ince, as his successor.[93] In Montgomeryshire the High Sheriff, who had attempted to obey both parties, was punished[94] and Sir John Price, who had resisted the Royalists, saw fit to turn Royalist himself. With north-west Wales loyal, all North Wales and its March now represented a secure Royalist base.

At the same time, a parallel development was occurring in distant Cornwall. There the local peace treaty made in August was shattered in September by a body of regular Royalist horse led by Sir Ralph Hopton, fleeing from the disaster in Somerset.[95] Once at Truro Hopton behaved with the same tact as Charles at Shrewsbury and Chester. He voluntarily stood trial on a charge of disturbing the peace and, perhaps aided by a packed jury, obtained his acquittal. The local Royalists were now free to indict their opponents of the same offence, and when these failed to appear, to call upon the High Sheriff, one of their party, to enforce their appearance. For this purpose the Sheriff, according to custom, raised an irregular levy of local people. The Cornish Parliamentarians fled the county, and in this manner it was secured by the Royalists. The Sheriff's levies, however, refused to remain in arms indefinitely or to wage offensive warfare, and so to mount a local war effort the Royalists had to raise regiments of regular soldiers with their own money.[96]

On 13th October, as his adherents were winning control of Cornwall, Charles commenced his march towards London, although the Lancashire regiments and those of Owen, Price, Stradling and Carbery had not yet arrived. It is possible that his haste was impelled by a growing lack of provisions around Shrewsbury or by the risk of a drop in morale consequent upon inactivity. He marched to Wolverhampton and then to Birmingham.[97] His behaviour in Staffordshire was notably harsher than it had been in the Marches; apparently the memory of Uttoxeter rankled. He sent a peremptory warrant to Lichfield for arms and money[98] and ordered the trial of certain persons who had offended his soldiers.[99] Likewise he was reported to have imposed a £2,000 fine upon Birmingham, as upon Nantwich.[100] He continued his march deeper into Warwickshire, and Stradling and the three Lancashire regiments joined, increasing the Royalist army to about 14 000 men.[101] The sluggish intelligence system of the Parliamentarians at Worcester relayed the news of the King's advance, and they moved eastwards to intercept him, leaving garrisons in Worcester and Hereford. Like two great blind moles the rival armies quested across Warwickshire for six days, unable to locate each other,[102] hindered perhaps by bad roads, but perhaps by the indifference of the local people. Upon the sixth day they collided, at Edgehill.

Two large areas had now felt the impact of civil war. One had been conquered and subjected to military rule, the other had undergone the opposite experience, the construction of a field army from predominantly local resources. Yet the involvement of the whole community in the war was by no means achieved. Whole areas remained virtually unaffected by these proceedings, and nowhere had an entire population been mobilised to participate in a war effort. As yet local communities stood apart from the war, while only activists of varying levels of commitment involved themselves in it. The consequence of the Edgehill campaign was to commence this final integration.

CHAPTER THREE
After Edgehill

As is well known, against all men's expectations both the battle and the campaign of Edgehill proved inconclusive. Parliament retained London while the King settled at Oxford, a city of great public buildings set in the centre of the kingdom among rich countryside capable of supporting his army. He and his enemies had proved themselves too evenly matched for either to achieve a decisive victory. Therefore as winter drew on both sides turned to the provinces once more, to recruit fresh strength to enable each to return to the conflict with a greater chance of success.

For Charles, the first and most obvious source of such strength consisted of the regiments which had not been fully recruited when he commenced the campaign. These joined him one by one. Price's arrived in November.[1]* Owen's experienced initial difficulties because of the shortage in north-west Wales of the money needed to raise it[2] but by December was at Worcester on its march.[3] Herbert's came to Oxford about three months later, though still short of weapons.[4] The biggest single addition to Charles's army, however, was the 2 000 foot and horse regiment which the Marquis of Hertford brought to Oxford on 9th January.[5]

Hertford had left court in July, armed with a grandiose commission as supreme commander of all Royalist forces in south Wales and most of southern England.[6] His mission had been to secure the West Country. It was he who presided over the Royalist attempt to win control of Somerset, which resulted in his small army being chased out of the county. By late September his horse, under Hopton, were, as shown above, in full flight for Cornwall. Hertford and the foot

---

* Notes for this chapter are on p. 212.

soldiers were pushed back to the Bristol Channel. The only obvious escape was by boat, to Royalist Glamorganshire. Hertford took it; he and his few hundred foot landed at Cardiff and were made welcome there.[7] Once safe, the Marquis was concerned to rescue his reputation by accomplishing in South Wales and its March what Charles had achieved in the north, the dual task of securing the area and drawing its resources into the field army. To this end he held musters and raised troops all through October and November. No records survive of this process, nor to illustrate how the local potentates Lord Herbert and the Earl of Carbery came to accept the authority of a superior of whose very existence they may have been ignorant. This they did, though there was certainly friction between Hertford and Herbert.[8] Ultimately the Marquis's 'drive' was successful all over South Wales except in its most Anglicised portion, Pembrokeshire. From there gentry did join him,[9] but some of their fellows drew the county militia into Haverfordwest, Tenby and Pembroke and appealed to Parliament for aid.[10] The three towns had a long tradition of identifying with the interests of London, from where they had obtained help against their Welsh enemies in the Middle Ages. This may seem a little simplistic as an explanation for their behaviour in 1642, but no other seems admissible. At any rate the episode had no sequel, as Hertford was more concerned with the menace of his Parliamentarian neighbours to the east.

As described above, the events of September had left Parliamentarian garrisons in Hereford and Worcester. Of these the more active was that of Hereford, consisting of the Earl of Stamford and his regiment. These regular soldiers were too formidable for the Marquis to engage, but he and Herbert between them were too strong in Monmouthshire for Stamford to dislodge. Two pamphlets[11] survive describing bloody victories won by Stamford over Hertford. Their vivid detail makes it natural that every historian since J.R. Phillips's standard book on the Civil War in Wales should have swallowed them whole.[12] However, all Stamford's own despatches survive for the period[13] and prove that the pamphlets are totally fraudulent and that the situation was one of stalemate enlivened by raiding. Stamford's raids certainly did a great deal of damage, particularly that on Radnorshire which wrecked the local Royalist effort and captured its leader, Charles Price. Time however was against him. The establishment of the royal army at Oxford placed Stamford and his colleagues at Worcester in a dangerous position, lying as they were between the King and Royalist Wales. In November the Worcester garrison evacuated, the local Royalists reoccupied and Stamford was left nearly encircled and unable to raise enough money locally to pay his men. In early December he retreated to Gloucester, where he left his regiment, under his lieutenant-colonel, Edward Massey, to hold the city. He himself moved on to the West Country, and never returned. Hertford occupied Hereford, and made Fitzwilliam Coningsby, who had joined him, its governor.[14]

Hertford's achievement was really a triumph of co-operation. When he marched most of his foot consisted of Carbery's regiment:[15] the pay for his forces was apparently provided by Herbert,[16] their arms had been largely purchased from Bristol while that city was still neutral[17] and his enemies had retreated under the pressure of external events. Yet it was a triumph none the less. Most of South Wales had been secured for the King, and protected by garrisons at Hereford and Monmouth,[18] and a body of troops brought from it to the King.

They did not exhaust the total of soldiers brought to Oxford from the region that winter. Existing field regiments sent for fresh recruits from their home areas.[19] Colonels commissioned for new regiments at Oxford sent agents to Shropshire and Worcestershire to find men.[20] Field regiments originally raised elsewhere likewise turned to this region for additions; thus the Lancashire regiment of Charles Gerard acquired a Denbighshire company.[21] It is dubious, however, whether all these men, even in total, managed to compensate for the drain of men from the field army at the same period. None of the men who had volunteered to serve the King in the autumn could have expected the war to last more than a few months. Now, after hard fighting, they found it prolonged indefinitely. Many fled home directly after the horrors of Edgehill,[22] others followed to care for their families during the winter and desertions continued in the spring as pay at Oxford began to fall into arrears.[23] These did more damage than a mere shrinkage of the army, for they carried home stories of the realities of military life, of poverty, boredom and disease, to tell potential recruits.

In this situation, it was all the more vital that the security of Royalist territory be improved and communications maintained between it and the field army at Oxford. The reoccupation of Herefordshire and Worcestershire had provided a corridor between Oxford and Royalist Wales. This was enlarged in February, when at Hertford's suggestion Prince Rupert conquered eastern Gloucestershire and added it to the army's quarters.[24] The military base around Oxford was further extended as detachments of the army moved into nearby areas of Berkshire, Buckinghamshire and Wiltshire. In the autumn the Earl of Newcastle raised a regular army in north-east England, and in December he brought this south to secure York, sending a detachment to occupy Newark.[25] To commence a line of posts between Newark and Wales, two Midland Royalist activists, Henry Hastings and Sir John Digby, were sent home in the winter from the field army to their respective shires, Leicestershire and Nottinghamshire. There they set about raising troops to put into strongpoints.[26]

The administrative task necessitated by these military developments was to provide some regular means of supporting troops to hold counties within corridors between blocs of territory and upon the fringes of those blocs. As the King had no legal right to impose taxes himself to support garrisons, he depended upon 'voluntary' local taxes agreed within each county by his supporters. Such a system was arranged in Oxfordshire on 21st December, when the gentry agreed to provide a regular sum to the detachments of field army horse quartered in the shire, to prevent them from plundering for food. This was at first regarded as a loan, but within a month it had become settled in the manner of a local rate.[27] Newcastle made a similar arrangement with the Yorkshire gentry in late December, to support his own army.[28] In Cornwall an official county-wide tax was not agreed until April, but during the winter individual Royalist colonels had imposed regular levies on groups of villages to maintain their regiments.[29] It remains to examine in detail how this system arose in Gloucestershire and the Marches.

It was accomplished in Royalist Gloucestershire on 6th February, when at Prince Rupert's request Lord Chandos led thirteen gentry in approving a plan to raise £3,000 immediately and £4,000 per month thereafter to support occupying troops.[30] The same system was already in force in Herefordshire, where Coningsby had been left by Hertford to raise a regiment of foot and one of dragoons to guard the county.[31] A monthly tax was somehow agreed to support them, although till it came in he relied upon loans from Hereford citizens.[32]

The best documentation of this process at work derives from Worcestershire. There Charles had placed the surviving leaders of the summer firmly in command. Russell was made governor of Worcester and High Sheriff, Lyttleton was made governor of the other walled town, Bewdley,[33] and Sandys was commissioned to raise regiments of horse and foot.[34] In addition Charles commissioned a Scottish veteran, Sir James Hamilton, to raise a horse regiment in the shire for the field army, appointing Russell his lieutenant-colonel to make Hamilton more acceptable to the local people.[35] On 17th December

Charles wrote to Russell telling him bluntly that the High Command had no money to spare for local forces and authorising him therefore to arrange a local 'contribution' to keep these troops from plundering.[36] Russell called a meeting to discuss a scheme for voluntary contributions[37] and then utilised the Epiphany Sessions to revive the summer device of employing the Grand Jury as a county Parliament. This obediently agreed that £3,000 per month would be levied from Worcestershire to pay local troops. A Treasurer was appointed to receive it and Russell to dispose of it, not in his military capacity as governor but in his civilian role as High Sheriff, head of the permanent county community. Collection was immediately commenced.[38]

In early March Charles capped all these arrangements by reconstituting the active Royalist gentry of the 'corridor counties' Herefordshire, Gloucestershire and Worcestershire as Committees 'for the guarding the county' with precise directions as to how to regulate their taxes and garrisons. They were expected to meet at least weekly.[39] The King may well have been pleased with their achievements, as they had set about reorganising an area which had been drained by the Parliamentarians. These had consumed much of the available local money in their occupation and confiscated the weapons of Royalists and of the militia.[40] On the other hand, the Parliamentarians may have done much to make rule by Royalist gentry palatable. They were strangers, and their troops had defaced churches, plundered and treated the local people as natural enemies.[41] This conclusion seems borne out by the fact that the Royalists faced their worst problems in this period not here but in precisely those areas where the royal army had been raised in the autumn.

In Shropshire the Royalists at first attempted to defend the county by calling up all the horse traditionally owed by the gentry for its defence. The gentry failed to co-operate[42] and in December a different scheme was promulgated, to raise 1 000 dragoons to defend the county by the subscriptions of thirty-three Royalist gentry, including all the local leaders. Sir Vincent Corbet, who had been captain of the moribund county horse, was made their colonel.[43] Charles approved this[44] and the scheme was extended to provide for the maintenance of the dragoons by a general levy upon the shire, settled by meetings within each hundred.[45] Yet by January only 298 had been raised, by the money of the Royalist leaders themselves.[46] The other subscriptions had simply failed to appear.[47] Likewise warrants to raise more money for the militia were ignored.[48]

A basic problem lying at the root of such failures was that the county itself was too large a unit for the horizons of the average man. As an alternative to the grand schemes of the county leaders, local people set up their own defence systems to protect their individual settlements. Thus Bishop's Castle corporation instituted an alarm network against plunderers[49] and the young men of Bridgnorth began to drill to protect their town.[50] This sentiment at least benefited Ottley at Shrewsbury, where the corporation agreed to levy £450 in the winter to improve the town's fortifications.[51] Ottley however wanted more; a commission from Charles as governor, to give him absolute power in Shrewsbury. The King was reluctant to grant this, fearing that such power would offend the corporation, the traditional rulers of the town, and disenchant them with Royalism. Ottley persuaded the corporation to recommend him, and Charles yielded in February.[52] Soon after Ottley was at odds with the corporation, having laid a tax upon the citizens without its consent.[53]

In January, at the King's command, the Denbighshire gentry agreed to raise and maintain 400 foot to garrison Denbigh, Ruthin, Llangeriew and Llangollen. William Wynne of Llanvase, leader of the disarmed militia, was made colonel.[54] These men were raised, and armed from family magazines, mainly Wynne's, though few munitions could be found for them.[55] The Flintshire gentry agreed to raise a local dragoon force under Sir Thomas Hanmer, though there was a notable inclination among them to 'stand neuters'.[56]

This last factor was crucial in Cheshire. There the Royalists had only obtained power in the autumn by the intervention of the King's army. That army had now marched away, taking with it the troops of the Cheshire Royalists. With diminished resources they were now expected to consolidate their hold upon the county. At first they relied upon the militia and upon a mutual aid agreement with the Lancashire Royalists,[57] who were in a worse predicament, with Parliamentarian garrisons at Manchester and Blackburn. The Lancashire connection, however, brought trouble when the Lancashire Royalist potentate, the Earl of Derby, who was nominally Lord Lieutenant of Cheshire, commissioned Orlando Bridgeman as supreme commander there.[58] Presumably the Earl wanted a henchman in control of Cheshire who would use its resources to aid the struggle in Lancashire. Bridgeman was not however one of the group of noblemen who had run the county since the summer, and these resented his appointment. Moreover he was a Chester man,[59] and his rivalry with the lords represented a clash between the interests of city and county.

Bridgeman set about the work of consolidation. In Chester he was supported by a set of aldermen led by the Gamull family, who had bought trading privileges in the city which Parliament would extinguish.[60] These obtained a corporation order on 6th December for a levy to complete the city magazine and fortifications, phrased delicately to avoid naming a particular enemy.[61] Bridgeman and Derby seem at the same time to have asked a local tax of the county[62] and to have ordered the disarmament of suspect gentry.[63] These two manoeuvres in unison produced disaster. The gentry concerned, led by Henry Mainwaring of Kermincham, rose and gathered a large force, comprised of most of the former neutralists plus, probably, anybody who did not want to pay tax. All the retrospective sources call them Parliamentarians, as they later became, and at the time Parliament was eager to claim them as compatriots. Doubtless there were genuine Parliamentarians among them. But there is no evidence that at this period Mainwaring and the leaders regarded themselves as acting for Parliament. In the summer they had been militant neutralists, and their behaviour in December was perfectly in accord with this position.

Mainwaring's troops rapidly overran eastern Cheshire, and on the 10th they occupied Nantwich, the strategic heart of the county.[64] A handful of regulars might have broken them, but Bridgeman had no regular soldiers. The militia, demoralised by the divisions in the Royalists and in the county community, disintegrated.[65] The Royalists were left with little more than Chester and the private garrisons of the lords, like Earl Rivers's at Halton Castle.[66] Their fellows in neighbouring counties promised aid but Bridgeman, with reason, doubted their ability to perform.[67] His solution, produced in co-operation with one of the lords, Kilmurrey, was to propose a proper local peace treaty to his opponents. They accepted, and it was signed at Bunbury on 22nd December. Both sides agreed to disband most of their troops and only to raise them again in unison, to escort 'foreign' soldiers of either party firmly through the county. Cheshire had effectively contracted out of the war.[68] At best Bridgeman had, after a fashion, secured the flank of Royalist North Wales. At worst, he had bought time. The treaty caused fury in Parliament[69] and among Royalists in Cheshire and elsewhere.[70] The King, however, was persuaded to approve it.[71]

Events in Staffordshire followed yet another course. Through the autumn it had preserved the neutrality which Cheshire was struggling to achieve, apparently without effort. Gentry sent private aid to Charles at Shrewsbury while declining to raise their county for him.[72] This position was tested in November, when a party of Yorkshire Royalist horse under Sir Francis Wortley crossed the Staffordshire Moorlands, the high bare area in the north-east of the county. Although barren, this at the time harboured a thriving plebeian population, and these Wortley's troopers plundered, to survive.[73] The reaction of the county community was to hold a Special Sessions of the Peace on 15th November, which decreed that 800 foot and 200 dragoons should be raised in the shire to deal with any future incursions. The order was signed by twenty-six gentry, who included most of the future local Royalist and Parliamentarian leaders, plus Lord Paget who had so recently raised his regiment in the shire.[74] The Cheshire pact had been created to end the war in that county. The Staffordshire pact was intended to stop it ever breaking out.

This Charles would not tolerate. On 26th November he ordered the High Sheriff to suppress the neutralist army and to garrison Staffordshire in his name instead.[75] Next he selected a minor Staffordshire gentleman, Thomas Comberford of Comberford, who had joined him, made him governor of Stafford and colonel of a regiment of horse[76] and sent him north around the New Year guarded by Wortley's troopers. The neutralist army ought in theory to have destroyed them, but the local people had obviously been just as lax in this matter as in any other expensive scheme, for it had not been raised. They occupied Stafford, the Mayor being favourable to them. How they won over the Mayor is not known, nor how the Mayor won over the townspeople, although his accounts contain tantalising references to payment for bundles of proclamations and to a distribution of beer among local people 'when Sir Francis Wortley was coming'.[77] They were assisted also by Sir Richard Leveson MP and Sir Robert Wolsely MP, the new High Sheriff, former neutralists.[78] These men may have been driven over to Royalism by Parliament, which had declared them enemies and ordered Wortley's plundering to be compensated out of Leveson's estates.[79] By the end of January Comberford and Wortley were established in a fortified Stafford and the former was raising his horse with money lent by the towns people.[80]

They had forgotten the Moorlanders. These people had no intention of permitting the county to be dominated by their plunderer Wortley, allied with yet more potentially predatory horse. In early February they sent a demand to the Royalists at Stafford demanding the withdrawal of these regular soldiers and their replacement with a small garrison of local men.[81] When this was rejected they rose, and assaulted Stafford. They could not take the town for lack of cannon and proper weapons, but they could prevent Comberford from fetching in supplies, and their numbers and the remarkable determination of their leaders made them formidable.[82] Comberford appealed for aid to the nearest active Royalist soldier. This was Henry Hastings, a younger member of a great Leicestershire family, who had been in the summer one of Charles's most fervent, and notorious, followers. After fighting at Edgehill he had, as mentioned earlier, been sent home with the title of Colonel-General to secure the East Midlands, and gathered at his family castle of Ashby-De-La-Zouch a small but mobile army, which had operated as far as Cheshire.[83] It had touched the fringe of Staffordshire in January, when Hastings had garrisoned Tutbury Castle against his Derbyshire opponents.[84] Now he prepared to march to Comberford's aid.[85] Meanwhile a third centre of Royalist power had come into being in the county, when the Derbyshire Royalist potentate, the Earl of Chesterfield, retreated to Lichfield with a small force and settled there. Cheshire had fallen into chaos and resolved it with a neutrality pact. Staffordshire had produced a neutrality pact, and fallen into chaos.[86]

The opposed experiences of these two neighbouring counties highlight a general danger in the study of the Civil War, that of treating the various county neutrality pacts of 1642–3 as a single phenomenon. These pacts fall, in fact, into three different categories. The first is typified by the Staffordshire agreement, and was earlier given the label of 'militant neutralism',[87] signifying the determination of members of a county community to oppose attempts to involve that community in the national conflict. The Cheshire declarations of the summer of 1642 were of this nature. Something similar must have been agreed in Wiltshire, symbolised by a petition sent to the King by the county's leading gentry in October, begging him to make peace.[88]

These pacts contrast violently with that of Bunbury, which was negotiated by committed Royalist activists as a tactical ruse to secure a deteriorating military position. It was a tactic which had already been attempted in two nearby counties, Lancashire and Yorkshire, where the Royalist partisans had likewise given their best men and arms to the royal army and were left to face their local opponents with much diminished resources. The King's departure from York in August had left his supporters there caught between emerging Parliamentarian forces in the East and West Ridings. They signed the treaty with their opponents in September, at the same time as they were asking Newcastle to march to their aid.[89] In Lancashire, the punishment of Nantwich in September for its resistance to the Royalists had caused the citizens of Manchester to ally, at last, with the local Parliamentarians. It was a reluctant alliance, based upon fear of punishment by the Lancashire Royalists for having refused them the town magazine. The first reaction of the Royalist leader, the Earl of Derby, was to attack the town. The second, when he had been repulsed and had sent his troops to join the King, was to offer a county peace pact.[90] Parliament's relentless hostility to these treaties was perfectly rational, as such pacts would prevent it from attacking the Royalists in the counties concerned while they were at a disadvantage. By the time Bunbury was signed the Yorkshire treaty had collapsed and the Lancashire negotiations been broken off as a result of pressure put by Parliament upon its supporters. Nevertheless, these treaties should not be divorced from their context in a general local climate of hostility to the war. The two treaties which were actually signed, in Yorkshire and Cheshire, reached that stage because the Royalist activists were not negotiating with men who, like themselves, had already been engaged in arms for one of the parties. The York Royalists found a favourable reception for a peace pact not among the Parliamentarians of the East Riding, who had exchanged shots already with the King's soldiers, but with those of the West, who were only just arming. The Royalists in Chester, as shown, were dealing with men to whom the label 'Parliamentarian' should be applied with caution.

The third variety of local peace pact had affinities with both the previous two. It consisted of a pacification negotiated between two opposed sets of partisans when they had discovered that complete control of the area they were contesting could only be achieved after a prolonged and destructive struggle, which they were unwilling to undertake. The most spectacular example of this kind of pact was the truce signed in late February 1643 by the Royalist forces based in Cornwall and the Parliamentarian forces based in Devon, after they spent a winter locked in fierce and inconclusive combat. The truce provided for a conference at Exeter to unite the counties of Cornwall, Devon, Somerset and Dorset in a neutral Association, standing outside the partisan struggle.[91] Smaller versions of this scheme had been discussed in the Midlands during the winter. In December the rival partisans in Nottinghamshire, having armed against each other, held several talks aimed at producing a demilitarisation.[92] In January Henry Hastings proposed to his Parliamentarian opponents in Leicestershire an undertaking by which each refrained from raiding the other's portions of the county.[93]

Whatever the exact nature of each pact, they all focused attention upon a general problem. It was the same that had occurred in the summer; how to make a war effort attractive, or even acceptable to the bulk of the population in each locality. Nobody was more conscious of this problem than the King himself. Hence his High Command was most anxious that local commanders continued to distribute the bundles of propaganda material sent to them from Oxford.[94] They were obviously dispersed quite far, for local people in eastern Herefordshire rejected a Parliamentarian warrant because they had 'His Majesty's book' against it.[95] Directed to the same end were letters like the one Charles wrote to Russell on 21st December ordering him to inform local people that the King well understood and regretted their sufferings at the hands of both armies in the autumn and that he promised strict attention to all laws. He meant this seriously, because Russell was ordered to ensure that the promise was kept.[96] Similarly he issued a proclamation to troops in the 'corridor counties' instructing them to obey all regulations and behave well towards civilians.[97] Another proclamation publicised the fact that the Shropshire gentry who contributed to support the county dragoons were to receive a gold medal each.[98]

Ultimately all these efforts were in vain, because nothing could induce the bulk of local people to volunteer the sacrifices necessary to fight a war which they neither wanted nor could comprehend. If any of the Royalist leaders realised this unpalatable fact they could not publicly acknowledge it. The only way out of the impasse that was ideologically safe was to ascribe the torpor of the local war effort to sabotage by concealed Parliamentarians. In the first months of 1643 the witch-hunt began. It was apparently most intense in Shropshire, where Ottley's soldiers dragged suspects to prison and then ransacked their houses. Men went in fear of being denounced by spiteful neighbours.[99] The Shrewsbury citizens were instructed to swear individually to oppose Parliament. Refusal to swear carried the death penalty.[100] A similar oath was opposed on Chester,[101] where the leaders suspected the common people of being 'poisoned',[102] while a big trial was staged at Worcester in the same period of people accused of plotting against the governor.[103]

Whatever the Royalists had to fear from concealed foes, they certainly had reason to fear the external enemy. Parliament was assembling a formidable army for the approaching campaigning season of 1643, to be launched against the Royalist military base at Oxford. To ensure that this blow would be fatal, it had also to send smaller forces to break open and destroy the huge Royalist hinterland of Wales and the Marches, which serviced the royal army and which the King's adherents had spent the winter fortifying. To accomplish this, it possessed advanced bases at Gloucester and Coventry and an isolated stronghold at Manchester. If it could drive a line of fortified posts from Coventry to Manchester, it could run troops up and down this, striking at whichever point of the Royalist area seemed weakest at any one time. The Royalists themselves, however, had an interest in aggressive strategy. They had already linked Wales to Oxford: now they needed to link it securely to the Royalist North. This entailed completing the chain of posts which men like Hastings and Sir John Digby had begun to construct in midwinter between Shrewsbury and Newark. The two projected military corridors, Royalist and Parliamentarian, crossed in Staffordshire. This unfortunate county was about to become the centre of a highly complicated and deadly game of chess, with mastership of England as its prize.

Parliament made the first move, striking at the weakest point in the Royalist defences, Cheshire. It empowered its champion of the summer, Brereton, to wage war there, equipped him with a body of horse and sent him north on about 4th January.[104] By the 19th he was near Stafford, and disrupted a local meeting called by Comberford.[105] The mere news of his coming was enough to sink the Bunbury treaty. Mainwaring's group, put to the test, did not relish the prospect of helping Royalists fight Parliamentarians. They proposed individual resistance to Brereton instead, and Bridgeman lost all faith in the pact.[106] He appealed to neighbouring Royalists for help, and by the time Brereton entered Cheshire on about 25th January had succeeded in securing Chester with about 1 000 foot, much of it from North Wales.[107]

As it happened, Charles himself had no more faith in the Bunbury pact than anybody, and made his own move. Against Brereton's horse he decided to set Aston's, who being Cheshire men might be more acceptable to the local people than any other field army unit. Aston was made Major-General in Cheshire, ordered to link up with the Shropshire dragoons and secure the county, and despatched from Oxford on the 19th.[108] By the 25th he was in Shropshire, only to find Corbet's dragoons scattered and already ordered by Charles to aid Comberford. It took him three days to remedy this situation, and by then Brereton was in Cheshire.[109] Both he and Aston now raced to gain Nantwich, which Mainwaring had evacuated under the terms of Bunbury. Brereton won by a margin, but the citizens, faithful to the Bunbury pact, refused to aid him. On the 28th Aston arrived, and the two forces joined battle. To steady the fresh dragoons, Aston divided them up among his horse, a fatal mistake as when Brereton charged the dragoons broke and carried the horse with them.[110] Aston lost many men and weapons, but even more in prestige. The citizens of Nantwich threw in their lot with the victor, who fortified the town. Mainwaring's party, apparently deciding that neutralism was now untenable, joined him there and became, finally, Parliamentarian.[111] It was a decision they later regretted, for Mainwaring himself was sacked by Parliament in 1644 for 'disservice'[112] and most of his colleagues followed him into retirement, reinforcing the impression that their alliance with Parliament was late and hesitant.[113]

During February both sides skirmished and attempted to gain strength. To secure his rear, Brereton established contact with the Moorlanders, who by now had been driven back by Hastings, and sent them officers to train them.[114] Sir John Gell, the Derbyshire Parliamentarian leader, likewise wooed them, sending a cannon.[115] Thus an alliance began to form between Moorlander and Parliamentarian. Brereton was himself however in need of experienced officers and faced with the problem of welding his troops and Mainwaring's into a single force.[116] His difficulties nevertheless were nothing to Aston's. This gentleman had continued with his horse to Chester, leaving Corbet's dragoons at Whitchurch to watch Nantwich. At Chester he and the lords arranged a local tax to support his horse. Unfortunately the Royalists now held only those parts of Cheshire surrounding the city, and these could not support both Aston's horse and the city garrison. Bridgeman obtained a royal warrant appropriating their money for the latter, and soon the horse were plundering to survive.[117] Bridgeman compounded this action by appealing to the King for an expert to advise him upon the defence of Chester. Charles sent Sir Nicholas Byron, as he had to Warwickshire before. He arrived on 14th February, equipped with a commission as Colonel-General of Cheshire.[118] Aston's authority had been divided.

On the 25th Brereton garrisoned Northwich, and cut the Royalists off completely from eastern Cheshire.[119] As Bridgeman had appropriated the western districts, Aston's forces had to break through to the east to survive. By 10th March Aston had gathered some Welsh foot and some militia to join with his horse for the task. The whole force was mutinous for lack of pay, and although the foot were led by a Denbighshire veteran, Robert Ellis, neither men nor junior officers were trained. Nevertheless Aston seized Middlewich, between Northwich and Nantwich, hoping that Corbet's dragoons would keep Nantwich busy. In fact they had by now gone home, and Aston's men were attacked upon both sides. They bolted, leaving their weapons and Ellis to be captured.[120] It was a decisive victory for Brereton, but also for Bridgeman. Aston was ruined; he and his regiment were recalled to the field army and never employed prominently again. His allies the Cheshire noblemen became exiles at Bridgeman's court. Brereton had secured the county, but Bridgeman had secured the city, and effectively covered the flank of Wales. Neither possessed the resources to dislodge the other. It was a stalemate in some measure honourable to both men.

Meanwhile Parliament had launched its second offensive. On 31st December it had appointed Lord Brooke its Commander-in-Chief in Warwickshire and Staffordshire[121] and he arrived at Coventry in late February with 400 foot and 200 horse to conquer this area.[122] In January the Coventry Parliamentarians had garrisoned Kenilworth Castle to tighten their grip on northern Warwickshire.[123] To oppose them, Charles had settled Brooke's arch-enemy Northampton at Banbury with the title of Colonel-General of Warwickshire and a powerful force.[124] This dominated the southern districts, with an outpost at Stratford-upon-Avon. Brooke's first move upon arrival was to take Stratford and clear Northampton's men out of the county.[125] He then garrisoned Maxstoke Castle[126] and drew troops out of the existing garrisons to recruit his foot to about 800.[127] On the 28th he invaded Staffordshire.

There Hastings had accomplished a great deal. He had repulsed the Moorlanders, defeated incursions by Brereton and Gell, garrisoned Rushall Hall and Eccleshall Castle and persuaded some gentry to agree to a local army supported by a local tax. Charles had rewarded him by adding Staffordshire to his Midland command.[128] Brereton and Gell however now co-operated to keep him busy while Brooke picked off the main Royalist strongpoints, beginning with Lichfield.[129] There the Earl of Chesterfield surrendered after a week's siege, and the town received a Parliamentarian garrison. It was a triumph for Brooke, but a posthumous one, for a bullet fired from the defences had pierced his brain.[130]

Charles determined to compound this blow to Parliament by sending Northampton to undo his deceased rival's work. The Earl drew out of Banbury two horse regiments and swept north in early March. Brooke had weakened his garrisons in Warwickshire too much for them to intercept Northampton's party.[131] In Staffordshire Gell had taken over Brooke's army, Brereton having returned to Cheshire to face Aston. Gell's forces added to Brooke's made up about 1 000 foot and some horse, plus 300 Moorlanders, half of them armed. Hastings had more horse but fewer foot. He garrisoned Tamworth Castle to balance Lichfield, and awaited Northampton.[132]

The two united at Coleshill and attacked Lichfield.[133] Gell in turn united with Brereton, fresh from his victory at Middlewich, and advanced. The two composite armies met near Stafford on 19th March, on Hopton Heath. Northampton charged at the head of his men, and perished fighting heroically. Like Brooke, he bequeathed victory to his followers, for Brereton and Gell, though unbroken, suffered such losses that they retreated and divided, returning to their own shires. Hastings was left in possession of the field in Staffordshire, with 1 000 superb horse, to which he added 1 000 properly-armed foot and a further 1 000 armed with clubs.[134]

Charles now played for checkmate. On 29th March he detached Prince Rupert from the field army with 1 200 horse, about 700 foot, four cannon and a huge supply of munitions[135] and sent him to join Hastings and destroy the Lichfield garrison, Brereton and Gell.[136] On his march Rupert drove a Parliamentarian force out of Birmingham. In the process the town and its people suffered so much damage that an outcry was provoked in both London and Oxford.[137] Charles felt constrained to appease civilian opinion in general by publishing a letter to Rupert ordering him to behave more gently.[138] The Prince linked up with Hastings and reduced Lichfield in two weeks.[139] Obedient to his uncle's warning, he gave the garrison good terms, and replaced it with Royalists under Richard Bagot, late of Paget's Foot.[140] Bagot was a local man, and therefore supposedly more acceptable to local people. He was however a younger son, not a prominent gentleman, and his proved ability, rather than his standing in the community, must have weighed with Rupert.

The Prince, with a splendid army, was now ready for Nantwich. It is doubtful if Brereton could have resisted him. But he was not put to the test, because at that moment Rupert was recalled. Parliament had just launched its main field army against the King, and Charles needed every available man.[141] The Prince hastened back to the royal army with all the troops withdrawn from it that spring. Hastings, reduced to his own local force, took it to campaign in the East Midlands leaving Staffordshire secured by its Royalist garrisons. A hush settled upon the county, the contesting generals being dead or departed. For the time being the Royalists had won, and created their corridor to the North. But until they eradicated Brereton, it could never be safe.

Staffordshire, which had been the most determinedly neutral county in the region, had become its chief battlefield. This fate was symbolic. As Rupert rejoined his uncle, and the Parliamentarian field army attacked Reading, the attempt to bind the four western counties in a neutral Association collapsed under the weight of Parliament's disapproval, and the local partisans returned to their struggle. The attempted pacifications in the Midland counties had proved abortive long before. All over England overt opposition to the war, which had been so powerful and widespread, was at an end. Military 'fronts' had been created. Within these zones every propertied man was taxed to support the war effort, and counties behind them were expected to make regular contributions. Put to the test, the gentry who favoured neutrality had simply not been coherent and determined enough to oppose both the two traditional branches of government. It has been said that the summer of 1642 witnessed the triumph of provincialism.[142] If so, the following winter witnessed its defeat. There had been only one decisive victor in the fighting of those months: the war itself.

PART TWO
The grandees

Introduction

As the campaigning season of 1643 opened, Charles must have been pleased with the work of his local supporters in erecting garrisons to protect his territory and providing the financial support for them. Something was still missing, however, in most Royalist areas; a controlling hand capable of drawing upon the resources of several counties to provide a strong enough force to defend all of them, and of co-ordinating military administration and solving its problems over a comparably wide area. In Oxfordshire and adjacent counties such control was provided by the royal Council of War, a mixed body of soldiers and civilians which dealt with problems arising from the quartering of the royal army in this area.[1]* In the North it was represented by the Earl of Newcastle, based at York with the title of Lieutenant-General of the six northern counties and a formidable army, to which the Catholic community of the north-east, forseeing a grim future at the mercy of Parliament's extreme Protestantism, had contributed considerable support.[2] Lancashire, though nominally within Newcastle's command, was in fact controlled by its own Commander-in-Chief, the Earl of Derby. In late winter he had strengthened his position by raising a regular army, again with great assistance from the local Catholics.[3] In Royalist Wales, the Marches and the West, however, such figures were missing.

They were now to be provided. On 4th April Charles created three Lieutenant-Generals for Wales and the Marches, and on the 25th a fourth was appointed for England west of, and including, Wiltshire and Hampshire.[4] The latter was the Marquis of Hertford, who was thus given a chance to reverse the disaster of the previous

---

* Notes for this introduction are on p. 215.

summer. He was provided with a section of the royal army and sent into the West to link up with Hopton's army advancing from Cornwall, and conquer the whole area. Lord Herbert was given south-east Wales and its March, comprising Herefordshire, Monmouthshire, Breconshire, Glamorganshire and Radnorshire. The Earl of Carbery was given the south-west, Carmarthenshire, Cardiganshire and Pembrokeshire. All the rest of the region, consisting of the six counties of North Wales plus Cheshire, Shropshire and Worcestershire, was placed under Lord Capel. These three generals were expected to raise local armies and clear their commands of enemies.

Charles now had six regional generals to preserve and extend his territory. Together, they represented an ideological, as well as a military, system. Five were the greatest Royalist magnates of the areas committed to their care. The sixth, Capel, was a powerful noble from eastern England, and was appointed to an area which possessed no obvious native leader. All these generals, then, were great aristocrats and amateur soldiers, men who would command respect by virtue of their inherent status in the community rather than by powers conferred upon them by war. They would command military governors drawn from the gentry of the locality surrounding their fortresses, assisted by their fellows on the Commissions of Array. In this manner Charles hoped to preserve harmony within his war machine and between that machine and the surrounding population. He also hoped to limit the encroachment of the war upon traditional values.

Again, to avoid producing a book of interminable length and impenetrable detail, it is proposed to make an analysis in depth only of the fortunes of the three grandees in Wales and the Marches, and their servants. In a concluding section their achievement may be compared with that of their colleagues. The careers of the three commanders are not chronologically consistent. Herbert had been in action for months before he was formally raised to his Lieutenant-Generalcy, while Carbery was not to take up his command for many months more. Yet their experiences, like their identity, formed a coherent pattern, and merit their treatment as a group.

CHAPTER FOUR
Herbert

With the departure of the Marquis of Hertford, Lord Herbert was able to come into his own as a local commander. He had never been eclipsed, for even during the time of Hertford's presence the Parliamentarians had ranked them as equal enemies, and Charles had honoured Herbert by creating his father Marquis of Worcester.[1]* Further honours had included a grant of the customs of Bristol, whenever that city were captured, and the confiscated Welsh estates of his local rival, the Earl of Pembroke.[2] Herbert possessed, in fact, one asset which made him impossible to ignore – his family was the richest in the kingdom. As well as making his support worth cultivating in a national cause, this gave him an incomparable advantage as a local commander. On Hertford's departure, Charles immediately confirmed him as Commander-in-Chief in south-east Wales and its March, with absolute authority over Monmouthshire.[3] The local Royalist commissioners were ordered to make some arrangement with him to deliver him money from their respective counties to support the army he would raise.[4]

He was assisted in this enterprise by the drain of troops from the field army back to their native areas. Price's entire regiment was actually ordered home in early 1643, perhaps to alleviate the pressure on resources around Oxford, and became part of Herbert's command. The dues of the local clergy were earmarked to support it.[5] Howell Gwynne, formerly captain in Stradling's Foot, became Lieutenant-Colonel in the new foot regiment which Herbert raised for himself.[6] The natural resources of Herbert's area represented yet another advantage. Unlike Charles in the previous autumn he pos-

* Notes for this chapter are on p. 215.

sessed enough time to forge new armaments if existing weapons were in short supply. At this period there were five ironworks in Glamorganshire and Breconshire, capable of turning out twenty tons of iron per week each, and more in Monmouthshire.[7] Herbert's forces were soon acquiring newly-cast cannon, armour and pike-heads.[8]

His only serious problems at this period derived from local rivalries. Within his own county of Monmouthshire he had trouble with Thomas Morgan of Machen, a Commissioner of Array formerly in his rival Pembroke's faction, who refused to serve under him. In Glamorganshire likewise the Commission was divided against itself.[9] The best-documented of these quarrels occurred in Herefordshire.[10] There Fitzwilliam Coningsby had obtained leadership simply because alone of the local activists he had joined Hertford, instead of the King, at the Parliamentarian invasion, and had thus been the obvious man for the Marquis to leave at Hereford as Governor. After the Royalist reoccupation, however, all the local leaders returned, joined at last by the county magnate, Viscount Scudamore. The Viscount had so far been completely inactive in the war, marking time at London and even after joining Charles he showed a pronounced mildness towards Parliamentarians.[11] Yet having finally elected to enter the war he was not prepared to see his traditional local leadership exercised by Coningsby. First he attempted to have his rival ordered away into the field army with his newly-raised regiment. Charles and Herbert both refused to concur with this, confirming that the regiment was intended to defend Herefordshire. Next he drove a wedge between Coningsby and Herbert, persuading the Commissioners of Array to interpret Charles's instruction to give money to Herbert, by delivering him the entire county tax. With the clergy dues already given to Price, this left no public money to pay Coningsby's men. Coningsby stubbornly drew upon his own fortune and that of his officers, and in this manner recruited his regiment to 700 men, equipped them, laid up a magazine in Hereford and so remained in control there.

By 5th February Herbert's army was sufficiently ready for him to call a council of war at Hereford in order to concert plans for a campaign.[12] Two potential opponents existed. One was at Brampton Bryan Castle, where Lady Harley, cut off from her Parliamentarian husband in London, had decided that she preferred to risk a siege rather than accept a Royalist garrison which might abuse her home.[13] A mere detachment seemed sufficient to reduce the place, and this task was given to the Radnorshire Militia, stiffened by some of Coningsby's men. The Militia, however, refused to leave its own county unless Herbert led it in person, so that Coningsby was left to undertake the work with his detachment alone.[14] Herbert himself was undertaking the other, much more considerable, enemy, the city of Gloucester. Rupert's conquest of the Cotswolds had left Gloucester in the position of an isolated but dangerous Parliamentarian enclave within the 'Cavalier Corridor' between Oxford and Wales. If it were captured, the corridor would be completely secured. Nobody was more conscious of this fact than the citizens themselves, who showed signs of wishing to forestall the inevitable siege by coming to terms with the Royalists. Unfortunately for them Edward Massey took seriously Stamford's parting instructions to him to hold the city. Instead of retreating southward he pulled back into Gloucester his outposts on its eastern side and instituted a mixture of free quarter and loans to maintain his troops indefinitely.[15] Clearly he was expecting his enemy to come from the east, and to be Rupert. The only Royalists to materialise from that direction, however, were a detachment from Worcester under Russell, which occupied Tewkesbury.[16] The main threat was in fact to come from the west, across the Forest of Dean, and was represented by Herbert.

Herbert invaded the Forest on 7th February[17] with a force of about 1 500 foot and 500 horse, including most of Coningsby's regiment[18] and, apparently, the best of Herbert's own foot and Price's. Most of the available arms in the area were given to it, including those laid up by Coningsby at Hereford.[19] Coningsby, Price and the remainder of the three regiments were left behind to guard Herbert's command in his absence. His brother, Lord John Somerset, led the horse of the expeditionary force[20] while an English veteran soldier, Sir Richard Lawdey,[21] commanded the foot. At Coleford they routed Massey's western outpost, losing Lawdey, who fell in the attack.[22] He was replaced by another 'foreigner', also a veteran, Sir Jerome Brett. Clarendon completely misrepresents this episode by describing the Parliamentarians as 'a rabble of country people, being got together, without order or an officer of name' [23] Corbet, who knew the men personally, makes clear that they were a body of regulars, under a Colonel Berrow.

There is now a gap in the contemporary records of over a month, and the retrospective sources telescope events to exclude this period. All[24] recommence on 24th March, to portray Herbert's attack on Gloucester as deadlocked. He and his brother had left the army, which was quartered at Highnam, near Gloucester, around the mansion of Sir Robert Cooke, a Parliamentarian. Its pay was met at least partly out of a tax which had been imposed on the Forest of Dean.

Nemesis was rapidly approaching it, for it had become caught up in a complicated series of moves between King and Parliament to match those which were being enacted in the same period at the other end of the Marches, in Cheshire and Staffordshire. Just as Parliament had sent Brereton and Brooke to strike at the Royalists in that area, so on 11th February[25] it made a veteran soldier, Sir William Waller, its Commander-in-Chief in Wiltshire, Gloucestershire, Worcestershire and Shropshire, to drive a wedge into the southern end of the region. Waller marched west with about 2 500 men. In early March he was held up in Wiltshire, but eventually emerged from there victorious, and made for Gloucester, which had already been reinforced by 200 foot sent from Bristol. His army was ferried over the Severn by Massey at dusk, and guided through the night by Cooke himself towards Highnam House. At dawn on the 25th Herbert's army there found itself caught between Massey to the east and Waller to the west, encircled and outnumbered. It fought till its ammunition ran out and then surrendered. The men were released on a promise never to fight Parliament again, but their weapons and horses were lost for ever.

Herbert's remaining soldiers in Dean fled into Monmouthshire. His family left Raglan Castle garrisoned but themselves fled as far as Swansea, intending to take ship if Waller pursued them.[26] The Royalists at Tewkesbury retreated.[27] The siege of Brampton Bryan was called off.[28] On 4th April Waller advanced to Monmouth[29] and in the succeeding days to Chepstow and Usk, the Royalists retreating before him. He failed, however, to find any supporters in Monmouthshire. The Parliamentarian press[30] claimed that certain leading gentry, including Morgan of Tredegar, joined him. Corbet[31] however states only that some gentry promised aid but on Waller's appearance 'did not perform' and Waller's own despatch[32] speaks only of the difficulty of the terrain. In any case, the expedition had to be rapidly called off, because of the appearance of an enemy in its rear.

As ever, Charles had answered a Parliamentarian thrust with a counterstroke. On hearing of the disaster at Highnam he detached yet another section of the field army, comparable to those sent north under Northampton and Rupert at this period. It was given to Rupert's younger brother, Prince Maurice, and he was ordered westward to deal with Waller. He advanced to Tewkesbury, which had been reoccupied by a horse brigade from the field army under Lord Grandison, presumably Maurice's vanguard. There he concerted plans to catch Waller in a pincer of the sort in which Waller himself had caught Herbert's army. On the 9th April he detached a flying column of 80 horse and 100 dragoons and sent it into Monmouthshire under Sir Richard Cave. Cave's mission was to gather the foot left behind by Herbert when he had marched on Gloucester, and close in upon Waller from the west while Maurice did so from the east. Cave managed to add some of Price's regiment to his horse, and reoccupied Monmouth on the 11th. Waller was already in retreat towards Gloucester, aware of his danger, but Maurice and Cave almost caught him between them in Dean. Aided by the terrain, nightfall and his own skill he just succeeded in cutting his way through to Gloucester.[33]

There he attempted to regain the initiative by ordering Massey to storm Tewkesbury. This Massey did, advancing in the middle of the night and surprising the garrison Maurice had left there.[34] Both Waller and Maurice converged upon the town with their main forces and skirmished outside it.[35] At this moment, however, Maurice was recalled to the field army, just as Rupert was from Staffordshire, to enable Charles to face the main Parliamentarian forces. Waller suddenly found himself once again master of the field in the region round Gloucester. He determined to exploit this situation by striking at Hereford.

An excellent record of the situation there has survived in the independent but totally reconcilable accounts left by two of the protagonists, Cave[36] and Coningsby.[37] After Waller's escape to Gloucester, Maurice had made Cave temporary Commander-in-Chief in the area of Herbert's Lieutenant-Generalship, with instructions to unite its remaining Royalist troops into a bulwark against any further Parliamentarian incursions. Cave called a meeting of the commissioners for Herefordshire, Monmouthshire and Glamorganshire at Abergavenny, where they agreed to unite in a formal Association for mutual defence. A muster of the forces of those counties was appointed at Hereford upon 15th April. The most eminent person present at the Abergavenny meeting was Lord Herbert himself, who here re-enters the records. Precisely what the Lieutenant-General had been doing for the past month is a complete mystery. The mere fact that Maurice had needed to appoint the stranger Cave effective commander in Herbert's region indicates that the latter had been either absent or totally ineffectual.

Herbert and Cave went to Hereford together for the muster of the 15th. About 300 soldiers came in, but in general the Royalist troops in the area proved to be demoralised and disintegrating. Even some of those who attended the muster, from Herbert's own regiment, melted away the following day. At Hereford itself the price of Herbert's aggressive strategy now became apparent. Because all the county tax had been delivered to him none had been spent on fortifying the town. His expedition had consumed most of its munitions, arms and garrison. Coningsby had resigned the governorship in ill health and disgust, and Price was acting in his place, though this arrangement had not been officially recognised. At this uniquely unpropitious moment, on 22nd April, Maurice recalled Cave and his horse and extinguished his command, and Waller advanced.

Here, if at all, was the time for Herbert to behave like a leader. His reaction was immediate; he declared that he was going to seek aid at Oxford, told Cave to act in his stead, and vanished despite the appeals of his colleagues. Cave, likewise begged to stay, unwillingly obliged. He became the unofficial adviser of an unofficial governor, with the ex-governor Coningsby still in the town and at odds with Viscount Scudamore and the other local leaders present. Nobody had any legal control over the foot soldiers, who were completely inexperienced and rapidly became disorderly. The citizens refused to stir themselves for the stranger Cave. The Worcestershire Royalists were busy escorting a convoy to Oxford. When Waller arrived on the 25th and blew in a gate with his cannon resistance seemed pointless. Cave's horse marched away to join the King, the foot fled, and all the Royalist leaders formally surrendered, to save the town from a sack.

Almost without effort, Waller had captured not only Herefordshire but the entire local Royalist war machine, personified by Cave, Price, Viscount Scudamore and his heir, Coningsby and his heir, Dr Rogers, Croft and the other active gentry.[38] Of these, Cave and Price showed their mettle almost immediately by escaping to Oxford. The Coningsbys, Croft and the other gentry were imprisoned at Bristol until July, when Rupert stormed the city and released them. The two Scudamores were taken to London, where they gave their parole not to escape and lived quietly till the end of the war. Cave, who had shown more gallantry than anyone else in the episode, reached Oxford only to find himself court-martialled for the loss of Hereford. Coningsby, on his release, was placed under some censure for the same event. Both were exonerated but neither given any prominent position again. Lord Herbert, who deserved more blame than anybody else, was protected by his wealth and importance from official criticism and went on to further honours, as will be described. This injustice combined with the detention of the Scudamores to effect a complete change in the nature of Herefordshire Royalism. None of the original leaders of 1642 returned to the shire except Croft and some of the lesser gentry, and these never occupied a dominant position there again. Waller issued a certificate[39] noting the meek compliance of the Mayor of Hereford with his wishes, and the citizens in general responded tamely to a second Parliamentarian occupation. Three rapid reversals of fortune and the removal of the leadership had completely eradicated the spontaneous Royalism of 1642. Herefordshire, which had been one of the most enthusiastic Royalist counties, was becoming one of the most exhausted.

Waller did not linger there long, as having advanced so far from Gloucester he was vulnerable to a Royalist counterattack of the sort that had nearly trapped him in Monmouthshire. His expedition was a highly successful smash-and-grab raid and his stay at Hereford was devoted to laying his hands upon as much cash as he could extract before he retreated.[40] He likewise issued an oath to be taken by all the inhabitants of the county by which they promised never again to oppose Parliament.[41] Having thereby ensured as much trouble as possible for future Royalist administrations, he retired to Gloucester in early May, carrying with him the money he had collected and the remaining county munitions. On 29th May he attempted to repeat the same trick at Worcester, launching his army upon the city when Russell was absent at Oxford. The Royalists there, however, had been expecting such an attack since April and were much more numerous, united and well-supplied than those at Hereford, as will be illustrated. The assault failed, and Waller retreated to Gloucester.[42]

From there he marched away, almost immediately, to meet a Royalist advance in Somerset. With him went the Tewkesbury garrison and many of the Gloucester soldiers. These, like all of Waller's army, were not to return, for in July the whole force perished at the battle of Roundway Down. Massey, left behind, had the satisfaction of being officially confirmed, at last, as governor of Gloucester, though its citizens 'thought well of a man nearer home'.[43] He must have had the additional satisfaction of contemplating Herbert's command, which only a few months before had seemed so formidable, defeated, exhausted and demoralised.

CHAPTER FIVE
Capel

Arthur, Lord Capel, was born the heir of one of the richest squires in Essex and Hertfordshire. By 1640 he was the foremost man of that latter county, and its leading MP. In 1641 he joined the nascent Royalist party in Parliament, and Charles rewarded him with a peerage.[1]* On the coming of war he became one of the King's foremost supporters and high in his favour, being made one of the Council of War[2] and colonel of a horse regiment.[3] His appointment as Lieutenant-General was public knowledge by 15th March[4] and by 23rd March he was in Shropshire to take up his command.[5] He had been despatched from Oxford with his own horse and sixty barrels of gunpowder, match and bullets to make that command more effective. With him was a veteran soldier, Michael Woodhouse, who had been commissioned as commander of his foot forces but whose specific mission was to raise a new foot regiment to reinforce the field army.[6]

How Capel viewed his command is unknown. Objectively, it appears to have been the most daunting of the three Lieutenant-Generalships. Its area had been drained of many military resources already by Charles's army and further recruitment in the winter. Cheshire already harboured a formidable enemy. Shropshire and Flintshire had shown a disturbing lack of enthusiasm. North-west Wales was notoriously poor; Anglesey had difficulty finding twenty-four men with £4 per annum for jury service, and its richest gentry could only raise £300 each at short notice.[7] Its remoteness tended to produce a localism even more accentuated than elsewhere. One of its few gentry with a wider viewpoint, John Griffith of Llyn,

* Notes for this chapter are on p. 216.

had suggested to the King that certain cannon existing in Caernarvonshire could be more profitably employed elsewhere. His fellow Caernarvonshire commissioners henceforth regarded him as a public enemy and talked of seizing his estates.[8] In such an atmosphere Capel, as a stranger, was at an obvious disadvantage.

Nevertheless, he possessed certain long-term advantages which might prove potent if he were an able leader. As an outsider he at least stood above traditional local quarrels. His command already possessed a team of able local officers, Ottley, Corbet, Lloyd, Bridgeman and Sir Nicholas Byron, who were prepared to give him loyal support. The appearance of two more in north-west Wales provided him with some much-needed collaboration in that area. One of these was John Williams, Archbishop of York, one of the most adroit ecclesiastical politicians of the pre-war era. Always suspect to Charles, he had abandoned his see at the outbreak of war after a disastrous attempt to advance the royal cause in Yorkshire and fled home to his native Caernarvonshire.[9] Once there, however, he set about trying to rebuild his career by making himself indispensable to the Royalist war effort. The other man was Thomas Bulkeley of Baron Hill, the second gentleman of Anglesey. The principal gentleman of the island was Sir Thomas Cheadle, its High Sheriff and keeper of its great fortress, Beaumaris Castle, Bulkeley's traditional enemy. Bulkeley intended to use the war to win sufficient royal favour to topple Cheadle.[10]

Capel's other advantage was that his region contained excellent potential for the manufacture of armaments. In particular the Clee Hills and Coalbrookedale areas of Shropshire produced excellent iron, which was processed at the forges of Bouldon and Leighton.[11] On Capel's arrival Ottley had already begun manufacturing muskets, and one ton of shot and one of grenades were ready at Leighton.[12] Within a month Capel had enough ordnance to present Rupert at Lichfield with three spare cannon and a convoy of shot[13] and in August a warship at Chester was equipped with four new Shropshire guns.[14] In the course of 1643 one Francis Walker cast nearly £1,000 worth of artillery in Shropshire for the field army[15] and doubtless more were made there. Shot, however, was useless without gunpowder, and of this the area was seriously short. Capel's initial convoy was rapidly dispersed to local garrisons, and to Rupert, and he had to deplete Chester's already low supply.[16] Charles ordered powder mills to be established at Chester and Shrewsbury, but these were slow to commence production.[17]

Capel's venture itself made a slow start. In late March he was forced to return to Worcestershire to ensure that the county was well defended against Waller.[18] By 1st April however he was at Shrewsbury, concerting plans with the Shropshire Royalists.[19] To conciliate local opinion he published a proclamation on the 3rd[20] promising to punish plunderers and to pay his troops out of the wealth of local Parliamentarians to ease the burden on the region. The Welsh gentry were ordered to find men for Woodhouse's new regiment, which to conciliate them was publicised as the Prince of Wales's own.[21] To launch any expedition of his own Capel had at first only his horse, the Shropshire militia and Corbet's 100 remaining dragoons,[22] which by the 4th he had combined into 1 400 men.[23] These were forced into action almost immediately by the appeals of the Lancashire Royalists who were besieged by their local enemies in concert with the tireless Brereton. Rupert, now before Lichfield, ordered Capel to aid them.[24] He established an advanced base at Whitchurch and invaded Cheshire, drawing Brereton back. Weeks of confused skirmishing ensued in the broken country between Chester and Nantwich.[25]

By 2nd May he had gathered a large force at Whitchurch, and was replacing the militiamen in it, whom he condemned as 'soldiers of place' unfit for field service,[26] with regulars. These included Wynne's regiment from Denbighshire and a Caernarvonshire company drawn out of the Chester garrison.[27] Capel hoped that these would continue to be supported by their native counties, pointing out to the Welsh that they could protect their homes more effectively by keeping the enemy in the Marches. This was precisely the sort of argument that local men could not comprehend and the money ceased to arrive.[28] Charles tried to assist by granting Capel the rents of his North Welsh estates. The tenants agreed to pay four years' dues in advance, but this money came in slowly.[29] At Shrewsbury Capel did persuade the corporation to vote £500 for his army, £130 for the town defences, which were still ruinous in places, and a regular £120 per month to pay the garrison.[30] When however he asked the town to raise a dragoon troop to add to that garrison, as with Corbet's force, most sponsors defaulted.[31]

The reluctance of the north-west Welsh at least to endorse a policy of self-defence at a distance was not entirely narrow-minded. One of the great strategic failures of the King at the opening of the war had been his inability to secure the Navy. Hence Parliament commanded the seas, and although none of its warships had yet appeared off the coast of North Wales the area was vulnerable to a seaborne attack. Capel himself was aware of the danger, and in May attempted to meet it by arranging the repair of the great medieval castles of Con-way, Beaumaris and Caernarvon.[32] Here Bulkeley and the Arch-bishop seized their chance. The inevitable clash between the former and Cheadle had come, with Cheadle refusing to act with Bulkeley's faction among the commissioners and preparing to denounce them to the King. Williams recommended to Bulkeley that he pre-empt his rival by joining himself in presenting Capel with a quantity of gunpowder. Capel was suitably grateful.[33] The two men became contacts of his and of his officers in their area, and recommended by them. Williams was allowed to repair Conway Castle at his own expense, and his nephew was eventually appointed governor.[34] Bul-keley was first allowed to erect a fort,[35] then created a Viscount for his services[36] and finally given charge of Beaumaris Castle. His rival was for ever eclipsed.

They chose their present well, for in May Capel had desperate need of powder. Brereton had begun to run circles round him. Firstly Capel made a rather half-hearted assault on Nantwich.[37] Bre-reton left the town strongly defended to keep him busy and slipped into Staffordshire. There he contacted a group of local Parliamen-tarians who had by now emerged in the county, reinforced them and encouraged them to attempt Stafford. Comberford was absent, the Royalists were expecting nothing after the past month's relative peace, and the attack was made at 3 a.m. The town fell almost with-out a blow, although the castle held out. A garrison of local Par-liamentarians was installed, and Brereton and the remainder swept on through the county, capturing Royalist convoys.[38] Hastings, who might have counterattacked, was busy in the East Midlands and Bre-reton swiftly returned to keep Capel busy. In June the Coventry Par-liamentarians reduced Tamworth Castle and carried munitions to secure Stafford.[39] Its castle was evacuated by the Royalists in July.[40] Parliament had at last achieved its corridor to Lancashire, though the Royalist one to Newark was not severed while Bagot held Lichfield. Staffordshire had ceased to be a county community. It had become a military crossroads, through which rival convoys were run from one fortress to another.

Back in Cheshire in late May Brereton continued to torment Capel. On the 21st he marched to help the Lancashire Parliamen-tarians finally defeat their opponents. When Capel lumbered after him, he suddenly dodged past Capel's army and destroyed its base at Whitchurch and another recently established at Market Drayton, plundered the homes of local Royalists and returned to Nantwich loaded with captured weapons and money.[41] The episode must have been particularly damaging to Capel's prestige in Shropshire, and a Parliamentarian newspaper[42] claimed that a faction there subsequently petitioned the King to replace him with the local Lord Newport, the same who had bought his peerage in October, though there is no confirmation of this. Capel himself attributed his failures to the quality of his troops, and appealed to Rupert, fruitlessly, for musketeers from the field army.[43] The Parliamentarian press[44] claimed repeatedly that he had been reduced to pressing men to fill up his own army and this does seem to be proved by one of Ottley's papers[45] which complains of disorderly conscripts.

On 12th June Parliament trebled Capel's problems by ratifying two grand commissions.[46] The young Earl of Denbigh was made Commander-in-Chief in Warwickshire, Staffordshire, Worcestershire and Shropshire, and voted £6,000.[47] Sir Thomas Myddleton MP, an Anglicised Welshman with estates in Denbighshire, was made Sergeant-Major-General in North Wales and he and his friends advanced £5,000 to equip an invasion force.[48] If these two cooperated successfully with Brereton, Capel's command would be annihilated. Conscious of this, he spent June attempting a consolidation of his existing territory. Shrewsbury had already been placed in the charge of a committee consisting of Ottley and other local activists plus a professional sailor turned soldier, Sir John Mennes, who had accompanied Capel from Oxford.[49] A country tax of £4,500 per month was at last imposed on Shropshire, though as might be expected only a portion came in.[50] Every Shropshire gentleman was ordered to equip two horsemen and send them to Capel's army by 19th June, or be deprived of Royalist protection against plunderers.[51] He instituted a standing committee at Shrewsbury consisting of one commissioner from each county in his command to improve liaison within it.[52] He sent letters countersigned by the King to the Welsh counties ordering them to settle local taxes to support home guards.[53] He was reported as planting a new garrison in Oswestry, to guard the approaches to Wales.[54] At Chester a citizen regiment had been raised by Alderman Francis Gamull MP, and on 6th June Bridgeman and Mayor Ince called up every able-bodied man.[55]

As always, expensive local defence schemes produced disappointment and acrimony. The Caernarvonshire commissioners declined to join the liaison committee.[56] The Denbighshire gentry refused to impose a local tax, believing the Crown rents and proceeds of Parliamentarian estates sufficient to support the county troops.[57] Those of Flintshire followed suit.[58] The Denbighshire commissioners had indeed sufficient difficulty in calling up their existing militia, for whom they had now made new weapons.[59] Disorderly meetings, their purpose now unknown, had to be suppressed in Anglesey.[60] By late July Capel was complaining that his main enemy was not Parliament but local indifference.[61] He obtained a letter from the King authorising him to punish any gentry who seemed slack in supporting him, and published it.[62] On the 27th he ordered every man in his region to take an oath to oppose Brereton and Myddleton.[63] The High Command expressed concern that Ottley showed more attention to reprinting and dispersing Royalist pamphlets.[64] A fresh purge of secret enemies was instituted. Some victims offered themselves, such as one John Jones at Flint who was pedantic enough to challenge the legal right of the Royalists to impose local taxes. It was only a matter of time before the local commissioners broke down the door of his lodging and dragged him to jail.[65] At least one loyal Royalist, however, found himself confronted with some of Capel's soldiers who informed him that they regarded him as a suspect, took his horses and had to be bribed not to plunder his house.[66] The parishioners of Clungunnis got rid of their parson, who had supported traditional religious customs of which they and Parliament disapproved, by denouncing him as a Parliamentarian.[67]

Capel's new concentration on defence at least spared him further military humiliations. He was able to destroy a party of Brereton's men who raided inland Flintshire in June.[68] Brereton wasted the summer in an abortive attack on Chester and a siege of Eccleshall Castle, though he did reduce Halton Castle, one of the remaining outposts of the Cheshire Royalists.[69] Time however was on his side, for he needed only to await Myddleton and Denbigh. By the end of July Myddleton was in Staffordshire with a small army, seven cannon and forty carts of munitions.[70] Brereton went to meet him. This was Capel's last chance to attempt Nantwich, and he took it. He despatched a hurried and rather vague appeal to the commissioners of north-east Wales and Shropshire for carts, workmen and irregular soldiers, which they tried desperately to oblige.[71] The irregulars, armed with clubs, he expected the gentry to recruit among their tenants, and some did; thus Sir Henry Thynne of Caus Castle brought thirty.[72] By these methods he assembled a large but motley force and on 4th August attacked the town. After his cumbersome preparations it could not but be ready for him, Brereton had left it well defended and Capel's semi-feudal army cannot have been of high quality. Not surprisingly, the assault failed.[73] It was an expensive failure. The cost of the expedition was divided among the various counties, and the share of Denbighshire alone came to £162.[74]

Nevertheless the immediate consequences were undramatic. The Earl of Denbigh was delayed in taking up his command by a charge of disloyalty[75] and he launched no campaign that year. Brereton and Myddleton united on the 10th,[76] but they could not push westward until they had reduced Eccleshall Castle, which guarded the approaches to Shropshire. This they besieged fruitlessly through August until Hastings, in whose command it lay, relieved it. He was however beaten back in the process of revictualling it and left a Danish mercenary as its new governor. The garrison refused to serve a stranger and deserted, leaving the wretched Dane to surrender on the 29th.[77] The siege had nevertheless provided Capel with time for further defensive measures. The Denbighshire gentry at last agreed to a tax, albeit temporary and very localised, to support 224 musketeers to guard the bridges of the river Dee.[78] At Chester Bridgeman now possessed a second experienced soldier,[79] Sir Abraham Shipman, to assist him, and this gentleman ordered the garrisoning of Hawarden Castle to cover the approaches to Flintshire.[80]

The loss of Eccleshall, however, had exposed Shropshire. This was all the more serious because Parliament now sent to join Brereton and Myddleton its Shropshire gentry adherents who had fled to London a year before. One of them, Thomas Mytton, had raised a foot regiment there, and this he brought north in August with his colleagues.[81] On 9th September Brereton, Myddleton and Mytton advanced into Shropshire, and on the 11th they settled Mytton's regiment in the town of Wem, which they all spent the rest of the month fortifying.[82] Capel did not possess the strength to attack them. Woodhouse had at last raised his foot regiment, to a strength of 700, but it was urgently required for the field army, and he led it there.[83] At the battle of Newbury he was knighted for his courage.[84]

At the end of September, however, the King's campaign ended, and he was able to revert to his traditional tactic of balancing an enemy reinforcement with one of his own. Woodhouse's regiment was withdrawn from his army again. Richard Herbert was made governor of Ludlow[85] and his regiment likewise detached. Both were armed and given large supplies of munitions from the Oxford magazine[86] and sent to join Capel. In Worcestershire they seem to have been joined by a former field regiment, Sir John Beaumont's, which had been guarding that county. Capel's dream of a force of field army regulars was now answered. He gathered round them the best of his existing troops, such as Wynne's regiment, to make up a total force of 3 000 by 14th October. He was sufficiently confident then to refuse reinforcements he had previously begged from Hastings.[87]

On the 18th he took the field with all his troops and six cannon. Avoiding the Parliamentarian concentration at Wem he moved up to Whitchurch and from there attacked Nantwich. As usual he was repulsed, and Brereton and Myddleton marched to relieve the town, leaving only Mytton and his 300 foot to hold Wem. Capel fell back to Whitchurch and then suddenly dashed upon Wem. It was a manoeuvre worthy of Brereton himself, and indicative that Capel was learning generalship. Unfortunately it failed. Against all expectation, Mytton's garrison fought so ferociously that they held off the Royalists until Brereton and Myddleton returned. For Capel it was more than a failure, it was a catastrophe. Wynne and Beaumont were killed, the Royalist army fled, battered, back to Shrewsbury. Shropshire, which had been a Royalist stronghold, was now divided territory and the Parliamentarians were left masters of the field.[88]

This victory was precisely what the Parliamentarian leaders had been needing. Myddleton at least had imagined that upon their appearance the local people would throw off the Royalist yoke and flock to their banners. In reality, they had proved as indifferent to Parliament's cause as they had to Capel's. Not a single man had come in from Shropshire to Wem. In Wales Myddleton's own tenants cited Capel's Royalist oath as their reason for refusing to join him. In truth, had men flocked in he could not have paid them. The money with which he had left London was now spent, and the Royalists had already squeezed Shropshire so thoroughly that none could be found around Wem. The only solution seemed to lie in the conquest of more territory, and this was now made possible.[89]

With Capel's defeated army in southern Shropshire, the obvious point to attack seemed north-east Wales. Denbighshire was now defended by some horse under Mark Trevor, a local man but a veteran soldier recently returned from Ireland,[90] and some foot, perhaps the remnants of Wynne's, under Ellis, Aston's commander at Middlewich, who had been freed by an exchange of prisoners. Flintshire had at last raised a home guard, under Roger Mostyn of Mostyn and a Colonel Davies. Both counties, however, were demoralised by the death of Wynne.[91] In early November Brereton collected detachments from his allies in Lancashire and Staffordshire to make up a field army of about 1 500 regulars plus some Cheshire militiamen. He and Myddleton left Mytton to hold Wem, with an outpost at Tong Castle to increase his hold on north-east Shropshire.[92] They then stormed Holt Bridge and crossed the Dee into Denbighshire, Trevor and Ellis fleeing before them. Myddleton was left at Wrexham to recruit, and Brereton went on to occupy all the strongholds of Flintshire. The troops of Mostyn and Davies dissolved and Hawarden Castle, caught unsupplied, surrendered. Chester was thus encircled, and Brereton prepared to besiege it. The Royalists possess-ed no hold in north-east Wales now except Holt Castle, which was already besieged. Their frontier was withdrawn to Denbigh and Conway. At the former William Salusbury of Rug repaired the castle and the Merionethshire Royalists promised 100 musketeers to protect the country at his rear. Conway Castle was strongly fortified now by Archbishop Williams. Behind these strongpoints they hoped to hold the north-west, but this was a barren area compared with that which had been lost. Nor could they do anything to help Chester.[93]

One factor in their predicament was certain: that they expected no help at all from Capel. A Parliamentarian newspaper[94] reported that the citizens of Shrewsbury had clashed with his soldiers after the Wem disaster because he had refused to punish a trooper who had commandeered a horse from a leading citizen. This is substantiated by a blunt remark of Archbishop Williams,[95] that Capel now dared not leave Shrewsbury for fear that the townspeople would destroy the Royalist garrison as soon as he departed. Williams went on[96] to say some hard things in general about him, accusing him of cowar-dice and strategic ineptitude. He had, in fact, by now acquired a military reputation similar to that of the Grand Old Duke of York, and like that gentleman, had an unfortunate propensity for becoming the subject of popular ballads. The best of these runs:

> The Lord Capel with a thousand and a half
> Came to Barton Cross and there they killed a calf
> And staying there till the break of day
> They took their heels and fled fast away.[97]

This sort of jingle is a more potent slur than any formal propaganda. It outlives generations. It was a dramatic sign, if any were needed, of how deep Capel's failure ran.

CHAPTER SIX
Carbery

Of all the regions under study, south-west Wales is the most destitute of Civil War records. Not a single relevant family collection survives, and for information on local Royalism the historian depends entirely upon scanty and ambiguous corporation documents and reports made to the rival High Commands. Thus Richard Vaughan, 2nd Earl of Carbery in the peerage of Ireland, must remain the most shadowy of the three Lieutenant-Generals. He was the greatest resident magnate of the south-west, seated at Golden Grove in Carmarthenshire, and must therefore have played a considerable role in early Royalist activity in that region. Yet so impoverished are the records that his name does not feature in connection with the Civil War until 10 January 1643, when a regiment raised by him appeared at Oxford with Hertford.[1]* Even then he does not appear to have accompanied his soldiers in person, because his brother, Henry Vaughan, was given a knighthood upon the regiment's arrival,[2] presumably for leading it to the King. Thereafter it was certainly designated 'Vaughan's'.

Royalist interest in Carbery's region seems to have quickened in late March at about the time of his actual appointment as Lieutenant-General. On the 24th Charles knighted two Cardiganshire gentry at Oxford,[3] Walter Lloyd and Francis Lloyd MP, and on 1st April he expelled five Pembrokeshire gentry from the county bench,[4] replacing them with Carbery and other Royalists. Identical instructions[5] were issued to the commissioners of the Earl's area to those issued to Herbert's, ordering them to provide him with money for a local army. The only extant local source for this period, the

* Notes for this chapter are on p. 219

Haverfordwest Mayor's Accounts,[6] seems to show a corresponding activity in the area itself, for on the 29th March Carbery sent the town corporation a letter. Its import is unknown, but some weeks after the Earl himself visited the town and was entertained. The corporation subsequently wrote a loyal letter to him at his base at Carmarthen. A little time later, on 6th June, the local Parliamentarian gentry visited the town and were accorded an equal welcome.

Scanty as this information is, it does suggest strikingly that in south-west Wales, a year after the formal outbreak of war, civil war had still not been properly achieved. The area contained both Royalists and Parliamentarians, who were aware of each other's existence but preferred not to acknowledge the reality of conflict. Even more strikingly, the rival High Commands were certainly aware of this situation but did nothing about it. Charles, as said, knew the names of his opponents in Pembrokeshire. Parliament received a petition for aid from these men in May, and gave orders in principle for an expeditionary force to be sent to the county.[7] In practice, however, neither party sent any troops there, nor urged its local supporters to greater efforts. It appears that at this stage of the war they were both too busy with more considerable strategic objectives to be much concerned with what was, or rather was not, happening at the far end of Wales.

This situation began to alter as the summer wore on. Firstly Lord Herbert and his commanders in south-east Wales took to blaming the presence of Parliamentarians in Pembrokeshire for the laxity of the war effort in their own region.[8] But more fundamentally, the entire strategic situation was altering. Despite their mutual efforts of the previous winter King and Parliament were proving too evenly balanced for yet another year for either to defeat the other. Thus each began, as in the previous autumn, to make an effort to recruit new strength for the next year. This time each went beyond the English provinces. Parliament signed a treaty with the Scots, who had their own quarrel with Charles, to obtain an army from them. Charles in turn took steps to withdraw to England the army he had sent to quell the Irish rebellion in 1641. His deputy in Ireland, the Marquis of Ormonde, was instructed to arrange an armistice with the rebels, which he achieved in September 1643. The troops sent in 1641 could now be shipped back across the Irish Sea. This operation made that sea, and the harbours facing it, of great importance. Pembrokeshire projected into its centre, and whoever controlled this county was suddenly in a position to influence the entire course of the war.

Lord Herbert seems to have commenced moves for an offensive

there in July, when he suggested to Rupert[9] that an easy way to win
the area would be to break Parliament's control of the sea itself, upon
which its supporters in Pembrokeshire depended for relief. The
Prince's capture of Bristol had given the Royalists a small fleet, and
Herbert proposed that this be used for the purpose. Some of it was,
for in August Parliament published a letter[10] from the captain of one
of its warships, reporting that he had called at Milford Haven on the
7th to find two Bristol ships moored there under a newly-appointed
Royalist admiral, Barnabas Burley. These had just arrived and were
in the process of calling upon the local gentry to join them. The
Parliamentarian took them by surprise, captured Burley and his
ships, and instructed the gentry to remain loyal to Parliament. The
incident is substantiated by the accounts of that universal alehouse,
Haverfordwest corporation,[11] which entertained some refugees from
one of Burley's ships. Parliament's reaction was to order[12] that a
squadron of its ships should henceforth call regularly at the Haven.

The only hope now for a Royalist occupation of the area lay in an
overland attack, and here Carbery was at last called upon to fulfil his
role as Lieutenant-General. In many ways it was not an easy role.
His area was notably lacking in military resources, possessing no
iron and little money. In the 1570s the average subsidy money paid
by a gentleman in Surrey had been 25s., and in Rutland 40s. In Carmarthenshire it had been 14s. and in Cardiganshire 9s.[13] On the
other hand, if the example of Haverfordwest were general, the very
indifference of the area to the war might work to Carbery's advantage, for its communities might prefer to submit to his authority
rather than endure bloodshed. This possibility the Earl set out to
exploit, and in the first six months of his campaign secured most of
his objectives by an expenditure of ink rather than blood.

This process commenced on 18th August when he summoned the
Pembrokeshire gentry to Carmarthen, and persuaded twenty-four of
them to sign a declaration[14] recognising his authority and promising
him to help secure Pembroke and Tenby and to raise £2,000 to pay
his forces. Their only caveat was that he appoint as governors of
the two towns men acceptable to the local community. Within two
weeks Tenby was Royalist. On the 30th its Mayor and thirty-one
leading citizens signed a second declaration[15] promising to obey
Carbery and refuse to assist Parliament. The Parliamentarians were
later to attribute[16] this capitulation to the machinations of a local
gentleman, Roger Lort of Stackpool Court. He was said to have
been Hertford's Treasurer in the winter and to have led the Pembrokeshire gentry who joined Carbery. He was credited at this junc-

ture with performing the role of Ottley at Shrewsbury, of working upon the Mayor of Tenby until that individual had decided to receive the Royalists.

Haverfordwest, as anticipated, presented even less difficulty. On 3rd September its corporation wrote to the Royalists at Tenby informing them that all known Parliamentarians had withdrawn to Pembroke. On the 4th they received a letter from Carbery, on the 5th the Mayor attended him at Tenby and a few days later the Earl entered Haverfordwest, to a great welcome. He was accompanied by a foot company under a captain Butler, perhaps a member of the local gentry family of that name. This remained to garrison the town, and a levy of £100 was ordered from the citizens. On 3rd October the newly-knighted Sir Francis Lloyd arrived from Oxford, received the money ordered for the garrison and set about repairing the fortifications.[17]

This left only Pembroke, by now regarded as the main Parliamentarian centre, and here the evidence becomes problematical. It hinges upon three bulletins in the official Royalist newspaper, *Mercurius Aulicus*. The first,[18] dated 24th October, is a reprint of yet another declaration, drawn up by Carbery and signed by all the principal Pembrokeshire gentry, promising to victual neither Parliamentarian ships nor the town of Pembroke. Appended was a report that the corporation of Pembroke, on receiving this missive, had promised Carbery to keep their town for the King and give no aid to Parliament. The second[19] is the newspaper's New Year's Eve roll-call of the year's Royalist conquests, which includes Pembroke. The third[20] is a report that Pembroke had reneged on its promise, so that on 11 January 1644 Carbery commenced measures to besiege it.

By themselves, these reports tell a coherent story, but it is one that has never been included in a history of the war. The reason for this is that they have never recovered from their condemnation by J.R. Phillips, author of the classic work on the war in Wales. Phillips treated them with suspicion as they appear in a partisan source, which is perfectly correct, but as such he rejected them out of hand, which is not. His objection to the declaration was that it contains the names of former Parliamentarians, and to the other two items that since Pembroke remained Parliamentarian it could never have passed through a stage of being Royalist. In fact, a good case can be made for accepting their evidence as genuine.

Firstly, there is the sequence of military events. From August to October Carbery had conducted an intensive, if bloodless, campaign to secure the strongholds of Pembrokeshire. They had been secured, in succession, and Pembroke was the logical culmination of the campaign. The declaration reprinted by *Mercurius Aulicus* would be a stratagem typical of Carbery, and appears at precisely the time one would expect it. The same newspaper had earlier accurately reported the capitulation of Tenby and Haverfordwest, events corroborated by independent evidence. Furthermore, on 17th November Charles appointed[21] Carbery governor of Milford Haven, the great inlet dominated by Pembroke. As the King did not appoint men governors of fortresses yet unconquered, he must have believed the Haven to have been Royalist, and as he only accepted official reports of conquests, he must have been informed of its submission by Carbery himself. There is evidence[22] that Carbery was at Oxford in this period, and he would hardly have left his command if his work had been uncompleted. On 25th October he had been promoted to an English peerage, and this reward likewise would suggest a total success.[23] Further, if he had not believed that Pembroke was Royalist, it would be difficult to explain his inactivity between October and January.

What precisely, then, could have happened in Pembroke? The answer seems to lie in the changing nature of the local Parliamentarian leadership. The gentry who had signed the original plea to Parliament in November 1642[24] were Sir Richard Philips of Picton Castle, Wogan of Whiston and an individual signing himself simply 'Owen', who was probably the single most important local gentleman, Sir Hugh Owen MP. By 1643 both High Commands identified the Parliamentarian leaders as Owen and Griffith White. Of these, Philips, Owen and White appear among the signatories of the declaration against Pembroke. Owen certainly later joined the King at Oxford.[25] None of them feature again as Parliamentarian leaders. Instead, in January 1644, the entire local resistance to the Royalists becomes personified in one man, John Poyer. He was a very distinguished citizen of Pembroke, Mayor the previous year and captain of the town militia for sixteen years,[26] but his name does not so far feature in the war. From 1644 onwards, however, his name is synonymous with the Parliamentarian cause in Pembrokeshire, although as his correspondence in the Bodleian's Tanner Manuscripts makes clear he had many enemies within his own party, and his own town. In 1648, when he was on trial for his life, some of these enemies published an indictment[27] of his career. This stated that Poyer had originally achieved dictatorial power in Pembroke by quarrelling with the reigning Mayor, gathering a mob and seizing the castle. A.L. Leach, in his standard history of the war in Pembrokeshire, attributes this incident to 1642, but the statement itself gives no date, and if Leach's solution is correct, then it is odd that Poyer goes unmentioned until 1644.

All this evidence suggests a particular sequence of events: that in October 1643 Pembroke, like the two other towns, succumbed to the pressure of Carbery's diplomatic campaign and repudiated Parliamentarianism. This action was carried out, as at Haverfordwest and Tenby, by the corporation led by its Mayor. At Pembroke, however, one extraordinarily powerful and politically conscious personality, Poyer, overthrew this decision upon his own initiative. In doing so, he brought about, at last, the true opening of civil war in south-west Wales.

It opened, as said, on 11th January, with a gesture typical of Carbery, yet another declaration signed by local gentry, this time from the whole area. It was produced at Carmarthen, and authorised the Lieutenant-General to employ the militia of all three counties in reducing Pembroke and to assess their gentry for horse to the same purpose. Carbery's succeeding actions, and their result, are portrayed only in the reports of his Parliamentarian enemies[28] but these are detailed and corroborated by subsequent events. To reduce the town he possessed the militia and whatever regulars he might raise, plus cannon and munitions from Bristol and the services of an engineer and of his brother Henry, both detached from the field army. The £2,000 he had requested had been raised, and collected by Lort,[29] and he had received a further £400 from the Treasury at Oxford.[30] A local tax of £4,000 was now agreed by his counties to support his army in the future.[31] The tactics by which he employed these resources were ones of attrition. Rather than risk a direct assault upon Pembroke, he put his troops into Haverfordwest, Tenby and every castle and mansion around his objective, and into a new fort constructed upon the opposite side of Milford Haven. By this blockade he hoped to starve out Poyer.

At this moment, on 23rd January, the long-awaited Parliamentarian naval squadron sailed into the Haven – six warships under Captain Swanley. Swanley considered the situation and offered to evacuate Poyer. His offer was refused. Poyer had found a soldier, Rowland Laugharne, a local man and a Parliamentarian who had once served abroad under the Earl of Essex, now Parliament's Commander-in-Chief.[32] Even with 200 armed seamen borrowed from Swanley, Laugharne had only 300 soldiers, but he was determined to take the offensive. Numerically, the Royalists outnumbered him, but he possessed the classic advantage of interior communications and could pick off the encircling garrisons one by one. This is precisely what occurred. He began with the nearest Royalist mansions and proceeded on 22nd February to cut off and storm the fort across the Haven. The shock of this was so great that Carbery's principal officers evacuated Haverfordwest, retreating to Carmarthen. Laugharne was able to clear the remaining enemy garrisons from the Haven, and on 6th March he attacked Tenby. His troops assaulted by land while Swanley's ships attacked from the sea, and between them the town was stormed. The last of Carbery's garrisons in Pembrokeshire now surrendered, and Laugharne tendered to the inhabitants of the county an oath to serve Parliament.

A Cardiganshire Royalist, John Vaughan of Trawscoed, drew the appropriate conclusion,[33] that the disaster had resulted from Carbery's tactics of attrition. His dispersal of troops to garrisons had left no mobile field force to relieve those garrisons if the besieged took the offensive, because he had discounted the possibility of their being reinforced from the sea. Unfortunately, the results of that miscalculation were still in operation.[34] All Carbery's regular soldiers had been disarmed, leaving him with no forces with which to wage war. The local people were too impressed by his defeat to lend him further aid. Not merely Pembrokeshire but his whole command was open to his enemies. His reaction was that of Bridgeman in December 1642: to offer a local peace treaty. The time for such local initiatives, however, was over, and the offer was rejected. Carbery himself was recalled to Oxford and accused of misconduct. He was exonerated[35] but never took up his command again. His officers, including Sir Henry Vaughan and Lloyd, returned to Oxford with him. The ambitious Lort defected to Parliament.[36]

In April Laugharne prepared to conquer all south-west Wales. He offered a formal alliance to the gentry of Carmarthenshire and Cardiganshire, which they refused. On the 11th he mustered the Pembrokeshire militia outside Haverfordwest, only to learn that it refused to do more than defend its own county. This failure left him only with his regular force, by now recruited to nearly 800 foot and 140 horse, many of them formerly Carbery's soldiers. Small as it was, his opponents were even weaker. The Mayor of Carmarthen had 100 foot to hold his town, and Vaughan of Trawscoed was trying to fashion the remaining Cardiganshire militia into a garrison for Cardigan. Their main hope lay in Herbert Price, who had wintered at his native Brecon with his regiment, 400 strong, and 150 horse. Price came to Carmarthen, full of hopes of a general Royalist counter-offensive against Laugharne. He found, however, that the local gentry were too demoralised by Laugharne's victories to aid him. He may well have been reminded of the situation at Hereford a year before, and when Laugharne's superior forces advanced upon Carmarthen he withdrew. The town, and county, fell to Laugharne. Soon Cardigan followed.[37]

A few months before, Carbery, alone of the three Lieutenant-Generals, had seemed to have achieved a total success, and redeemed the King's choice of these grandees as his local commanders. Now his military career, like theirs, had culminated in disaster. Although the most delayed of the three failures, it was the most absolute, for he had lost not merely an army, or a county, but the entire area committed to his care.

CHAPTER SEVEN
Russell

Although Worcestershire was nominally included in Capel's command, there are good reasons for treating its fortunes in this period, and those of its leading Royalist Sir William Russell, as a separate study. Firstly, as shown, Capel barely concerned himself with the county, being preoccupied with North Wales and its March. Secondly, the Civil War material for Worcestershire is unusually rich, and as such deserves a treatment in depth. Thirdly, the Worcestershire Royalists occupied a position of peculiar responsibility and difficulty, for their county was the vital centrepiece of the Cavalier Corridor between Oxford and Wales. Up it travelled the regiments marching to assist beleaguered Royalists in the northern Marches. Down it passed the recruits to fill up the field army and the armaments from the Shropshire furnaces to equip it. It was moreover an industrial area in itself. There were notable ironworks around Dudley and Stourbridge,[1]* especially at the latter where the Foley family were founding a celebrated industrial fortune. Their works were reported[2] to have been employed in casting bullets for the Royalists as early as August 1642, and they accepted subsequent commissions. Brereton captured some Foley cannonballs bound for Lichfield in 1643[3] and a hundred were ordered by the King for Sudeley Castle in 1644.[4] Between them the Worcestershire and Shropshire forges produced tons of pig-iron, pike-heads, cannonballs and grenades, and many cannon, which were carried from Worcester to supply the field army at Oxford. From February to June 1643 alone five such convoys made the journey.[5] Russell spent £1,074 upon the manufacture and transport of armaments in the course of his governorship.[6]

* Notes for this chapter are on p. 220.

Fourthly, the nature of the Worcestershire material poses a particular, and vital, historical question. By far the most important Worcestershire source is the so-called 'Diary' of Henry Townshend of Elmley Lovett,[7] a mixture of transcripts of documents and personal notes left by one Royalist commissioner. The notes are mainly in the form of a journal of current affairs, sometimes national and sometimes local, recorded without overt comment. There is, however, one exceptional outburst, occurring in the papers from the very end of the war. It is Townshend's verdict upon that war, and his own part in it:

And those not only in the first commission but also in this last hath continued very sedulous to preserve their county from tyranny and oppression of the soldier. Though all in vain. The powers of punishment lying in the Governor as Commander-In-Chief, and the commissioners being only as councillors and subordinates, few barbarousness, plunderings, nay high insolencies against the commissioners themselves punished...all those which generally lie under the obedience of the Parliament, the soldiers are regulated, punished by their Committees. The country people live in quietness and safety, paying their contribution and taxes, which is to them beyond all other considerations.[8]

This may be paraphrased as follows: the local Royalist war effort depended upon the civilian commissioners, drawn from the local gentry. Effective power was however increasingly concentrated in the hands of the military commanders and their troops, whose excesses alienated the support of the local community, thereby cutting off support for the Royalist war effort at its roots and rotting it from the inside. It is tempting for the historian to extend this picture, and suggest that it may represent a convincing explanation for the failure of the whole Royalist cause, and the outcome of the Civil War. Not surprisingly, this explanation has been put forward, particularly in one recent thesis,[9] which relies heavily upon Townshend.

In many ways, the whole of the present work is intended to test such a view of the war. Because of the peculiar importance of Townshend in propagating such a view, however, I propose to investigate his particular assertions in detail in this section, by investigating Worcestershire itself in the period in which the commissioners, including Townshend, enjoyed their greatest local power.

Russell was the man upon whom the responsibilities of Worcestershire's position lay most heavily. He occupies a fitting place in the age of the three grandees, for like them he was a man without military experience, given great powers by virtue of his permanent standing within the community. As governor of Worcester he was responsible for the defence of the shire, and as High Sheriff he was responsible for its expenses, for he received the local tax. Those expenses were considerable. Apart from the armament convoys he had to pay for the recruitment and maintenance of Hamilton's horse, in which his own troop alone cost £52 per week, and for a dragoon regiment.[10] Huge sums were also paid to support Royalist regiments passing through the county, £100 to Owen's in December, £200 to Maurice in April.[11] Russell met all these expenses, and others, but very few of them from the new local tax. Some money was gained from that collected, but not delivered, for pre-war taxation interrupted by the war,[12] but the bulk of it represented *ad hoc* donations from Royalist sympathisers.[13] This was a wasting asset, and unless the regular tax were soon collected in full, expenditure would soon exceed income.

This became the principal preoccupation of the Committee 'for the guarding the county' which Charles commissioned in March,[14] and on which Russell collaborated closely with his fellow commissioners, including Townshend. The local tax was found to be hampered firstly by particularist sentiments even within the county unit. Thus Russell had to refuse a petition from Worcester to pay for its own expenses and contract out of the general tax, although he attempted to conciliate the city by permitting it to raise its share in the manner of a municipal levy.[15] Secondly, there were the inevitable disputes concerning alleged inequalities in the assessment of the tax.[16] But the most serious problem was that the bulk of the tax was simply not being paid, and the summoning of individual defaulters did little to remedy this problem.[17] Charles, in the proclamation accompanying the constitution of the new committees, had granted the commissioners emergency powers to ask the governors of Hereford and Worcester to send soldiers to demand arrears. On 30th March they enacted these, and directed Russell to sent out his horse, the officers to be responsible for the collection of the money.[18] In doing so they signed the death warrant of their own, civilian, control of the war effort. Charles's hopes of an administration acting in co-operation with the community had been stillborn. The civilians had proved themselves incapable from the beginning of ruling without the assistance of the sword.

The need for money became greater in the course of the summer, when the High Command began to manipulate the county's manpower resources in such a way as to place a greater strain upon it. Hamilton's horse and dragoon regiments, now complete, and a foot regiment he had also raised in the shire, were ordered into the field army.[19] To compensate, Russell was commissioned to raise completely fresh regiments of horse and foot in his own name, which he did by August although not to the strength of Hamilton's.[20] By this time Sandys had also raised his horse and foot regiments, to full strength, and a few dragoons. How all these were recruited or fitted into the payment system is not known. The Sandys family fortune played a part, and the captains of the three regiments included Sandys's uncles John and William and his nephew Thomas.[21] His brother Martin commanded yet another regiment, raised out of the Worcester citizens to defend the city, although this was obviously a part-time force as its members were only half exempt from paying tax, and regulars were wholly.[22] Russell's regiments were regarded as a permanent defence for the county, but Sandys's were frequently deployed with the field army. In addition to all these soldiers, a field army regiment under Sir John Beaumont, the same who was to fall at Wem, was ordered into the county in April to reinforce it against Waller,[23] and remained there.

Paying these men and fitting the various units into pay arrangements would have been difficult work even if the local tax had been regularly paid and administration orderly. As it happened, the former was in arrears[24] and the latter disrupted by Waller's presence at Gloucester, which kept the Worcestershire Royalists in a state of emergency for two months.[25] His attack when it came revealed grave weakness in the fortifications of Worcester[26] and an expensive programme of fortification had to be commenced to which the whole county contributed labour and money.[27] Under these conditions the soldiers' pay must have been chaotic, and it is not surprising to find the King writing an angry letter to the commissioners – his first – on 15th June,[28] noting that the Worcestershire troops were unpaid and disorderly.

The events of late summer could not have improved the situation. As will be more fully described below, the King launched a major attack on Gloucester in August, using the entire field army and several local detachments, including Russell's and Sandys's regiments.[29] When the Parliamentarians achieved their famous relief of the city in September this huge composite army, numbering up to 20,000 men, retreated into Worcestershire for over a week, waiting to pounce on the relieving force as it re-emerged. The county had to find tons of bread and cheese to feed it,[30] and apparently failed because the hungry troops took to sheep-stealing.[31] Local commerce was completely disrupted. To pay the army Charles asked for a loan of £7,000 from Worcester and its county, raised by extra taxation. The commissioners replied that under prevailing conditions they dared not impose such taxation on the county.[32] The city corporation offered to try to raise £2,000 and did try,[33] but could not find the money, an unfortunate sequence of events as the High Command had a long memory for promises.[34]

Charles's patience with the Worcestershire Royalists, wearing thin in June, could not have been improved by this experience. One more straw was needed to break it, and in October the commissioners provided that. They quarrelled amongst themselves. The dispute is rather mysterious. It took the form of an attack upon Russell by Sandys and Sir Ralph Clare of Kidderminster.[35] The charges themselves are not enlightening, as they are very wild and comprise every public vice a man can possess, from trivial misdemeanours to capital offences. There is no evidence to show how the commissioners as a whole divided. It was not a straightforward clash between the civilian and military arms, as Sandys and Russell were rival colonels. Sandys complained that Russell paid his own regiments but not Sandys's,[36] while Sandys's men refused to recognise Russell's authority.[37] Resentment of Russell had been certainly brewing among the commissioners as early as March, when they had commented adversely[38] upon the new importance to which he, who had been their equal, had been raised by his twin posts of High Sheriff and governor. Perhaps the clash represented pre-war rivalries. Russell had been an enemy of Sandys's distant cousin Sandys of Fladbury.[39] Russell came from south Worcestershire and his opponents from the north, and there was, and remains, a traditional rivalry between the two regions. But the documents of the incident themselves suggest that the terrible administrative problems of the year, and the pressure of royal displeasure, had simply been too much for the amity and understanding between the local leaders. Russell, being the most isolated of them by his position, had suffered worst.

As a result of the dispute the High Command agreed to an inquiry into Russell's accounts. What they thought of the resulting report[40] is not recorded. To a modern scholar its most striking features are the emphasis upon 'the great arrears' on the local tax, the huge amount of this tax, probably the bulk, that was collected by Russell's soldiers and the large quantity of this that was immediately used by them for their own support, without coming into account. The Royalist troops in Worcestershire had been living virtually sword to mouth. The whole document, though it occurs among Townshend's papers, is an indictment of his view of the war. It proves, together with the sources cited earlier, that there never was an ideal period when beneath the rule of their commissioners 'the country people' of Worcestershire lived 'in quietness and safety, paying their contribution and taxes', for the military to destroy. The taxes never were properly paid, because the people would not pay them. The soldiers always took a large proportion of their money by force, because the commissioners themselves told them to do so. If the troops were insolent to the commissioners, it was because they had no reason to be grateful to them.

The affair ruined Russell. The charges against him were dismissed, and he kept his regiments and his place among the commissioners, but the King clearly felt that under the circumstances his continuation as governor was impossible. His brief period of prominence was over, and he faded into the background of the local war.

Conclusions

In Wales and the Marches, the rule of the three Royalist Lieutenant-Generals had proved a direct contradiction of Charles's expectations. Their armies had been defeated, and the communities in their care left demoralised, divided and hostile to the war. Left to their own devices, as in Worcestershire, the lesser local leaders had proved an equal disappointment. This failure becomes more significant when a brief summary is made of the fortunes of the other grandee generals.

In Lancashire the Earl of Derby met with a disaster as complete as any in Wales. His army was broken, he quarrelled with his subordinates, and by June 1643 the whole county, save one garrison, was lost to the enemy.[1]* Hertford's fortunes at first sight seem to present a complete contrast. In May 1643 the troops sent with him from Oxford linked up with the Cornish army, in June they conquered Somerset and part of Wiltshire and in July they joined more units of the royal army in wiping out the Parliamentarian western forces under Waller at Roundway Down and storming Bristol. However, Hertford himself played little part in these victories. His army was led in practice by his subordinates Hopton and Prince Maurice,[2] he was not present at Roundway Down and he failed to attend the Council of War which planned the storm of Bristol.[3] Nor did he even make a prepossessing figurehead, as by the time that Bristol fell he was disliked both by his soldiers and by the local gentry.[4] He adhered to the principal already observed in the Marches, of entrusting Royalist territory to the care of prominent local gentry, but this policy also proved defective. The commissioners of Cornwall soon quarrelled as bitterly as those of Worcestershire, and the High

* Notes for this chapter are on p. 220.

Sheriff, like Russell, had to face an enquiry into his accounts.[5] Likewise in Devon and Somerset the local gentry responded sluggishly to the appeals of their Royalist neighbours.[6]

The Earl of Newcastle, out of the six grandees, was the only one to achieve a genuine personal success. On 30th June he broke his local opponents on Adwalton Moor, and went on in the remainder of 1643 to conquer most of Yorkshire, Nottinghamshire, Lincolnshire and Derbyshire. Nevertheless, even his achievement has been considered flawed. It was noted, then and ever since, that he faced opponents considerably weaker in numbers and resources than himself, that it is a tribute to the skill of those opponents that they postponed defeat as long as they did, and that the excessive caution with which Newcastle followed up his victories may have cost the King his chances of an outright victory in 1643. In general he has been accused of the same lack of energy and dilettante attitude to war which was so apparent in colleagues of his such as Hertford and Herbert.[7]

In general, Charles's principles in appointing generals for their social position rather than their skill and dynamism had proved faulty. The potential disadvantage of such leaders in the field had appeared outweighed by their potential advantage in reconciling local people to a war effort. The disadvantage had, in the event, been fatally real, the advantage illusory. The grandees had proved a false solution to the central problem of how the war could and could not be fought. It is with the precise nature of this problem that the next section of this work will be concerned.

PART THREE
The Royalist war effort

CHAPTER EIGHT
The machinery

A **proper** history of local Royalist administration will never be written, because the documents upon which to base it have not survived. In contrast with the hundreds of leaves of Parliamentarian committee papers preserved in the Public Record Office and elsewhere I can discover only three items to illustrate the machinery by which the Royalist war effort was carried on. One is the Docquet Book of the Clerks Of The Chancery,[1*] containing a list of the various kinds of committee set up and the dates of their creation, although not the names of all their members. The second consists of a series of minutes kept of meetings of the Worcestershire Committee 'for the guarding the county' in March and April 1643,[2] containing the names of those present, the business discussed and the decisions made. The last is the Order Book of the Glamorganshire Committee 'for the guarding the county',[3] comprising the instructions issued by that body between July 1643 and November 1644. It is proposed here to combine these sources with all the incidental evidence in other Royalist documents to produce at least a summary of the existing knowledge upon the subject, a skeletal portrait which may be revised if further evidence materialises or that surviving is better interpreted.

The basic instrument of all local Royalist administration was the Commission of Array, which merely empowered the recipients to raise the armed men of their county for the King and imprison his opponents. In effect however it created a wartime administration, for it defined a set of men whom the King could entrust with tasks concerning the war effort as they arose. Commissions of Array continued

* Notes for this chapter are on p. 221.

to be reissued for the north Welsh counties until April 1644.[4] In the West Country, north and south-west Wales, Cheshire and Shropshire they seem never to have been superseded and, under the more cumbersome title of 'Commissioners of Array and of the Peace', the men named in them remained the rulers of their counties throughout the war by authority of the Commission, carrying out specific tasks upon an *ad hoc* basis, according to specific orders. They were obliged to require a quorum of three at their meetings, but not to meet within any fixed period nor to keep a record of the business transacted.

Elsewhere the Commissions of Array were replaced by a more precise instrument. In early March 1643, as said,[5] the Royalist leaders in Worcestershire and Gloucestershire were reconstituted by new commissions[6] as committees 'for the guarding the county'. These were distinguished from the old Commissions of Array by a new set of instructions as to administrative procedures with which they were associated,[7] by their higher quorum of five and by the direction that the commissioners should meet at least weekly and in a fixed place. In March such a committee was also set up in Wiltshire, to strengthen the Royalists' shaky hold on that county,[8] and in April one was set up in Oxfordshire, the royal base.[9] In June the new type of committee was commissioned in Herefordshire and the other counties of Lord Herbert's command, as part of an attempt to strengthen it after the disasters of the spring.[10] This last group of committees was associated with a further formalisation, that the commissioners keep a written record of their transactions.

In view of the less nebulous nature of the committees 'for the guarding the county', it seems no coincidence that they, rather than the Commissioners of Array, have left the only records of actual transactions. Both these seem to indicate that the new committees were active and important bodies. That of Worcestershire sat twice as often as required, with never less than eight commissioners present. Russell, Clare and Sir Rowland Berkley of Cotheridge, who represented some of the oldest and wealthier members, were the only regular attenders and in all some fourteen gentry took part, so that a large proportion of local Royalist leaders were actively involved. It is possible that after the initial period of its existence, which its minutes represent, the interest of its members waned, but a letter of August 1644[11] was signed by nine of them in their official capacity. The Order Book of the Glamorganshire committee shows that it met almost daily in the summers of 1643 and 1644, though less frequently in the intervening winter.

By contrast, in North Wales, the Commissioners of Array had occasional difficulty in finding a quorum,[12] but this was partly a consequence of the sub-division which primitive communications forced upon them. Thus in Denbighshire five commissioners met at Denbigh and four at Ruthin, while a tenth, who lived between these places, attended both gatherings.[13] In Anglesey likewise four met at Beaumaris and two at Newborough, a situation which sometimes produced problems such as the occasion in April 1643 when an invitation from one set to the other for a general conference arrived after the date intended for the meeting itself.[14] Even in more advanced areas some form of regional delegation of tasks was necessary. The Glamorganshire committee 'for the guarding the county' sat at Cardiff, and had to entrust all matters concerning the Swansea area to three 'western gentry'. Its sibling at Worcester broke into subcommittees to enable its members to decide disputes concerning the monthly tax arising in their respective native districts.

This last comment indicates the main purpose of all these committees. Though the task of the Commissioners of Array was to 'secure' their counties and that of the later committees was to 'guard' them, both became in essence financial bodies. They had direct control of the militia but the realities of warfare meant that the defence of the county would come to depend on regular soldiers, over whom the commissioners as a body would exert power indirectly, through their function as the troops' paymasters. This role is made clear in the instructions issued by the King to the committees 'for the guarding the county', which are almost entirely concerned with financial duties.

The greatest of these was to confer with local garrison commanders to ascertain how much money their soldiers needed and then to supply it out of the county tax. A set of Townshend's papers[15] illustrates the process by which this tax was, officially, levied in Worcestershire, and the more incidental evidence from elsewhere indicates that the Worcestershire procedure was general for the region. A meeting of gentry initially agreed that a local tax would be levied. The Clerk of the Peace thereupon wrote to the various High Constables of the county to notify them of the fact. They in turn wrote to the village constables, informing them of the sum due from each village. These men then called upon the most respected villagers to assess themselves and their neighbours to determine how that sum would be shared out among the inhabitants. The proceeds were to be delivered by the assessors to the constable, who would hand them over upon a fixed day to his High Constable at Worcester. Each High Constable gave them to the Receiver, who gave them finally to the High Sheriff, a Royalist commissioner. The commissioners in time compiled a register of the tax owed by each settlement.[16] Villagers who felt themselves unfairly assessed were instructed to pay the sum demanded for two months and then sue the commissioners for redress.[17] Such complaints became a major problem of the Commissioners of Array or Safety in Worcestershire,[18] Glamorganshire[19] and Monmouthshire[20] and were probably so everywhere.

The second duty specified in the royal instructions was to call the wealthier local men together and appeal to them for voluntary donations, which were then to be forwarded to the King at Oxford as local expenses ought to be met from the tax. This was the means by which the royal army had been paid in the autumn, and for the first year of the war it continued a very effective source of money. Russell's accounts[21] showed such donations to have represented by far his largest single means of income. They also powerfully suggest that little of this money could have been sent to Oxford, as his other sources of income had yielded so little that without it he could not have hoped to have met his expenditure.

The third important duty given to the new committees concerned what was officially only a potential source of income; they were expected to make a list of local Parliamentarians, with the value of their estates, and to await further instructions upon the matter. The coy tone of this direction indicates the marked reluctance which the King displayed to order a general seizure of his opponents' estates, presumably as this would represent an assault upon private property. His local supporters had no such qualms concerning such an obvious check upon their opponents' resources. In December 1642 the Cornish Royalists distrained the local rents of the Parliamentarian Earl of Salisbury,[22] and in the following month their Herefordshire colleagues distrained Lady Harley's rents[23] while Ellis seized Myddleton's family castle at Chirk.[24] Such practices first became officially recognised by both sides in Cheshire. In early February the Royalists there were reputed to be seizing the estates of those who refused their oath.[25] Parliament riposted by granting its supporters in Cheshire and Lancashire the right to 'sequester' Royalist estates, meaning to divert their proceeds into Parliamentarian funds.[26] By 8th March Charles had given the Cheshire Royalists an equivalent power.[27] Within a month seizure of Parliamentarian property was sufficiently common all over the northern Marches for Capel to order it to cease without his personal command. He did however sanction sequestration in principle by promising that he would pay his troops from the proceeds.[28] In July the Glamorganshire committee 'for the guarding the county' issued an order[29] for the seizure of the estates of all disaffected persons, and the sale of their goods.

Nevertheless, the King gave formal sanction to these measures very slowly. In July he empowered the leading Royalists of Oxfordshire, Somerset and Carbery's command to make a list of their enemies' estates, but warned them to dispose of them only 'as His Majesty from time to time under his Sign Manual shall direct'.[30] In the autumn he gave the same power to certain Commissioners of Array and 'for the guarding the county' in Worcestershire, Berkshire, Buckinghamshire, Lord Herbert's counties and the various Royalist-held shires in western and southern England.[31] Not till January 1644 was a Royalist committee, that of Gloucestershire, empowered to seize estates at its own will.[32] By then, however, the Royalists in Glamorganshire had been freely disposing of sequestered property for months. Either they had taken these powers without reference to the court or had been granted them by a royal letter which has not survived. Whether by the one means or the other, the sequestration of their opponents' estates seems to have become a general activity of local Royalists by 1644.

If the legal basis of Royalist sequestration machinery is obscure, the machinery itself is even more so. In March 1644 Charles set up a separate committee to carry out the seizure and administration of estates in Worcestershire, composed of gentry quite different in identity and junior in rank to the Committee 'for the guarding the county'.[33] This distinct body endured till the end of the war.[34] Similarly a separate committee existed in Cheshire.[35] Both, perhaps significantly, were counties where the local Royalist leaders had been divided amongst themselves. In Glamorganshire, by contrast, the Committee 'for the guarding the county' continued to handle all business concerning sequestrations, and there and in Monmouthshire and Radnorshire the King contented himself with instructing certain existing commissioners to report to him upon how the profits were being employed.[36] No evidence upon this question exists for the other counties in the region.

It is almost unnecessary to say that, with the sequestration machinery itself so shadowy, the question of its efficiency is unanswerable. It can at least be said that its profits were never the largest source of income to the Royalists in any county. Nor were the Royalists impressed with the proceeds of sequestration. The Glamorganshire committee 'for the guarding the county' commented sourly upon the 'noise' of expectation concerning these proceeds, compared with the money that actually emerged.[37] The warrants of

Russell's committee were opposed by his enemies on the committee 'for the guarding the county' because of alleged technical errors.[38] The Cheshire sequestration committee reported that only four of its members were prepared to devote any time to its work, and the estates under its care produced little, because Sir Nicholas Byron claimed some rents as his private perquisites while others had been adroitly signed away by their Parliamentarian owners to younger sons who were technically loyal Royalists.[39]

Nevertheless, Royalist sequestration activity was not totally ineffectual, nor, given the Royalists' chronic shortage of funds, were the sums raised insignificant. The separate Worcestershire sequestration committee was diligent and bold enough to detect some rents assigned from one Parliamentarian's estate to a member of the committee 'for the guarding the county' and demand them from him.[40] The Glamorganshire committee 'for the guarding the county' took care to exploit the natural resources of sequestered lands, such as coal deposits.[41] The Royalists gained £2,250 from the Harley estates in 1643,[42] and £600 from the Warwickshire manors of the Earl of Middlesex, which lay in disputed territory.[43] Russell received a total of £761 from 'delinquents' in the same year, and a considerable quantity of corn and other provisions.[44] The High Sheriff of Cornwall gained £658 from the same source in that year.[45]

It is equally difficult to make any definite comment upon the severity of Royalist sequestration procedure. The King certainly urged his commissioners to proceed humanely, sequestering only half the possessions of offenders and leasing these where possible to the existing tenants.[46] He intervened personally to protect the annuity held by a spinster in the Herefordshire estates of the Earl of Essex.[47] Given their need for money, it is doubtful whether his servants were so scrupulous. The charity normally offered by them to the owners of sequestered estates was that of making peace with the payment of a fine. Thus the aged Sir Edward Powell, immobilised by infirmity in London, lost his Herefordshire lands to the sequestrators and only retrieved them by paying the equivalent of eighteen months' rent. He never regained the goods confiscated from the manor house.[48] The Glamorganshire Committee 'for the guarding the county' took £6,000 from three men as bonds for their good behaviour.[49]

In this connection it is interesting to consider the belief that the surviving sequestration records can throw light upon the motivation behind the war. It has been pointed out[50] that the Glamorganshire Committee states that most of the owners of sequestered property in the county were 'separatists and non-conformists'[51] and argued from this that religious conviction determined political allegiance in the Civil War. There is a great deal of evidence for this equation in the case of individuals, some of which has been cited earlier, but there is a danger involved in using the Glamorganshire Order Book to support it. As stressed above,[52] religious non-conformity was in itself equated with Parliamentarianism by the Royalists. The Order Book makes reluctance to 'become conformable to the Church government' in its existing form an automatic ground for sequestration.[53] Thus any man who supported ecclesiastical reform in Royalist territory was vulnerable to the sequestrators, whether he actively supported Parliament or not. This interpretation would explain the willingness of certain Glamorganshire non-conformists to promise co-operation with the Royalists in order to regain their property.[54] It is supported also by Richard Baxter, who claimed[55] that his Puritan father was maltreated by Royalists in Shropshire although he was 'so far from meddling on either side, that he knew not what they were doing'.

The meeting of Charles's Royalist Parliament at Oxford in early 1644 gave three more duties to his local supporters. One arose from a legal device employed by this body to vote the King money without calling into question its right to impose taxation; the writing of letters endorsed with the Privy Seal to wealthy Royalist gentry all over England requesting the loan of a specific sum of money, assessed in accordance with the individual's reputed means. These 'Privy Seal letters' were expected to raise a total of £100,000 to pay the field army for the coming campaigning season.[56] The High Sheriff of each county was requested to forward the proceeds to Oxford.[57] In December he was given the more strenuous duty of interviewing those gentry who had not given the money, who were apparently numerous, and reporting their excuses.[58]

All these efforts would be useless, however, if there were no field army left. By the winter of 1643–4 pay failures and hard service had produced a worse rate of desertion than ever before[59] and ensured that there would be few volunteers to replace those who had fled. Impressment had begun piecemeal in the summer, granted by Charles to individual colonels such as the new Earl of Northampton to fill up their regiments in May,[60] and employed by local Royalists as a matter of course. In May the Cornish commissioners used it to prepare for an offensive[61] and Capel was apparently recruiting his army by this means.[62] In July the Glamorganshire commissioners found men for the Gloucester campaign by this method.[63] In November the royal Council of War advised the King to impress recruits for his forces on a county basis,[64] and during the next two months he officially constituted the most important existing commissioners of Oxfordshire and its neighbouring counties, Staffordshire, the southern and western shires and those of Herbert's command as impressment committees, to recruit men for their respective areas.[65] Likewise he ordered the commissioners of North Wales to fill up Ellis's regiment, specifying the quota of men due from each county.[66] The work of the Royalist Parliament was to make this system universal. On 11th March it voted that 6 000 foot soldiers should be impressed instantly to fill up the field army.[67] A fixed quota of conscripts was demanded from each Royalist county and impressment committees were set up in each. Their full membership is not recorded, but they included the leading Commissioners of Array or 'for the guarding the county'.[68] Likewise in April Charles ordered the local armies of South Wales to be filled up, specifying both the number of men from each county and the size of the county taxes to be raised to pay them.[69]

Finally, the Royalist MPs resolved to follow the example of their enemies in London and impose an excise upon merchandise, the proceeds to be sent to the central Treasury at Oxford.[70] New committees of three men were empowered in May 1644 to administer the tax in the English counties, Wales having presumably too little trade to make the machinery worth while.[71] They were composed of minor gentry and aldermen of the cities where the tax was liable to produce most. The cities of Worcester, Exeter and Bristol possessed their own committees, while the excise in Oxfordshire and four neighbouring counties was administered by a single committee of important courtiers seated at Oxford. In Devon, Cornwall and Worcestershire the county excise committee was composed of leading members of the Commission of Array and the committee 'for the guarding the county'. Not even circumstantial evidence survives to explain these differences. There is equally little information upon the overall profitability of the tax; it definitely raised large sums in Worcester in 1644[72] but seems to have failed in unspecified counties in the Marches,[73] while in Somerset some of the leading Royalists opposed its collection, for reasons which remain unclear.[74] Its political consequences will be considered in a later chapter.

By June 1644 the complexity of local administration had increased to a degree that made some form of regulating mechanism desirable, particularly in financial matters. The accusations levied against Russell and the Sheriff of Cornwall had highlighted the need for a regular and reliable system of accounting. Charles commissioned a report upon the problem, and this[75] recommended the establishment of a new committee in each county to check the accounts of all money received and spent in his service. These committees were duly established in early June.[76] Their potential for creating local ill-feeling seems obvious, but Charles apparently deliberately defused it by selecting the membership of the new bodies in every case from existing Commissioners of Array or 'for the guarding the county'. Even this precaution sometimes failed, for example in Montgomeryshire where the accounting committee was composed entirely of members of Sir John Price's faction, to the fury of the rival Herbert bloc.[77] In Glamorganshire by contrast the accounts were taken with apparent goodwill on the part of all concerned, and published to the county community in general at each Quarter Sessions.[78] As quarrels tend to leave traces it is likely, but not certain, that Glamorganshire was the more typical example.

This, then, is all that can at present be said about the mechanisms which legalised that collection of tasks comprising the war effort. The most striking impression gained is how great a burden the system placed upon a few individuals, the activists who had responded to the original Commissions of Array. The isolation of these men is easily camouflaged by the role they were to play in the second half of the war, soon to be portrayed, when they would appear the representatives of their local communities against outsiders and defenders of the interests of those communities. Indeed, they represented a social elite, each being a wealthy landed gentleman and the head, or heir, of his family.[79] The war had indeed made them the legal leaders and guardians of communities which they had been born to lead. Yet, at least in the English counties, they represented only a fraction of the gentry who had been the natural leaders of those counties before the war. They were exceptional men, who had, from loyalty or ambition or both, made a commitment which most of their colleagues had avoided or opposed. In doing so they had risked ruin or a death on the scaffold, and they were indeed to lose huge sums of money and their local and national power as the consequence of their choice. For a time, however, that choice won them an absolute predominance within their counties, and when wielded by men like Ottley and Russell that power could fall heavily indeed upon their former neighbours. It was the double tragedy of these Royalist commissioners that not merely would they lose the war but that before they did so the war itself would render them impotent. They had become entangled in a machine which did not answer to the realities of that war. Their power was about to fall to a different sort of man, whom these realities had themselves produced.

CHAPTER NINE

The task

The intention of the following chapter is to answer a question developing out of the previous two: why the machinery constructed for the maintenance of the war effort failed to achieve its purpose, so that wherever there is evidence the local taxes imposed are invariably shown to have fallen into arrears almost from their inception.

The best approach to this problem is to consider Clive Holmes's study of the Parliamentarian Eastern Association,[1]* the great supply-base of the Parliamentarian war effort just as the area studied here supplied Charles's army. For the present purpose, the most significant of Professor Holmes's discoveries is that local indifference to the war effort and huge arrears upon the county taxes were as much a feature of wartime administration in the Eastern Association as in the Royalist counties. This picture is duplicated in Professor Everitt's famous book upon Parliamentarian Kent.[2] The difference between the Royalist counties studied here and Kent and East Anglia is that in the latter the arrears were eventually gathered in by the steady work of the county committees, so that in the long term the taxes were paid in full. Thus the machinery designed to maintain the Parliamentarian army performed its task in these counties once it had been given the time and the lack of disturbance to settle down. The beginning of this process can be seen in Royalist Worcestershire in the peaceful early months of 1643. On 25th May the total tax due from January to April was more than half unpaid. That for January, however, was by then only £657 short of the £3,000 demanded, while the February tax was £954 in arrears, and the arrears increased until April, when only £54 of the tax due that month was yet paid.[3] These figures suggest that the arrears were being slowly made up month after month just as they were in the Parliamentarian areas

* Notes for this chapter are on p. 223.

cited. In the Royalist counties, however, this process seems to have been interrupted, and the taxes never made up in total. It is not difficult to suggest an explanation for the difference. One need only imagine the Parliamentarian commissioners attempting to settle down to work in an Eastern Association with strong Royalist garrisons at Norwich and Ipswich, continually raided from the East Midlands, subject to the constant passage of Parliamentarian armies and with a Royalist navy dominating its coasts.

The general military insecurity of the Royalist areas produced certain specific problems to bedevil the work of administrators. The first was the irregular levy. The eventualities of war ensured that the commissioners had frequently to impose emergency taxation to raise sums for specific purposes, over and above the regular county tax which was solely for the soldiers' pay. Thus the Worcestershire hundred of Doddingtree paid extra levies in 1643 to help cover the costs of the armament convoys to Oxford, the carriage of the mint installed at Shrewsbury to Oxford and improvement of the fortifications of Worcester.[4] Such extra taxation removed much of the money which would otherwise have gone to the regular tax.

Second, there was the emergency system of free quarter, described earlier.[5] It was suggested then that the Royalists managed to avoid this system in the opening moves of the war, although this belief is challenged by a letter from a Royalist peer[6] written on the Edgehill campaign, which contains the assertion that the horse in the royal army were already starting to resort to it. By March 1643 the local soldiers in Worcestershire were definitely using the system, because the arrears in their pay resulting from the slow appearance of the local tax had made this necessary.[7] By May Charles was granting the right to take free quarter to newly-commissioned colonels who lacked the money to make the initial payments to the regiments they were to raise.[8] In August it became the practice of the field army on campaign.[9] Thereafter, as shall be seen, it became virtually the rule in every county where there was a large number of soldiers, despite perpetual attempts to eliminate it. Occasionally these attempts were successful, such as in Shropshire in March 1644,[10] but the victory was invariably temporary.

At first sight the unpopularity of free quarter with both local people and the military commanders seems puzzling. It does not appear in itself a harmful system if the tickets given for it were discharged as the rules demanded. In the more turbulent areas they were probably not, but the accounts of the garrison at Ludlow,[11] set in a relatively peaceful Royalist district, show that there free quarter was regularly imposed and then paid off in full when more money came in. The vice of the system, however, was the same as that of the irregular levies; the cost of supporting a soldier frequently consumed all the available cash which a villager had to spare for the county taxes, particularly as troops sometimes demanded a high standard of accommodation.[12] Hence several petitions survive such as that from Lennox Beverley in Cheshire,[13] who had been so impoverished by quartering some of Capel's soldiers as well as paying tax that he was incapable of supplying any more money to the Royalist war effort. Free quarter, made necessary by the arrears upon local taxes, could itself become an impediment to the elimination of those arrears.

Free quarter at least left intact the mechanisms which produced money at village level. The consequence of the third spanner in the works of Royalist administration, the conscription of materials of war, was to remove these. From the beginning Charles had granted the officers of his field army rights of compulsory purchase of horses for the cavalry and horses and carts for the baggage train. So many horses were conscripted from Stafford during the King's stay there in 1642 that the corporation begged him to prevent any more being taken.[14] Three weeks later Charles decreed the death penalty for any former owner attempting to retrieve his horse or cart from the new baggage train.[15] On the army's march in October Rupert seized more horses for his cavalry, at least three, at Penkridge, without payment, for the owner issued a complaint.[16] When Charles ordered Aston to Cheshire in January 1643 he empowered him to conscript horses there to mount a new dragoon regiment.[17] In March a hundred draught horses were demanded from Worcestershire for the field army.[18] Horses and carts continued to be conscripted throughout the war in every part of the region where troops were stationed at the opening of a campaign. By April 1644 the governor of Lichfield was unable to seize horses in response to an order from Rupert because so few remained in Staffordshire.[19] Attempts to settle a regular postal service between Oxford and the Midlands failed because the horses were usually conscripted on the way.[20]

Horses and carts were the most obvious targets upon a farm for the military, but soldiers in the course of their duty did other damage to the basic resources of the countryside. A widow at Ludlow lost all the turf from her meadow, dug up to improve the fortifications of the castle.[21] At Shrewsbury Capel's horse overgrazed and ruined the town pastures.[22] In Monmouthshire other Royalist cavalry destroyed a year's crop of hay by grazing their mounts upon growing grass.[23] Soldiers gathering provisions carelessly took breeding animals from farmyards.[24] Such exactions not only struck at the roots of a local economy but unlike a tax they were capricious, striking one individual rather than another according to whether or not the troops picked on him. If a man were unlucky in this respect, the consequences could be frightful. One poor wretch near Ludlow lost his three horses in succession and then had his spade taken to dig new fortifications, leaving him with no means of breaking his land, a family to support, the local tax to pay and a soldier to feed and accommodate.[25]

All these problems were magnified when an army entered a district. Initially the royal army itself was maintained by a special levy upon each area in which it quartered. Thus tiny Hatherton paid £1 towards the upkeep of Charles's army encamped around Wolverhampton in 1642[26] and the various Worcestershire hundreds contributed money to his forces quartered in the county in September 1643.[27] Those towns which were honoured by a visit from the King or an important general fared rather worse, as etiquette demanded a handsome reception for their guest; even the modest settlement of Walsall presented Rupert with £20 in gold when he entered it in October 1642.[28] To provide for smaller forces on their march, Charles gave their commanders rights of free quarter, the certificates of which were to be redeemed by the local Royalist commissioners. Kidderminster paid Aston's regiment £28 on its journey to Cheshire, and presented the bill to Russell.[29] The total sum of money spent in this way could be considerable in a 'corridor county' like Worcestershire; Russell spent in all £1,813 in assisting the passage of 'foreign' troops in 1643,[30] and all this came ultimately from the pockets of the county. Furthermore individual generals imposed their own extra levies. Droitwich spent £312 on clothing regiments passing north in November 1643[31] and Charles demanded a thousand pairs of stockings from Evesham for his army in June 1644.[32]

All these exactions had some claim to legality, although in the case of conscription of horses that legality could be very dubious indeed. In addition, wherever troops were stationed or passing the countrymen ran the risk of being robbed by the soldiers for their private profit. This straightforward plundering could do terrible damage to a district. Townshend believed that the depredations of 700 horse sent to cover Worcester during the campaign of September 1643 caused more expense than the food bill for the entire field army then quartered in the shire.[33] Aston's horse, returning disgraced from Cheshire, pillaged the Droitwich and Bromsgrove area so savagely that it was completely unable to pay its monthly tax. In this case the Worcestershire commissioners complained to the King, and some of those robbed went to Oxford to reclaim their property from Aston's troopers, but there is no sign that these efforts met with any success.[34] Nor was plundering necessarily associated with troops crossing a strange county on their march, for as seen above Aston's horse and the local soldiers of Worcestershire robbed their own shires. Thus another vicious circle was set up within administration, for looting rendered the countryside incapable of paying the tax upon which the soldiers' pay depended, and pay failure drove the soldiers to loot. All these depredations were the work of 'friendly' soldiers; in addition counties on the border of the Royalist area suffered severely from Parliamentarian invasions specifically designed to destroy Royalist resources. Furthermore, the breakdown of order produced a new threat to property in the shape of Royalist deserters or ordinary criminals who wandered the countryside, sometimes in bands, demanding money and supplies on the pretence of being soldiers.[35]

Quite apart from all the specific tribulations listed above, the war produced a general loss of wealth in the Royalist counties studied. The importance of London in the English economy of the time meant that when Charles finally prohibited trade between Royalist and Parliamentarian areas in October 1643[36] he left the former with very little commerce at all, while his enemies preserved the capital's links with the eastern counties and foreign countries. Attempts to develop Bristol as an alternative entrepot were foiled by the Parliamentarian hold on Gloucester, which jammed the whole great trading system based on the Severn Valley. The most notable casualty of this situation, as will be seen later, was the North Welsh cattle trade, which had produced the little wealth that region possessed. Even local commerce was disrupted by the war, because fairs and markets provided tempting targets for plundering soldiers.[37] The mere presence of the field army near Evesham in September 1643 was enough to produce the cancellation of its fair.[38]

The central problem of Royalist territory was therefore that it was not merely a base but a battlefield in itself, and its wealthiest counties were also the most disturbed. This problem worsened as the Parliamentarian pressure upon the area increased. It ensured that the initial conception of the Royalist administration as entirely based upon committees of local gentry suffered ever greater impediments and produced a growing need for a different model. By late 1643 such a model was in action in Staffordshire, which represented the shape of things to come for the whole region as Warwickshire had done in 1642.

As described above, the result of the Parliamentarian campaign in May had been to turn Staffordshire into a no-man's land of rival fortresses. As such it posed all the problems of Royalist administrators elsewhere in an extreme form. The Royalist garrisons relied for their payment upon villages from which the local tax was regularly demanded for the garrisons of their enemies. In this situation, although the county was officially governed by the usual set of committees, Royalist administration became in practice conducted by the military governors of the main garrisons themselves, Tutbury Castle, Lichfield and Dudley Castle.

Each of these garrisons possessed a distinct origin and identity. Tutbury, as said, had been garrisoned by Henry Hastings in January 1643. Its governor was always one of Hastings's own officers and the fortress represented part of his personal military empire in the Midlands. It was given the tax of Totmanslow Hundred for its support. Lichfield was governed by Richard Bagot, appointed as described by Rupert, and given Offlow Hundred to support itself. Bagot recognised Hastings's authority as Colonel-General but conducted his daily affairs without reference to his superior. Dudley was properly speaking outside Hastings's control as it stood in a tiny detached portion of Worcestershire, and the castle was garrisoned at the King's command in March 1643 with Worcestershire soldiers.[39] Its position on a fictional island, however, made nonsense in this case of the county unit as the basis of wartime administration, and Charles soon allotted it the western Staffordshire hundreds of Seisdon and Cuddlestone[40] and neighbouring portions of Parliamentarian Warwickshire.[41] The situation of Dudley Castle would probably have led in any circumstances to confusions in the chain of military command. The personality of its governor, Thomas Leveson, ensured that these confusions would become a national issue.

Leveson was the squire of Wolverhampton,[42] and locally notorious before the war as a man of dangerous temper and devout Catholic faith. When the great fear of a Catholic rising swept England in 1642, one of the principal measures taken by the Staffordshire gentry to secure their county was to confiscate Leveson's weapons when he sent them to an armourer to be repaired.[43] Leveson's reaction was to thrash the unfortunate armourer and flee to France, abandoning his wife, with whom he was apparently on no better terms than with anybody else.[44] By May 1643, however, this alarming individual was back in England and successfully ingratiating himself with Charles at Oxford, for he was commissioned to raise a foot regiment. In June the same gentry who had tried to disarm him the year before received, with feelings which can only be imagined, a royal letter instructing them to regard Leveson as their protector. In July he was formally confirmed as governor of Dudley Castle.[45]

Almost immediately he quarrelled with Bagot. The latter had already suffered a diminution in the resources for his garrison by the allotment of portions of Offlow Hundred to hard-pressed Tutbury and the garrison Hastings had put into Rushall Hall. Now his soldiers, attempting to gather money from his remaining villages, found themselves clashing not only with Parliamentarians from Stafford and Tamworth but Leveson's troops, all on the same errand. Both he and Leveson complained to the King, who, failing to persuade them to settle the dispute themselves, referred it in October to their immediate commander, Hastings. Hastings's own reputation at this period was higher than ever at court, where he enjoyed the powerful friendship of Rupert, and he had just been created a peer. Leveson also stood very well with Charles, because his campaigns in Staffordshire since his appointment had made him a Royalist hero. Accordingly, the King recommended that Hastings settle the argument in his favour, and this the Colonel-General did, to the fury of Bagot.[46]

The latter had at least the satisfaction of seeing his own quarrel rapidly submerged in a much bigger dispute between Leveson and Hastings themselves. There had already been tension between these two in the autumn, created by Dudley's strategic position upon the borders of four counties, which resulted in orders often being sent to Leveson direct from the King to intervene in one or the other. If such an order conflicted with a direction from Hastings, duty and his desire for local independence both prompted Leveson to disregard the Colonel-General. The crisis was precipitated in January when the King made Leveson High Sheriff of Staffordshire in an effort to strengthen his hold on the south-west of the county with the Sheriff's ancient power to call up all able-bodied men at will in a local emergency as the *posse comitatus*. Leveson issued his warrants to muster the local population, only to see them disregarded because they had been declared invalid by Hastings, who saw them as a negation of his own authority in the county. Leveson lost his temper, complained to the King and wrote a furious letter to Hastings, who reacted by mobilising a faction in the Royalist Parliament to obtain a declaration negating Leveson's authority as Sheriff.[47]

The King's reaction was to refer the whole problem to Rupert,[48] who called the parties concerned to a conference to remove all grounds for dispute.[49] There southern Staffordshire and northern

Warwickshire were formally divided into separate hunting-grounds for Leveson and Bagot. Somehow the former was reconciled with Hastings, and in April 1644 Charles was able once more to ask the Colonel-General to arbitrate impartially between Leveson and Bagot in another quarrel, arising from alleged infringements of Rupert's judgment.[50] Further clashes occurred between the two governors until early 1645, but by then they had become capable of ending them without outside interference.[51]

At first sight Staffordshire seems to have represented an appalling failure of Royalist administration. The impotence of the normal administration controlled by civilians had left all local government to the military commanders, who had between them produced total anarchy, expending as much energy against each other as against the enemy. Yet the true significance of the county is that it represented, incredibly, a success story for the Royalists. Despite every apparent disadvantage – the collapse of the formal administration, the competition of Parliamentarian garrisons and their own mutual animosity – the governors of the Staffordshire fortresses fulfilled their duty to preserve their strongholds and to maintain, and even increase, their local power. By December 1643 Bagot had obtained only £384 in total from the local tax to which he was entitled, to set against an expenditure of £8,727 and the garrison's pay was in serious arrear.[52] By November 1645 the same garrison was being paid regularly every three weeks, and the proceeds of the tax represented seven-eighths of the expenditure.[53] Rupert had fixed the total strength of the garrison at 400 soldiers.[54] In December 1643 it consisted of 300 foot and 200 horse and in November 1645 the foot alone totalled 466. Leveson's garrison seems similarly to have increased in size, and like Lichfield it became powerful enough not merely to hold its own locally, but, as will be seen, to add hundreds of men to the field armies on campaign. Some Lichfield soldiers detached for such service were reported to be mutinous because of the 'plenty and ease' to which they were accustomed.[55]

Scores of such garrisons were to sprout all over disputed areas from the end of 1643, produced by the intensification of the local war effort by both parties. By the end of the war thirty-one had been erected in Shropshire alone. As the military 'front' moved, new garrisons were created but few existing strongholds were evacuated. Each major fortress threw out minor garrisons to strengthen its hold upon local resources, until in some areas they interlocked like spiders' webs upon an autumn field. Thus from Dudley Leveson put troops into the great houses of Chillington, Lapley and Patshull.[56]

The governors sent out warrants for the local tax, and for horses, carts and provisions, exactly as the commissioners would in more peaceful counties, and expected the local constables to deliver the proceeds directly to them.[57] If the constables did not respond, they ordered out their troops to enforce these warrants just as governors in sheltered areas often, as seen, ended up doing for the commissioners. A great deal of wealth was accumulated in addition to this by raiding enemy territory, which represented the principal activity of garrisons in the frontier zone. These raids could extend very far, and bore no relation to the actual distance of strongholds from each other. Parliamentarian Edgbaston Hall, whose men pillaged as far as Bewdley and Evesham[58] was almost visible from Dudley Castle. The Coventry garrison complained to Parliament that Royalists were levying money up to its very walls.[59] Birmingham suffered from its famous zeal for Parliament by being repeatedly plundered. Merchants upon the road were particularly favoured targets, and Hastings, Bagot and Leveson became known in the Parliamentarian press as 'the Rob-Carriers'.

At times relations between rival garrisons almost assumed the status of a great game. Parliamentarians from Stafford captured Bagot's favourite horses when they were being exercised, whereupon he offered £1,000 for their return.[60] On another occasion the governor of Tamworth Castle formally challenged Bagot to battle by letter; the Royalist kept the appointment but the Parliamentarian lost his nerve.[61] Nevertheless the pattern of raid and counter-raid was a deadly business. The object of each frontier garrison was to destroy the enemy's resources and protect its own, including the intangible resource of its prestige among the neighbouring population. 'The country observes the enemy to have the field from us,' wrote one Parliamentarian governor, 'and being clodheads merely sensible and sensual, suppose it will ever be so, and look not beyond the present, so that they will do nothing for our warrants.'[62] A governor who became a master of this sort of sparring would (literally) get his name into the newspapers and earn favour from his superiors and supplies for his garrison. The interminable struggles between garrisons became indeed the staple material of the newspapers of both parties, and fulfilled a vital function. If the general military news were bad or inconclusive it was only necessary to extol some brilliant exploit by a local governor to give the impression that the cause was still victorious. In this manner the activities of a ridiculously small and remote place like Rushall could assume the same importance in the minds of readers in London and Oxford as even more remote garrisons at Rorke's Drift and Lucknow would in the minds of a later generation of Englishmen.

There is one more consideration to be made upon the military governors; that they generally found their work rewarding. Not even in their worst rages did Bagot and Leveson contemplate resigning their posts, nor is there any recorded case of a governor voluntarily doing so. They had achieved something which most men desire but few obtain; power over all they surveyed. The only possible brake to this power was a distant High Command which demanded only that they wield their rule effectively. To enforce his will each possessed a body of regular soldiers, which he led in person and maintained like a private army. They resided in great castles and mansions, to which the local population brought tribute. They had become warlords, masters of chunks of territory which they ruled by the skill of their swords. They were English gentry turned feral, spiritual descendants of the robber-barons of the Middle Ages.

These men represented in miniature the solution which the High Command came to apply to the problems of the local administration. Charles had originally envisaged his war effort as being maintained by local populations working voluntarily under their natural leaders, their own gentry. By the end of 1643 he had abandoned this notion, and begun to commit the provinces one by one to the care of men of the sort who were ruling in Staffordshire. These new appointees had two qualifications, that they had already proved their loyalty and military skill in the field, and that they were not the natural leaders of the areas which which they were entrusted. The Commissioners of Array or Safety were all, as said, the heads or heirs of great families in the counties which they ruled. By late 1644 every piece of Royalist territory was in the power of military men who were with one exception either younger sons or gentry from districts distant from those placed beneath their rule. The exception was the Heathcliffe of Staffordshire, Thomas Leveson, a perfect parody of the traditional picture of a paternalistic country gentleman. The solution to the problem of Royalist administration was in fact unpleasantly simple; that the local populations had to be squeezed and squeezed again without mercy until they were forced to disgorge the money and provisions which the war effort needed but which they could not afford to supply. Local gentry would hesitate to ruin their neighbours; geographical and social outsiders would not suffer this handicap. They served the war itself, and their only loyalty was to their commanders.

CHAPTER TEN

The Parliamentarian comparison

In this narrative, the Parliamentarians inevitably feature as *dei ex machina*. To incorporate an account of their local war effort and its politics would result in a book of unnecessary length and expense, as the Parliamentarian war machine has now been analysed and portrayed in a number of excellent recent studies.[1]* However, any description of the Royalist administration would be deprived of much of its point if no attempt were made to illustrate the manner in which the King's machinery approximated to, and differed from, that of his enemies. This is the task of this chapter.

Parliament's war effort, like the King's, depended upon a series of county committees to carry out the functions of levying money and troops, and sequestering the estates of opponents and taking accounts, but the most superficial examination reveals important differences. The Parliamentarian machine was designed to be at once more formal, more complex and more arbitrary than the Royalist. Unlike the King, Parliament could make use (albeit, without the King, dubiously) of traditional powers of legislation and taxation. These were balanced by the weakness that whereas the King possessed unquestioned personal authority over his followers, Parliament was a huge committee of theoretically equal members, anxious to avoid entrusting power to any one man or small group of men. These differences were naturally reflected in the rival administrations.

The first contrast lay in the construction of the Parliamentarian machine. Whereas the growth of the Royalist administration was gradual and pragmatic, the Parliamentarian ordinances for the

* Notes for this chapter are on p. 224.

Assessment (24 February 1643), sequestration (27 March) and the Excise (22 July) created at three blows bodies and activities which the King brought into being county by county over many months. The Assessment Ordinance, for example, imposed a tax on property to support Parliamentarian troops, named committees in each county to receive it and instructed them to nominate collectors. It specified the varieties of property to be taxed and the total sum expected from each county, and empowered the committees to arrest and fine individuals to enforce collection. No ordinance made any concession to local sentiment or custom, nor claimed any precedent in law, nor permitted commissioners empowered by its terms any latitude to amend its provisions in any way.

With this boldness and arbitrariness went an emphasis upon central regulation and control. The King's soldiers were supported by voluntary contributions, though by the time of the Privy Seal letters these were becoming forced loans, and the local rates agreed in each county by the gentry. The only financial imposition made upon the provinces by the Royalist central authorities which was both general and compulsory was the Excise imposed by the Royalist Parliament, in imitation of that which the Parliament at Westminster had been demanding for nearly a year. By contrast, Parliament's soldiers were paid mainly from the Assessment, as established by the ordinance, and the forced loan principle had been established as early as November 1642 in the Fifth and Twentieth Part, a levy demanded from all who had refused to contribute voluntarily to Parliament. Central committees were established in London to co-ordinate the collection of the Fifth and Twentieth Part and the Excise, and the business of sequestration and accounting, and the local committees were seen simply as agents of these. To compare with the Royalists' employment of county Grand Juries to attest the imposition of rates, the Parliamentarian system made no use of such existing local bodies at all. As the representative of the people, Parliament declined to recognise rival representatives.

Parliament's twin desires, to enforce effective central control and to prevent the concentration of executive power in a few hands, resulted in a greater complexity in the formal structure of its machine. All the financial receipts of the Royalist High Command went either to the Exchequer or to the Treasurer-at-War. Parliament, as said, had separate central committees to co-ordinate the raising of the Fifth and Twentieth Part, the Excise and the proceeds of sequestration, and there was a separate treasury for each of these sources of revenue. The central committees for the Excise and accounting nominated their own local commissioners, but Parliament itself named those for other purposes. There was a central committee and county committees for sequestration, but victims wishing to compound had to journey to London and face a separate central committee altogether. In each county Parliament set up a further committee to eject Royalist clergy and provide support for Parliamentarian clergy fleeing from Royalist territory. Equivalent work was undertaken by the Royalist Commissioners of Array or 'guarding the county' as part of their general duties. Whereas these Royalist commissioners were empowered both to control the militia and to receive revenue, the Parliamentarian Deputy Lieutenancy, which was responsible for the security of each county, was in theory a separate body from the revenue-raising committees. Whereas the Royalist commissioners for accounting were led by the most prominent members of the existing committees, the Parliamentarian equivalents were specifically composed of men not already appointed to any office. Indeed, the function was rather different, for the Parliamentarian accounting committees were intended to check and pass the accounts of all creditors and debtors to Parliament, the Royalist equivalents to establish what became of the money collected and spent by Royalist officials.

Having made all these contrasts, it must be said that once the picture shifts to a local level virtually all the differences between Royalist and Parliamentarian administration disappear. Once in action, they displayed remarkable similarities. In practice Parliament itself encouraged the consolidation of the membership of all its various committees in each county to create a general all-purpose county committee on the lines of the Royalist committees for 'guarding the county'. Likewise it tried wherever possible to ensure that the Deputy Lieutenancy and the local committees consisted of the same men. So it came to pass in the majority of the Parliamentarian counties studied so far. As in the Royalist areas there were local idiosyncrasies. Cheshire retained four quite separate committees to perform separate functions. In Yorkshire the committee for ejecting ministers was separate from the county committee, while in Lancashire the Deputy Lieutenancy retained a separate identity. Likewise in Lancashire, Norfolk and Suffolk the local committees for accounting became trusted allies of the main committees, as they apparently did in most Royalist counties. In Somerset, Staffordshire and Lincolnshire they were used by factions against the main committee, as they were in Royalist Montgomeryshire.

Again, although the Parliamentarian ordinances made no concession to local circumstances, the committees they created adapted to them in other ways than in their degree of amalgamation and their internal politics. Like the pre-war JPs and the main Royalist county committees, the Parliamentarian committees in Cheshire, Yorkshire, Kent, Dorset and Essex divided into sub-committees to deal with separate areas of each county, formed of gentry from those areas. For all their detail, the ordinances left many aspects of administration unspecified, such as the principles upon which sequestration was to be carried out, or upon which the Assessment was to be levied. The answers supplied to these problems naturally varied between counties. In Buckinghamshire the Parliamentarian commissioners employed the model of existing local rates, as the Royalists did in Worcestershire when imposing their military rate in January 1643. In Kent they attempted an entirely new evaluation, of a fixed percentage in the pound on all incomes, a reform the Royalists were, as shall be seen, to undertake in their territory in 1644. In most Parliamentarian counties the Assessment was collected in the manner portrayed in Royalist Worcestershire, by local constables acting upon a division of the tax made by a few prominent householders in each village. In both Royalist and Parliamentarian counties impressment was likewise the work of local constables, acting on the directions of the most important county committees.

There were other similarities. For both Royalists and Parliamentarians the local unit of military administration was the Association of several counties, pooling their resources to support a regional army led by a single general. To match Charles's lieutenant-generals, Parliament appointed local major-generals like Waller, Denbigh, Myddleton, Lord Fairfax and the Earl of Manchester. Like Capel, the Earl of Manchester tried to work through an Association committee of representatives from the various county committees in an attempt to make their delivery of men and money more efficient, and like him was continually irritated by local inertia and self-interest. Capel had trouble with the citizens of Shrewsbury, Manchester had to put down a rebellion at King's Lynn. As the problems of military administration were much the same, so was the behaviour of the civilian commissioners. The Parliamentarian ordinances may have sounded more despotic than the King's declarations, but in practice, as seen, the behaviour of the Royalist commissioners in exacting money and quelling dissent was as ruthless as any of the measures permitted in the ordinances.

In general, therefore, the point made in the previous chapter stands. Any differences between the Royalist and Parliamentarian administrations were the result of experience rather than construction. When the embattled Royalist hinterland is compared with the relatively secure and peaceful Parliamentarian base in East Anglia or Kent, then some contrast in the working of administration appears. But when the Royalist counties are compared with those on the border of Parliamentarian territory, the contrast evaporates. There military commanders like Brereton and Massey dominated the scene, struggling against the indifference and hostility of the local population and attempting to make a working relationship with civilian commissioners and urban corporations as their Royalist counterparts did. It is to those counterparts, and their problems, that the story must now return.

PART FOUR
The warlords

CHAPTER ELEVEN
Vavasour

Sir William Vavasour was the younger son of an important gentleman of Yorkshire and Lincolnshire. He presumably had some military experience before 1640, when he was already a knight and commander of a regiment in the Scottish war. On the outbreak of civil war he was made a member of the Council of War and Lieutenant-Colonel of the royal Lifeguard, but this promising career was interrupted when he was captured at Edgehill.[1]* In April 1643, however, he escaped and arrived at Oxford to a hero's welcome.[2] This publicity added to his experience ensured him rapid employment; he was made a baronet and in June given the task of rebuilding Lord Herbert's demoralised command.[3]

Charles's regard for Herbert and his family fortune was too great to permit the Lieutenant-General to be publicly disgraced. He retained his command, and Vavasour was given the rank of Colonel-General under him, with the understanding that the latter would do all the actual work.[4] Charles did his best to provide an adequate legal framework for the task. The Commissioners of Array in the five counties were, as described, reconstituted as Committees 'for the guarding the county'. To provide the nucleus of a new local army the Herefordshire commissioner Henry Lingen and the Monmouthshire commissioner Sir Trevor Williams were authorised to raise new foot regiments and Vavasour commissioned to raise his own regiments of horse and foot. To fill the vacuum left in Herefordshire by the capture of its local leaders Lingen was also elevated to High Sheriff.[5]

In late June Vavasour settled down to work at Hereford, aided by

* Notes for this chapter are on p. 224.

Lingen and his fellow commissioner Sir Walter Pye,[6] and within a month he had collected and armed 1 200 foot and over 200 horse.[7] Despite this progress his relations with the commissioners in general had already been soured, over the vital question of finance. They had agreed local taxes for their counties, that for Hereford alone being £1,200 per month,[8] of which a proportion was to be sent to a central fund to support the Colonel-General's field army and the rest used to keep local garrisons. In his first month in command little more than £100 in all had come in to the central fund, and to keep his new army off free quarter Sir William relied upon Herbert's famous fortune, which was at last showing signs of strain, and loans from Hereford citizens.[9] In Glamorganshire at least this was clearly not the fault of the commissioners, who worked hard to raise money and speed men to Hereford. What had defeated them was the quagmire of local indifference in which they had to work. The local tax came in slowly, the sequestration of estates produced too little to redress the balance and even so prominent an individual as the Bishop of Llandaff, whose career was threatened by Parliament, defaulted upon the supplies charged upon him. Eventually the soldiers sent to Vavasour were, again, supported by private loans.[10]

The Colonel-General decided that a victory was needed to restore the faith of the local population in the Royalist cause. A soft option seemed to be at hand in the shape of Brampton Bryan Castle, where Brilliana Harley was still obstinately in control. Siege was laid upon 26th July, although it proceeded slowly because Vavasour lacked the heavy cannon necessary to bombard the walls, as he had not the money to pay for their casting.[11]

Within two weeks Sir William himself had departed, as Lord Herbert before him, for the much greater project of reducing Gloucester. The fall of Bristol on 23rd July had left the city completely isolated, with no powerful Parliamentarian strongholds nearer than Plymouth and Southampton. For long it had represented an appalling nuisance to the Royalists, endangering their links with Wales, pinning down the South Welsh army, destroying the Severn trade and preventing them from properly exploiting the riches of Gloucestershire. After the storming of Bristol its reduction would seem almost an anticlimax, but Charles took no chances. In early August he mobilised against Gloucester the biggest collection of troops he ever commanded in the field, comprising the entire royal field army plus most of the local soldiers of Worcestershire and of Vavasour's command. The effect upon the citizens was unequivocal. In the words of Massey's chaplain, they all turned 'infidels'.[12] Massey concurred with this, calculating that not one in ten of them was still 'cordial' to his cause.[13] Yet his soldiers remained loyal, and he prepared, as he had in February, to do his duty.

The King relied upon starvation and mining to reduce the city, and gave to Vavasour's army the role of closing up its western side. Sir William left Lingen with 700 men to carry on the siege of Brampton Bryan, and joined the King with 300 horse and 1 200 foot, mainly pikemen. Pye commanded the horse and the faithful Herbert Price helped lead the foot.[14] This force was increased to 2 000 within a few days by the arrival of the Glamorganshire militia under its High Sheriff, Richard Bassett, whom Charles rewarded with a knighthood.[15] To maintain Sir William's army in the field required a constant flow of money, weapons and recruits from his counties which their commissioners were hard put to supply. In Glamorganshire an order of the Committee 'for the guarding the county' to its 'western gentry'[16] to impress and arm eighty men from their hundreds met first with a plea to remit the order and then the reply that they could find only sixty suitable recruits, and even the loss of these weakened the local economy. Moreover only twelve could be armed, and these only with staves. The commissioners at Cardiff had to use their own family armouries to provide weapons. To provide money they tried desperately to hurry the collection of the county tax and improve the profits of sequestration, but remained perpetually short of the quantity needed. As Charles described the Glamorganshire commissioners as 'a president to others in testifying their zeal', their fellows in Vavasour's command must have fared worse.[17] Herbert certainly claimed later that his own fortune had been employed, yet again, to support Sir William's army before Gloucester.[18]

The siege of Gloucester has become part of the national epic. The story is well known of the terrific fight which Massey, with his 1 500 men, put up against Charles's huge army all through August until Parliament, reeling from its defeats, took heart and determined to fight on. Less publicised, but equally heroic, was the resistance at Brampton Bryan, where Lingen besieged Lady Harley. Still lacking heavy guns, he adopted the futile tactic of trying to frighten the formidable Brilliana into surrender, so that almost as many messages were exchanged as shots.[19] Both sieges were raised in early September by the appearance of the Parliamentarian army sent to relieve Gloucester. Charles retired, as said before, into Worcestershire, taking Vavasour's army with him. Lingen retired to cover Hereford, harassed by parties which the triumphant Lady Harley sent out to beat up his quarters.[20] The King sent a consignment of munitions to

Hereford,[21] and ordered the commissioners of south-east Wales to call up all local men and move this irregular force into Monmouthshire to protect their region.[22] He himself waited to pounce upon the Parliamentarians as they re-emerged from Gloucester. A week later they did, dashing for London, and Charles's army, including Vavasour's troops, streamed off in pursuit.

This pursuit, and the campaign of 1643, culminated in the appalling and indecisive carnage of Newbury, in which Vavasour's men suffered as badly as any others.[23] To his army, returning exhausted to its native region in October, was given the task of bottling up Gloucester through the winter, in the hope that a blockade might slowly starve Massey out. There was a genuine possibility that this might occur; the Parliamentarians who had relieved the city had estimated that a further 1 000 foot and £8,000 would be needed to keep it through the winter[24] and not till February was any such supply convoy ready to leave London.[25]

Initially, however, there was a danger that Sir William's command would itself be too demoralised after the recent fighting to make such an effort. He put 400 Welsh foot into Tewkesbury to fortify the town, but upon the first sally of the Gloucester garrison these mutinied and fled homeward.[26] Herbert now retired altogether to the court, leaving Vavasour without his local prestige to bolster his own authority and refused any control over the Lieutenant-General's own regiments, left at Raglan.[27] The Glamorganshire commissioners found it necessary to cut the county tax from £1,000 to £800 per month in December, and by January the King had written several letters of castigation to them concerning their neglect of the payments due from them to support Vavasour's army.[28] The Colonel-General himself was completely hoodwinked by a false offer from one of Massey's men to betray Gloucester. In his efforts to co-operate with what he believed to be the stratagem of the spurious traitor Vavasour marched around the city in January according to the directions of Massey himself, permitting the latter to take in supplies in safety and producing a rift between Sir William and local Royalists like Pye, to whom he could not confide the reasons behind his curious manoeuvring. At length Massey published the whole affair,[29] and made his enemy a national laughing-stock, a blow from which Vavasour's reputation never recovered.

Nevertheless, not all Sir William's endeavours at this period were as fruitless. Lingen raised a horse troop to guard Herefordshire and Hereford was garrisoned with 700 foot.[30] A new garrison was put into Goodrich Castle to strengthen the line of the Wye.[31] In the Forest of Dean Vavasour acquired a powerful ally in Sir John Winter, a Catholic courtier whose proprietorship of the Forest had been withdrawn by Parliament just before the war.[32] The King had not recognised the confiscation, and in September 1643 Winter finally fortified his mansion at Lydney in the Forest for the Royalists.[33] Charles added Dean to Vavasour's command, and authorised the settlement of a local tax there to support Winter's newly-raised troops, who were stiffened with the loan of Herbert's horse regiment.[34] Sir John soon proved himself a master of the art of garrison warfare, and his raids upon the Gloucester area seriously reduced Massey's mobility.[35] In December Charles gave the commissioners of Vavasour's command powers to press soldiers for his army,[36] and two of them, Pye and Croft, raised new foot regiments. A Colonel Wroughton raised some horse. In the same month units of the royal Irish army, released by the truce described earlier, arrived at Bristol, and three were assigned, after much haggling, to Vavasour's army. They consisted of about 100 horse and two foot regiments under Sir William St Leger and Nicholas Mynne, who had been Vavasour's Lieutenant-Colonel in 1640.[37] These men represented a real windfall, being veterans accustomed to hard service. They made a proper blockade of Gloucester possible.

On 1st February Vavasour mustered his whole army, about 2 600 strong, at Hereford and marched to Tewkesbury, equipped with a convoy of munitions from the Oxford magazine. There he left Pye's foot and Wroughton's horse to garrison the town. On the 2nd he continued westwards to Newent, and entrenched Mynne's foot in that town and neighbouring mansions. He retained St Leger's, Croft's and Lingen's foot and the Irish horse, reinforced by horse lent by Winter, as a mobile force and led it to operate between Gloucester and Warwick. Massey put detachments into four great houses in the Vale of Gloucester to preserve this rich area to feed the city. Though food continued to enter Gloucester, however, the encircling ring of Royalists ensured that money ran short, and Massey's soldiers began to desert.[38]

At the approach of the new campaigning season, the High Command made a considerable administrative effort to ensure that this situation continued into the summer. On 24th March Charles appointed Winter Commander-in-Chief of all Royalist forces in Dean, under Vavasour, and ordered the commissioners of Herefordshire and Monmouthshire to pay him £800 per month to add to the meagre tax which the Forest could supply. All Gloucestershire was added to Vavasour's command, and he was given the task of blocking up Gloucester from the east as Winter would from the west.[39] On 7th and 12th April the committee of Lords Commissioners appointed by Charles to supervise the needs of his Oxford base produced two reports upon measures to ensure the continuation of the blockade if Vavasour's army were called away. Tewkesbury and Lord Chandos's family castle of Sudeley were to be garrisoned by local recruits stiffened by a few of Vavasour's existing soldiers. Chandos was to raise the men for Sudeley and another powerful local gentleman, Sir Humphrey Tracy, those for Tewkesbury. Chandos was already colonel of a horse regiment, and this was to be quartered in the northern Cotswolds with three new troops commissioned from local gentry to range the area between the two garrisons. All these soldiers were to be supported by the tax of the hundreds in which they were stationed, plus the proceeds of local sequestrations and a dole of £320 from the Oxford Treasury.[40] In this manner it was hoped to release Vavasour's field army from the blockade, replacing it with local men led by local gentry and paid by local money.

The defect of the scheme was that it was too late. All through March the High Command had infuriated Vavasour by issuing him with conflicting orders, in obedience to which he and his army indulged in much fruitless marching in the Costwolds. He was at least able to maintain the pressure on Gloucester, and block the way of Parliament's convoy of supplies, which had by now reached Warwick and was awaiting an opening for its final dash.[41] At the end of the month, however, the great Royalist defeat at Cheriton in Hampshire made Charles call Vavasour's army into his own to protect Oxford. It became a permanent part of the royal field force.[42] Its disappearance left the country between Warwick and Gloucester open, and the Parliamentarian convoy got through, followed by a regiment of horse, while the Lords Commissioners were making their reports. Sudeley was duly garrisoned and Chandos's horse stationed nearby as the reports dictated, but it was a classic case of closing the stable door after the horse had bolted. Massey was now strong enough to take the offensive and in mid April he attacked Mynne at Newent. In this emergency Vavasour, though not his army, was sent back to the area. Massey's assault had been repulsed, but Sir William nevertheless ordered Mynne to withdraw to Ross-on-Wye and fortify himself there to protect Herefordshire.[43] The Colonel-General himself settled at Hereford to enact a grand scheme for a new local army and new campaigns.[44]

In reality his command was already extinguished, destroyed by court politics. Since December it had become obvious to everybody that Lord Herbert had retired permanently from the local war, and sooner or later would be replaced as Lieutenant-General by a command prepared to do some fighting. A field of three candidates rapidly emerged; Chandos, Viscount Conway and Vavasour himself. Sir William was at several disadvantages in this contest, being of inferior birth, of tarnished reputation as a general and possessing powerful enemies. The most powerful of these was Herbert himself, whose enmity was engendered directly by his equivocal military position, whereby he commanded in theory and Vavasour in practice. The High Command found it expedient to send orders directly to Sir William, whereas Herbert, disregarding the realities of warfare, felt they ought to proceed through himself. The crisis came when the King ordered the Colonel-General to appoint one man to command his horse and the Lieutenant-General ordered him to appoint another. Vavasour naturally obeyed the royal order and Herbert never forgave him.[45] Almost as inevitable was the enmity of Winter and Mynne, who criticised Sir William for misunderstanding the strategic situation and neglecting their needs, errors arising naturally from the size of the operation needed to contain Gloucester compared with the paucity of the Colonel-General's resources.[46] Against these Vavasour could muster the support of the Glamorganshire commissioners, who hated Herbert, and the powerful Tracy family in Gloucestershire, who presumably wished to assert their local independence against Chandos.[47] In addition he possessed one trump card, the friendship of Prince Rupert.

Vavasour determined to utilise his advantages and negate his weaknesses by promoting a subtle scheme to obtain the overall command for Rupert himself, preserving his own power as Colonel-General intact as Rupert's deputy. In the early months of 1644 he mobilised a lobby at court and in his counties to achieve this effect, to which Rupert consented.[48] Half the plan was achieved, and Rupert replaced Herbert. The latter, however, laid down two conditions for his voluntary resignation.[49] One was that his own home of Raglan Castle and the nearby fortress of Goodrich should remain under his personal command, supported by the local tax of the surrounding hundreds and outside the jurisdiction of his successor. The other was that Vavasour should be sacked. Both were granted, and Sir William never held another command. The King asked Rupert to appoint a new Colonel-General, remarking that Chandos seemed the most highly favoured candidate at court.[50] Rupert respected military realities more than court opinion, and chose instead the most experienced soldier upon the spot, the newcomer and outsider Nicholas Mynne. The effect upon Chandos and Conway was dramatic; within two months both had abandoned the Royalist cause and surrendered to Parliament.[51]

Vavasour's command had lasted nearly a year. If he had not improved the overall strategic position of his counties he had at least left them better defended. The military developments in this period were minimal, however, compared with the political. Sir William had taken command as a glorified example of the expert adviser, as Sir Nicholas Byron had been in Warwickshire, subordinate to a local potentate and using local resources upon his behalf. Mynne took command as the deputy of a foreign-born professional soldier, using troops raised and trained elsewhere to defend an area from which the greater local leaders had retired and the lesser remained as subordinates.

CHAPTER TWELVE
Maurice, Byron and Gerard

A few weeks after Vavasour took over Lord Herbert's command, a more spectacular break with the old order occurred, when, at the end of July, the Marquis of Hertford was replaced as Lieutenant-General of the West by Prince Maurice. To an extent the significance of the change was masked, as it had been in the case of Vavasour. The latter took command, in theory, as a subordinate officer of the local magnate. Maurice took full control of both the title and power of his former commander, but as a member of the royal family he too might be considered to deserve respect for his social rather than his military position. Nevertheless, it was obvious to everybody that the prince had been given this command because of his military experience and ability, and was a stranger not merely to the area he now defended but to England itself. It was equally obvious that Hertford was extremely unwilling to resign his command, and although welcomed back to court with great honour accepted his replacement with a bad grace.[1]* Maurice appeared to justify the decision, for he took up his new command with as much energy as Vavasour did his, and more spectacular results. In the course of the late summer and autumn the prince and his officers conquered most of Devon and Dorset[2] and in the following winter his Field-Marshal, Hopton, another able and experienced soldier, was given a separate force which extended the King's territory to include all of Wiltshire, much of Hampshire and, for a time, western Sussex.[3] Maurice left undisturbed the local gentry whom Hertford had made governors of fortresses but in appointing new garrison commanders he chose men of proved military acumen.[4] When an inexperienced local gentleman

* Notes for this chapter are on p. 226.

was made governor of Weymouth by the King at the request of Hertford, Maurice ensured that he was given the honour on the strict understanding that within a short time he would resign to make way for a veteran.[5]

Such delicacy was possible in an area where the Royalists were masters of the field. In the Northern Marches and in Worcestershire, areas where the local Royalists were exhausted and harried by their enemies, more ruthless tactics were employed. There, during the winter, power was transferred openly to two experienced strangers, John Lord Byron, and Sir Gilbert Gerard. Both were members of distinguished military families, the Byrons of Newstead in Nottinghamshire and the Gerards of Halsall in Lancashire. Three of Byron's brothers fought for the King with him, and Sir Nicholas was his uncle. At least six members of Gerard's family served alongside him in the royal army. Byron certainly, and Gerard probably, learned soldiering in the Netherlands, and both served Charles against the Scots in 1640.[6] Byron was made, as said earlier, the colonel of the first horse regiment raised for the royal army in 1642, and for his services as a cavalry commander the King rewarded him and his heirs in October 1643 with the peerage which was to end two centuries later at Missolonghi.[7] Sir Gilbert raised a foot regiment, led it to the royal army and made his name there by his defence of the Buckinghamshire outpost of Brill.[8] Both were protégés of Prince Rupert, and in November 1643 Rupert recommended them to the King as suitable for two commands in the provinces which the King was now seeking to fill. His suggestions were accepted. Gerard was made governor of Worcester, in place of Russell and to the exclusion of his rivals. Byron was sent north with an army to reverse the disasters resulting from the Earl of Derby's defeat and reconquer Lancashire.[9] Their respective fortunes may now be examined in detail.

When the Earl of Derby's army was destroyed in April 1643 his best officers escaped into Yorkshire, taking with them two horse regiments and one of foot. In the course of the summer they led these troops to join the royal army and served with it through the Gloucester and Newbury campaigns. At the onset of winter the High Command considered whether these troops, now quartered in Hampshire, might not be better employed in an attempt to regain their native county. The disappearance of these three regiments would reduce the burden of the field army on southern England while not significantly diminishing that army's strength, as after their long service they represented its weakest units. These were the troops, and this the task, given to Byron. He was permitted to add his own horse regiment, itself much reduced in numbers, to the expeditionary force.[10]

Even before this force departed, its object had become more complex. On 11th November the news of the Parliamentarian invasion of north-east Wales, and Capel's inability to stop it, reached Oxford. Charles ordered Byron to muster his little army immediately and to assist the Lieutenant-General in defeating the invaders while *en route* to Lancashire.[11] Byron appointed Evesham as his rendezvous, and his troops received there a large convoy of weapons and munitions from the Oxford magazine.[12] On 30th November they reached Shrewsbury with 1 000 horse and 300 foot.[13]

Events had by then moved ahead of both him and Capel, due to the appearance of a new and formidable Royalist army literally out of the sea. It represented the first of the shipments of Irish army units which Charles had ordered the Marquis of Ormonde to despatch to England following his truce with the Catholic rebels. The regiments posted in Munster were destined for Bristol, and landed there as described. Ormonde's own Leinster army was ordered to take ship for Chester.[14] These soldiers would, Ormonde warned, require a great administrative effort from the English Royalists whom they were to assist. There were no ships at Dublin capable of transporting troops, so that these would have to be sent from England. Furthermore the civil war had cut off the supplies from England upon which the Irish army had depended, and its soldiers were underpaid, underclothed and underfed. If these wants were not supplied when they returned to England, their loyalty could not be guaranteed.[15]

The High Command accordingly took measures to ensure their transportation and refreshment. A fleet of seven Bristol ships under Captain Baldwin Wake was despatched to Dublin to carry the troops over.[16] A proclamation was issued declaring the Irish currency in the soldiers' pockets to be legal tender in England.[17] As Capel had already drawn heavily upon the resources of north-east Wales for his campaigns, it was decided to squeeze those of the north-western counties to supply the troops when they arrived. The commissioners of Anglesey, Caernarvonshire and Merionethshire were accordingly instructed to provide a total of 1 300 suits and a proportionable number of shoes and stockings, plus food or money to maintain 4 000 men for a fortnight.[18] That ambitious duo Thomas Bulkeley and Archbishop Williams swiftly ingratiated themselves with Ormonde as they had with Capel, and set about assisting Bridgeman in collecting these supplies.[19] The Marquis reciprocated by sending cannon and powder from his stores to all three to strengthen their respective strongholds of Beaumaris, Conway and Chester.[20]

On 15th November Wake's ships appeared off the Flintshire coast, carrying 1 500 of Ormonde's soldiers under the command of Sir Michael Erneley. They comprised most of the foot regiments of Erneley himself, Sir Fulke Hunckes, Richard Gibson, Sir Robert Byron and Colonel Langley, plus some horse led by John Marrow.[21] On the 16th they came ashore. Brereton, preparing to besiege Chester, received the appalling news that hundreds of crack troops were pouring onto the neighbouring beaches to avenge the raw local levies he had just defeated. He attempted to persuade Erneley and his officers to defect to Parliament and the local population to resist the newcomers. When both efforts failed he and Myddleton fled back into Cheshire, leaving only a garrison in Hawarden Castle to show for their recent victories. Erneley marched triumphantly to Chester, leaving a detachment to reduce Hawarden, which surrendered after twelve days.[22]

In early December Byron, Capel and Erneley, each with his own army, met at Chester. They became the subject of a debate concerning their respective commands, conducted and decided hundreds of miles away at Oxford. It had originally been intended that Ormonde, himself a distinguished general, would cross with his army and lead it to the King. By 29th November, therefore, a commission had been prepared at Oxford appointing him Commander-in-Chief of all the forces he was sending into England, plus the existing Royalist forces in the area of Capel's command, where he was to land.[23] Doubts arose, however, whether the Marquis would not be better employed in Ireland, where his authority and experience were unique, than in England where another able general could do as well. The King eventually decided to instruct him to remain at Dublin, and to appoint Byron to lead the troops sent over.[24] Byron had originally been sent north with the title of Field-Marshal in Capel's counties and in Lancashire, which empowered him to lead his expedition but kept him firmly subordinate to Capel when in his area and to the northern Royalist leader, the Marquis of Newcastle, when in Lancashire.[25] It was now decided to replace the discredited Capel as Lieutenant-General with Ormonde, who would delegate his command to Byron as Field-Marshal.[26] The new commission was sealed on 19th December[27] and by it Byron became effective commander of North Wales and its March as well as leader of Ormonde's army. Capel arrived back at court on the same day, to an official welcome.[28] Like Herbert, his noble status insulated him from censure and he was soon given high civilian appointments, though no more military commands.

While this dispute was conducted, the local Royalist civilian administration was achieving one of its rare triumphs, in providing for the newly-arrived soldiers at Chester. The linchpin of this effort was Bridgeman, who made a personal tour of North Wales to ensure that the supplies ordered were gathered. He was able to provide Erneley's men with all the shoes and stockings they required and obtained cloth to cut into clothing for them. To pay them he raised £1,000 upon his tour and more money thereafter.[29] In early December the remainder of Sir Robert Byron's regiment and Henry Warren's, another 1 300 foot, crossed from Dublin to Chester and Bridgeman had clothing, shoes and stockings waiting for them when they arrived.[30] He ensured that these men, like Erneley's, received some regular money during their stay in Chester.[31] By these efforts the newly-arrived troops were kept relatively well behaved and loyal to the Royalist cause despite attempts by Brereton to win them over.[32] Byron's army also appears to have been provided for although Capel's clearly represented a strain upon resources in addition to the other soldiers, as the Corporation presented the Lieutenant-General with £100 worth of the city plate as a (successful) bribe to remove them.[33] The only administrative failure of the entire operation concerned Wake's fleet, which was intended by the Royalist leaders at Chester to take in supplies from Anglesey.[34] The island's gentry, led by Bulkeley, considered themselves incapable of providing the quantity of victuals Wake required, and the burden of maintaining his crews was given to Ormonde.[35] This was a minor flaw in an otherwise impressive achievement, for which Bridgeman was justly rewarded with the post of Attorney to the Court of Wards.[36] The appointment marked a shift in his career, for in January he departed to take his seat in the Royalist Parliament and never returned to the local war. He had no personal need to do so, for in a sense Bridgeman's war was already won, having secured him the pleasures of a life at court.

On 12th December Byron took the field, his army being refreshed and the burden upon Chester becoming serious. Reinforced by local soldiers, his army and the men from Ireland made up a splendid force of 4 000 foot and 1 000 horse, almost all veterans. This scored a remarkable initial success on the 13th, when a small detachment surprised and took the impregnable castle of Beeston. Its fall exposed all southern Cheshire, where the Royalist army stormed the lesser garrisons with a ferocity that earned its commander the nickname of 'the

Bloody Braggadocchio' in the Parliamentarian press. When his troops stormed a Parliamentarian garrison at Barthomley he ordered that no quarter be given the defenders, claiming that 'mercy to them is cruelty'.[37] Brereton obtained reinforcements from Manchester and on the 26th he offered battle at Middlewich, where he had routed Aston. If he hoped that the place preserved some luck for him he was wrong, for Byron's men destroyed his army with almost contemptuous ease. All the fruits of a year's hard and patient fighting were lost, as the Royalists overran the rest of Cheshire. Brereton and some of his adherents fled to Manchester. The remaining Parliamentarians retired into Nantwich, which was soon their only hold in the shire. The town proved too well defended to be stormed, and Byron settled down to besiege it.[38]

During this triumphant progress the High Command was attempting to strengthen the Royalist area in Byron's rear. In December it ordered the commissioners of North Wales to impress 1 250 men to repair the broken foot regiment of Robert Ellis, which was intended to guard the area. When they failed to provide this number, they received a royal rebuke.[39] When Capel had retired to Oxford he had left his army in Shropshire to protect mid Wales and its March. Charles ordered Bridgeman's former military advisers, Shipman and Sir Nicholas Byron, to proceed to the area to provide for its needs, and those of the local garrisons such as Shrewsbury.[40] As his reward, Sir Nicholas was to be appointed the first military governor of Chester, which he had protected for a year as the servant of the Corporation.[41] It must have been a bitter blow to him that although his commission as governor was signed he never took it up. On 14th January he was escorting some munitions from Shrewsbury to his nephew's army when a Parliamentarian party from Wem surprised and captured him.[42] In this fashion another familiar figure vanished from the local war.

Meanwhile Parliament was taking its own measures to oppose Byron. On learning of Brereton's defeat it had ordered to the area its nearest field army, that in Lincolnshire under Sir Thomas Fairfax. After a difficult march Fairfax's men arrived in Staffordshire in early January, only to be harassed by Byron's horse, which he had sent out under Marrow to attack the approaching Parliamentarians. Sir Thomas turned north, and joined Brereton and his Lancashire compatriots at Manchester, where he settled down to the difficult task of combining their quarrelsome forces with his own.[43] In the interim Byron continued to besiege Nantwich, and by late January the town's fall was daily expected. When this occurred, the Field

Marshal intended to fulfil his original design and recover Lancashire, securing all north-western England.[44] It is possible that the High Command had always intended the troops from Ireland to join him for this task.[45] Any discussion of the objectives of Charles and his councillors, however, is always bedevilled by their inclination to rapid changes of purpose, as seen in the matter of Ormonde's command and in the complaints of Vavasour. This in turn tended to create confusion among their subordinates. For example, Byron was convinced that he was eventually destined to fight the Scottish army invading England to support Parliament.[46] The King, on the contrary, had already ordered the Marquis of Newcastle, who was facing the Scots, to leave Byron's army in Lancashire and not to call it to his aid.[47]

To forestall any further moves by Byron whatsoever, and to save Nantwich, Fairfax led his composite army into Cheshire and arrived outside the town on 25th January, to find his opponents awaiting him. The ensuing battle was the biggest to be fought in the region. Fairfax's army was larger but Byron's of better quality, and the struggle was hard and protracted. In the end it was Byron's men who broke. The best study of the battle[48] attributes this result to a sally by the Nantwich garrison upon the Royalist rear, while noting that the ultimate fault lay with Byron himself, whose control over his men was much laxer than that of Fairfax. Sir Thomas is indeed often acclaimed as the best general of the entire war, whereas Lord Byron, as shall be seen later, was found wanting in other actions.

During the next month Fairfax patiently reduced all the new Royalist garrisons which had been created in eastern Cheshire and northern Staffordshire during the brief period of Royalist superiority. Brereton and Myddleton journeyed to London to obtain new materials with which to rebuild their battered armies.[49] Byron retired to Chester with the remnant of his own consisting of all the horse and over a thousand foot. Although they were enough to ensure the safety of the city, there was no possibility of the Field-Marshal taking the offensive again for a long period. All his officers except his brother Sir Robert had been captured, and the troops were demoralised. Their situation was worsened by the fact that the corporation of Chester had not been expecting their return, Bridgeman and Sir Nicholas Byron were both gone, and attempts to provide money and supplies for the soldiers were correspondingly chaotic. The soldiers, in turn, behaved badly and were soon hated by the citizens.[50]

Lord Byron's campaign was nevertheless, like those of Vavasour, not totally devoid of effect. While the Royalists held Beeston Castle their enemies would find it difficult to dominate western Cheshire once more and menace Chester and North Wales. Byron himself retained a body of seasoned troops to provide the foundation of a new army. Yet, as with Vavasour, the most important developments of this period were ultimately concerned with internal power. At Chester the native-born Bridgeman had been replaced as the leading figure by the Field-Marshal, an outsider. Although local gentry still controlled Shropshire, the King had entrusted the hastening of supplies there to two other 'foreign' military men. One Shropshire squire delivered a prophetic comment upon the latter development: 'this day we were all summoned to Ludlow by a sole commissioner cased with a colonel; if this may pass for current certainly the Array is extinct, and we are all slaves to the Generalissimo'.[51]

This was precisely the fear which was developing in the same months among the Worcestershire gentry. In mid December, as Byron was marching out to conquer Cheshire, Sir Gilbert Gerard took up residence as governor of Worcester. The feelings of the commissioners regarding his appointment may be likened to those of the frogs in the fable, who upon complaining of being ruled by a log found themselves ruled by a water-snake instead. Gerard found them as mutually hostile as ever, but unanimous in their resentment of himself.[52] The High Command guaranteed his unpopularity by associating him with additions to the already considerable burdens upon the county. First, it decided to increase the military strength of Worcestershire, and the obstacles in the path of any convoy attempting to break through to Gloucester, by moving units of the field army into the shire. Sir Gilbert's own regiment accompanied him to Worcester, while a Yorkshireman, Henry Washington, was made governor of Evesham and installed there with his dragoon regiment. Aston's horse were also quartered in the Evesham area.[53] Washington was reinforced by the local soldiers of Sandys and the former field regiment of the deceased Beaumont, now led by his Lieutenant-Colonel, Godfrey.[54] Russell's regiments apparently remained near Worcester. In addition Sir Gilbert raised some new horse in his own name.[55]

At the same time as the High Command provided Worcestershire with more soldiers to pay for, it attempted to tap the county's financial resources for its own ends. Gerard was instructed to put pressure on the corporation of Worcester for the £2,000 loan it had promised the King in September. He did so, and became much resented in the city.[56] The corporation was forced to send a deputation to the King asking him to reduce the amount demanded to £1,500 and presenting him immediately with £200, raised by a frantic appeal to the wealthier citizens.[57] In addition the royal Ordnance Department ordered Gerard to continue the convoys of iron from Worcester to Oxford, which had been halted by the growing scarcity of horses and carts, and to raise £600 in the shire for the Department's needs. Both these demands were fulfilled in January.[58]

During the same period the resources of the county were being depleted by enemy activity. A party of Parliamentarians settled near Alcester in November and began living off south-east Worcestershire. The local Royalists were too divided to agree upon a leader to mount an expedition against them.[59] In December some colleagues of theirs, under Colonel John Fox, established themselves near Birmingham, and commenced raids on the north-east.[60] Gerard found the Royalists at Worcester barely capable of defending themselves, let alone counterattacking; the fortifications were in disrepair, the regular garrison reduced to 200 foot by lack of pay and the citizen regiment slovenly and inefficient.[61]

All these problems combined to reduce Sir Gilbert to frustration and fury after a month as governor. He had arrived with dreams of raising 2 000 more soldiers and conquering Warwickshire.[62] Instead the most he could accomplish was to drive the enemy from the Alcester area in January,[63] for his troops rapidly became immobilised by lack of money. Only a tenth of the county tax, which was intended to support these soldiers, was gathered in December and January, with the result that the men received one week's pay in six.[64]

This situation produced a very dangerous impasse in relations between the governor and the commissioners. The latter believed that there were now too many soldiers in the shire for local resources to support, while Gerard believed that the answer lay in more ruthless exploitation of these resources. He concluded that the local Royalist leaders were themselves the main obstacle to efficient administration, and wrote ominously to Rupert, 'I confess myself altogether ignorant of the commissioners' powers, but if nothing can be done without them, I believe His Majesty's business will not be much advanced.'[65]

The approaching clash between governor and commissioners was not to occur. Gerard's command, like Byron's, was about to be subjected to the administrative acumen of a much greater personality than either, one who was to rationalise and control the changes taking place in local Royalist government.

CHAPTER THIRTEEN
Rupert

Prince Rupert was a younger son of the Rhenish Wittelsbachs, the most illustrious ruined family of his age. As such, it was a natural development that he would become a professional soldier, and with his brother Maurice he embraced that career from early adolescence. None the less when he joined his uncle in 1642 he was still only twenty-three, and although he had seen action he had not yet held a major command. It appears that his appointment as Charles's Commander of Horse was a gesture of courtesy, extended.to him as the King's closest full-grown male relative present at the time. If this were the case, Rupert soon proved himself worthy, commencing a string of brilliant actions which have established him as one of history's great generals. To the Parliamentarian pamphleteers he became a terrifying barbarian, with an uncanny taste in disguises and strange pets.

Like many men of genius, the Prince was clearly conscious of his talents and proud of them. This self-confidence combined with his youth and an over-serious nature to produce an inability to react reasonably to any disagreement with his views. At court, where his birth and his position both made him automatically a major figure, such a trait won him almost as bad a reputation among many Royalists as among the enemy. One of those alienated was Clarendon, who portrayed him in his History as a rough, blunt soldier with contempt for the opinions of any civilians from Clarendon downwards. Since then, although each generation pays yet more tributes to Rupert's personal dash and military brilliance, this character-study has received little amendment. The purpose of the present section is to test it, by studying the Prince in his hitherto disregarded role as a wartime administrator.

His assumption of that role commenced on 6 January 1644, when he was commissioned to replace the distant Ormonde as commander of the army, and the region, at that time commanded in practice by Byron. To raise him in status above other regional commanders he was given the title of Captain-General.[1]* His wish to command a regional army was inspired by the hostility he had aroused, as described, at court, which had worn his nerves to the point where he urgently desired to leave the royal army for a period.[2] By late January there were equally urgent strategic reasons for him to do so. Byron's defeat at Nantwich had exposed North Wales and its March to renewed enemy attacks. No help could be expected from the northern Royalists, as for the first time they were facing a superior opponent on their home ground. In early January the army promised by the Scots to aid Parliament had crossed the Tweed and driven the King's adherents in Northumberland and Durham into their garrisons. Newcastle's army had to march north to succour them, leaving the field in Yorkshire clear for Fairfax when he returned victorious from Cheshire. A powerful controlling figure like Rupert was now desperately needed in the northern Marches to repair their defences. With this task in mind his commission was enlarged on 5th February[3] to empower him to create and dismiss both civilian commissioners and military officers within his counties. The following day he left Oxford to take up the command, accompanied by his own crack horse regiment and some foot.[4]

From the beginning the Prince approached the role of administrator with an unprecedented energy and breadth of vision. Before he departed he despatched letters to the commissioners of every county in his command. Those of Cheshire, Shropshire and Worcestershire were ordered to call meetings of their respective communities to discuss administrative problems, and those of the Welsh shires were ordered to appoint members to attend the Prince at these meetings.[5] At the same time letters were sent to military governors such as Ottley at Shrewsbury,[6] demanding a report upon the condition of their garrisons.

Quite apart from these formal measures, Rupert gained a great deal of information from protégés of his own whom he had sent ahead of him into the area. These already included Gerard at Worcester and Byron at Chester, and in January he despatched to Shrewsbury the two experienced soldiers who had served Capel, Woodhouse and Mennes, to prepare the town for his coming. The reports

* Notes for this chapter are on p. 227.

of all four men were strikingly similar, conveying a sense of an approaching collapse of the local war effort which they attributed to the ineptitude of the local leaders. Gerard's letters upon this theme have been quoted. Byron rapidly developed a hatred of local people in general, referring to Ottley as 'an old, doting fool'.[7] At Shrewsbury, Mennes and Woodhouse found both Capel's horse and Ottley's 300 foot ready to disband for lack of pay, no money forthcoming and the townspeople obviously hostile. They attempted to introduce a new efficiency at once, hanging a guard for sleeping on duty and attempting to hang the town marshal for allowing a prisoner to escape. Ottley and the Royalist gentry responded by refusing to admit Mennes and Woodhouse to their meetings and appealing to Rupert for the marshal's life. Mennes in turn fulminated to Rupert against 'the insulting people, who now tell us their power, and that three of the Commissioners of Array may question the best of us, from which power good Lord deliver me'.[8] In this matter the local people were certainly legally correct, but then Rupert's officers might claim with equal justice that the legal authorities had failed in their duty.

This was the devil's brew that Rupert inherited. Given his character as portrayed by Clarendon and the reports received from his henchmen, it would seem reasonable to expect him to have solved these problems by a ruthless assault upon the commissioners and their powers. Instead, he attempted a complete overhaul of the administration in partnership with them. He arrived at Worcester on 8th February,[9] and on the 10th, presumably after the county meeting, issued a proclamation[10] 'with the consent of the Commissioners'. It enacted a suggestion of theirs, which Gerard had ridiculed, that the number of soldiers in the county be reduced to a level which it could support. There were to be 2 000 foot and 500 horse, and to pay them properly the monthly tax was to be raised to £4,000 for three months and then reduced to the old level, or lower if possible. Free quarter and plunder were to be ended on pain of court martial, and a Council of War was to sit weekly at Worcester to hold the courts martial. The prices to be paid for fodder and victuals were also fixed and so were the days on which garrisons were supplied, to ensure that their governors kept good accounts.

In addition the Prince ordered specific measures to improve the county's security. He decreed a new programme of fortification for Worcester, requiring 300 workmen.[11] Evesham, and Sandys' foot regiment which held it, were put under a Warwickshire gentleman, John Knotsford, freeing Sandys to lead his horse regiment.[12] These directions could not have pleased the citizens of Worcester who paid for the fortifications, and definitely displeased Sandys.[13] Nor could the administrative reforms solve the problem of arrears upon the tax, for all the factors contributing to those arrears remained. Nevertheless they completely removed the friction between Gerard and the commissioners, and produced an energetic drive to collect the tax both in county and city.[14] The Council of War sat, and executed plunderers.[15] A dramatic display of regular justice was made at the Easter Assizes, when Sandys's brother Martin, colonel of the city regiment, was tried under civilian law for the murder of a fellow officer.[16]

On 15th February Rupert advanced to Bridgnorth, and installed as governor another experienced soldier, Sir Lewis Kirke, a Londoner recently knighted for his performance as acting governor of Oxford.[17] On the 19th, he reached Shrewsbury.[18] By this time the local Royalists had stated their case to him by letter,[19] to balance the complaints of Mennes and Woodhouse. The root of the trouble lay in the fact that on Capel's departure the gentry had agreed to support his horse, 300 strong, for only a month longer. Upon the expiry of that time they had refused to pay more, leaving the Royalist commissioners to attempt to support them from their private incomes. These had proved so inadequate that the regiment had dwindled to 70 men.[20]

Rupert's solution was another large-scale reform, of which however only traces survive in the sources. To cope with the shortage of cash at Shrewsbury he ordered the garrison to be paid in kind.[21] The county tax was in future to consist of a levy of 6d. in the pound on all men's estates 'without partiality or excuse'.[22] Overall control of the shire was vested in a new commission, on which Mennes sat with the local leaders, although Ottley remained governor of Shrewsbury. This was to oversee all branches of administration and keep regular accounts.[23] It set to work, and by March had eliminated free quarter in the county.[24]

One incident at this period illustrates both the scrupulous fairness and the ruthless efficiency of Rupert's regime. Apley Castle was a mansion dominating the eastern approaches to Shrewsbury, and Capel had installed a garrison there. Its misbehaviour caused the owner to complain to the Commissioners of Array, who promptly threw him in prison, where he languished until Rupert arrived. The Prince appointed his Commissary-General to hear the case. The unfortunate gentleman was released and given the choice of garrisoning his home with local men, accepting some of Rupert's, or blow-ing it up. He chose the first, but soon lost the mansion to a sally from Wem. He was given no second chance. Rupert's officers recaptured his home and destroyed it.[25]

To represent him in North Wales the Prince appointed the local dignitary Sir Thomas Hanmer, balanced by another able outsider who had accompanied Rupert from Oxford, Dudley Wyatt.[26] These met the commissioners of each county and agreed new local taxes.[27] Rupert came to Chester on 11th March for two days, but his only recorded action there was to block the appointment of its MP, Sir Francis Gamull, as governor, which had been urged upon the King by the Royalist Parliament. Byron objected bitterly, arguing the dilatoriness of local leaders in enforcing military measures, and Rupert persuaded Charles to refuse the commission.[28]

While occupied in the mobilisation of local resources, the Prince was already laying the basis of a much greater project, the construction of a new field army. To this task the provinces could supply men and money, but to complete it he required the weapons, munitions and legal powers that only the High Command could donate. To obtain them involved prevailing, at a distance, in the tangled politics of a court where vital decisions turned upon whoever held the King's ear at the critical moment. Rupert's principal enemies there consisted of Lord Digby, the Secretary of State, and John Ashburnham, the Treasurer. To plead his case, he was represented by Lord Jermyn, the Queen's favourite, and a clever Welshman, Arthur Trevor, who sometimes worked for Digby.

In February and March the odds in this struggle were weighted against Rupert, as the court's attention was focused upon rebuilding the royal army itself, blockading Gloucester and mounting an important offensive in Hampshire. The royal Ordnance Department could not supply Rupert as well as these projects.[29] Meanwhile his arch-enemy Digby was active. He failed in an attempt to poison Ormonde's mind against the Prince[30] but did succeed in obtaining for himself and Ashburnham the ransoms of Parliamentarians captured in Rupert's territory, which had been promised to Rupert for his troops.[31] When the Prince attempted to consolidate his power in Wales by obtaining the old office of President of the Principality, Digby protested that the appointment could not be bestowed without its patent, which was conveniently mislaid.[32] In this delicate situation Rupert's fiery temper proved an obstacle in itself. He destroyed in a fit of pique an attempt by Trevor to bring about a rapprochement with Digby.[33] Trevor himself, a born intriguer, involved the Prince in a new and probably unnecessary quarrel by convincing him that the lack of response from the Ordnance Department was entirely due to the enmity of its keeper, Lord Percy.[34]

In some measure these disappointments were balanced by the acquisition of two foot regiments under Robert Broughton and Henry Tillier and a horse regiment led by Sir William Vaughan. These seasoned soldiers numbered 1 200 foot and 300 horse and represented the last major consignment of troops sent by Ormonde. Wake's fleet carried them over to North Wales in February, and as the Chester area was burdened by Byron's battered army they marched to Shrewsbury and joined Rupert.[35] These units, with his initial force and detachments from Leveson, Bagot and Hastings, represented the troops which he took to relieve Newark in March. The town, key to the Royalist East Midlands, was besieged by a powerful army, and the King ordered Rupert to its aid.[36] He relieved it on 21st March, in one of the most brilliant actions of the war, and returned triumphant to Shrewsbury on 4th April.[37]

During March and early April the Prince's officers won several minor victories to parallel his major success. They were aided by the departure of Fairfax for Yorkshire and the absence of both Brereton and Myddleton in London. The only Parliamentarian leader remaining was Mytton, and he was defeated by Rupert in a skirmish before the latter's departure for Newark. He sallied out again, but on 25th March Ellis and the newly-arrived Vaughan beat him decisively at Lilleshall. By mid April every Parliamentarian garrison in Shropshire except Wem had fallen, and Wem itself was blockaded and its troops deserting.[38] Gerard took the field, defeated his enemy Fox on 24th March, and reconquered northern Worcestershire.[39] Byron raided the Nantwich area, fortified Bangor-on-Dee to strengthen the defences of Wales, conquered inland Flintshire and moved into Shropshire to live off the country around Wem.[40] Woodhouse attacked Brilliana Harley's fortress of Brampton Bryan. Brilliana's courage had proved to be more resilient than her constitution. Her ordeals in 1643 undermined her health, and in the autumn she had died. Yet her garrison continued to thrive, and had put an outpost into Hopton Castle. Woodhouse's army now encircled Brampton Bryan and undermined the walls. The defenders were forced to capitulate, and the home for which its mistress had given her life was burned down. What happened at Hopton was infinitely worse. The castle was stormed and its garrison made prisoner. Woodhouse ordered that the captive men be bound and their throats cut one by one as they lay helpless. The face of the war was changing.[41]

Newark was as great a defeat for Lord Digby as for Parliament.

Rupert became the hero of the court and Charles was disposed to refuse him nothing. The Prince was made President of Wales and the areas hitherto commanded by the defeated Carbery and the supine Herbert were added to his command. Within this huge region, all Wales and the Marches, he was given absolute control of all civilian and military appointments and half the 'Privy Seal Letter' money, £12,000 in all.[42] The speculation of courtiers in the ransoms of Parliamentarians from that area was stopped.[43] The Ordnance Department dispatched a large convoy of munitions to Shrewsbury.[44] Rupert now possessed the materials with which to construct his field army.

One major problem remaining was that of its destination. Charles had apparently considered that the new force should quarter in the Marches to defend them and to reinforce the royal army if needed.[45] Rupert himself considered invading East Anglia.[46] Byron, however, was anxious that the Prince should complete the task in which Byron had been interrupted, the conquest of all north-western England. He convinced Rupert, and visited Oxford in late April to prevail upon Charles. He was aided by the importunities of two other generals, the Earl of Derby who begged aid for his besieged mansion of Lathom in Lancashire, and Newcastle, who was himself now besieged in York by Fairfax and the Scots. When the pressure upon York tightened the King agreed to let Rupert relieve both places, providing he left behind 2 000 foot to assist the royal army.[47]

The Prince commenced further administrative work to secure his command in his absence. He visited Worcester on 6th May[48] to confer with Gerard and the commissioners. They had hit upon the idea of using the county Grand Jury not, as before, as a formal mouthpiece but as a genuine sounding-board for local opinion. The Easter Sessions had produced a number of ideas for improving Rupert's New Deal, and Rupert approved them in a proclamation.[49] Treasurers appointed by the commissioners were to receive lists of the sums due to each garrison and visit the governors on a fixed day each week to go over their accounts with them. Soldiers were only to collect arrears if accompanied by the civilian tax collector, the local constable.

At Shrewsbury the Prince ordered the committee he had appointed in February to settle an arrangement with the corporation to support a garrison increased to 800 foot.[50] Ottley was at last deprived of his governorship, for unknown reasons, and replaced by one of Ormonde's colonels, Sir Fulke Hunckes. Kirke was left at Bridgnorth, Woodhouse made governor of Ludlow and Shipman of

Oswestry. Rupert appointed his friend and Serjeant-Major, Will Legge, governor of Chester with Gamull made Lieutenant-Governor to placate him. To administer Royalist Cheshire and north-east Wales the Prince created a committee on which Legge and Gamull sat with the local leaders, specifying that Legge's absence from any meeting automatically rendered it illegal. Marrow's horse were left to patrol the area, and a suburb of Chester was destroyed upon Rupert's express order to improve the city's defences.[51] To secure mid Wales he made Richard Herbert governor of Aberystwyth Castle and, uniquely, left his father in command of the Herbert family castle of Montgomery instead of putting in a proved soldier. Presumably this was a gesture of favour to Richard.[52] Horse were sent to quarter in Montgomeryshire to force it to pay its tax.[53] In Lord Herbert's counties Rupert placed Mynne in control, as shown above, with the able Lingen given Goodrich Castle.[54]

North-west Wales gave particular cause for alarm. A Parliamentarian fleet had, belatedly, appeared off the coast to prevent Ormonde sending over any more troops, and aroused fears of a seaborne invasion.[55] The internal condition of the area was also alarming. In Anglesey the feud between Bulkeley and Cheadle had flared up again.[56] Archbishop Williams delivered a petition from the Caernarvonshire commissioners to the King in April, complaining of the condition of that county.[57] Its problems were twofold. Firstly, the cessation of the cattle-trade with London and the already considerable drain of men into the Royalist armies had impoverished its gentry. Secondly, those gentry were now divided because the local MPs John Bodvel and William Thomas had used their position in the Royalist Parliament to obtain commissions to raise foot regiments. The two men had turned the new regiments into local power blocs by filling them with their own local supporters, who they insisted were now exempted by military status from the power of the commissioners.

Rupert faced these problems. He ordered a report[58] to be made upon the real possibility of a seaborne attack, which concluded that there was reason for concern. He sent a special questionnaire[59] to the Sheriff of Anglesey to determine the island's state of defence. A monthly tax of £200 was agreed there, at Rupert's new rate of 6d. in the pound from all men, half to be paid in kind. Bulkeley and his friends fortified Holyhead and Ormonde managed to send over a few horse to patrol the island.[60] The Prince ordered the repair of Harlech Castle and commissioned as governor William Owen, a local man but one who had proved himself in the field army where his brother

John was a colonel.[61] As Commander-in-Chief of the three counties he appointed Mennes.[62] Clearly aware of both the poverty of the inhabitants and their suspicion of strangers, he ordered Sir John to 'deal very gently and civilly' with them and to employ them as garrisons for the coastal strongpoints.

Three case studies illustrate the virtues and limitations of Rupert's rule. The first[63] is from Myddle, Shropshire, where the Prince entered an inn. He drank some ale, praised it, paid the landlord handsomely and exhorted his soldiers to follow his example. They listened and when he had departed they drank the inn dry and paid nothing. The second[64] is from Worcester, where Henry Townshend, the commissioner 'for the guarding the county', presented Rupert with a petition complaining of a dispute with the sequestration commissioners. The Prince was in such a hurry that he galloped off with the paper unread, but a few days later Townshend received a letter signed in Shrewsbury, bringing the case to the notice of the sequestrators and ordering them to account to Rupert for their decision. It is an anecdote worthy of Plutarch. Yet two years later Townshend had still not obtained satisfaction.

The third[65] is from Caernarvonshire. Rupert's chaplain, wishing to make a donation to his master at no cost to himself, adroitly signed over to him £50 lent by his wife six years before to the Caernarvonshire commissioner Owen Wynn. Rupert bombarded Wynn for two months with increasingly threatening demands until the wretched gentleman, lacking the cash, was forced to sign away two family annuities. The episode does reveal the Prince's desperate need for money to pay his troops, but it also raised doubt as to whether such a sum was worth the damage done to the Royalist cause by this hounding of a loyal local leader.

This last anecdote sheds light upon an obscure but possibly important phenomenon. The Royalist clergy had, as shown, been important agents in promoting the King's cause, and also represented a considerable source of funds.[66] Thus it became a source of concern to Rupert that by 1644 the growing impoverishment of the provinces had resulted in increasing non-payment of tithes and fees by parishioners to their priests. The complaints of the clergy caused him to issue a proclamation[67] ordering the dues to be paid on pain of court martial. This situation may have provoked a rift between the established Church and local populations, weakening the political influence of the Royalist clergy. No firm evidence, however, exists upon the matter.

While Rupert was conducting this administrative overhaul of his command, his brother was engaged in similar, if less thorough, work in the West. There the counties were relatively wealthy, recently acquired and free from attack, and problems of the magnitude of those which had faced Rupert were missing. Nevertheless, as in the Marches, the county taxes were not fully paid, garrisons could not receive their promised wages[68] and some machinery for overall regulation and supervision seemed desirable. Hopton attempted to supply this in Somerset before he departed on his Hampshire campaign, giving the Commissioners of Array precise instructions to observe and account for the payment of the county tax and the condition of the garrisons.[69] At Christmas Maurice sent his army into winter quarters and was able to devote time to reforms upon a larger scale. On 5th January Cornwall and Devon agreed to associate to apprehend deserters, collect arms, enforce payment of the local taxes and pool the proceeds to raise and pay a fixed number of men. A joint committee of commissioners from the two counties was nominated to administer the scheme.[70] By spring Dorset and Somerset had joined it.[71] With the aid of the new Association he refreshed and recruited the western army to enable it to commence an offensive at the end of March. Unlike Rupert, Byron and Vavasour, he made very little use of soldiers returning from Ireland in this work, though a few were incorporated in his army.[72] Instead two regiments shipped over from Munster formed the nucleus of Hopton's force for his eastward thrust in the winter while a third stormed and garrisoned Wareham to protect Royalist Dorset.[73] With these veterans holding the fringes of his territory Maurice was free to recruit fresh strength within it and to bottle up the remaining enemy garrisons at Plymouth and Lyme Regis. The first objective of his spring campaign was the reduction of Lyme.

For all his much greater efforts, by early May, when his brother had been in the field a month, Rupert was still not ready to take the offensive. Three-quarters of his great command had been secured, but the remaining quarter, in south-west Wales, represented a source of serious weakness. In the same weeks in which Rupert had been strengthening North Wales and the Marches, Carbery's soldiers had been crumpling before the victorious progress of Rowland Laugharne. The Prince could not afford to leave such an enemy in the rear of the areas he had secured and by the terms of his Presidency of Wales he was directly responsible for the counties lost by Carbery. Yet, with the campaigning season so close, Rupert could not march to the far end of Wales to deal with its problems in person. He took the obvious solution, and appointed yet another experienced soldier to undertake the task, Charles Gerard.

Charles Gerard[74] was Sir Gilbert's nephew, and the head of the Gerards of Halsall. Having learned soldiering in the Netherlands, he had raised a foot regiment in 1642 and led it to the royal army, where he became a distinguished officer and a member of Rupert's faction.[75] The commission with which Rupert equipped him to deal with Laugharne has not survived, but it seems to have allotted Gerard all South Wales and Monmouthshire, leaving only Hereford-shire and Gloucestershire to Mynne. This enlargement of Carbery's former area was necessitated by the fact that by this date the Royal-ists held nothing west of Aberystwyth, Brecon and Swansea,[76] so that Gerard needed the resources of south-east Wales to counter-attack.

On 8th May he left Oxford with his foot regiment, a horse regi-ment, and Carbery himself, to act as adviser.[77] He entered Wales, and rapidly increased his force to 1 000 foot, 700 horse and 200 dragoons. Although small, this army was nevertheless more power-ful than Rowland Laugharne's, and the latter did not await its impact. He abandoned Cardiganshire and Carmarthenshire, pulling back his soldiers into Tenby and Pembroke where the Parliamen-tarian navy could reinforce them.[78]

These tactics placed Gerard in a difficult position. Carbery's defeat had proved the futility of attacking the Pembrokeshire seaports while Parliament controlled the sea. On the other hand he could not tie down his field regiments indefinitely to the frustrating task of wait-ing for Laugharne to emerge, like a cat watching a mousehole. Yet if he returned to the royal army with his troops, his enemy would simply sally out and reoccupy the whole south-west. The solution to the problem was obvious but difficult; to strengthen the local Royal-ists until they could hold Laugharne unaided.

He commenced this task in a manner worthy of Rupert by ordering reports upon the munitions and weapons existing in his counties.[79] Upon his departure from Oxford the King had equipped him with a powerful administrative weapon, in the form of orders to the com-missioners to press 2 450 new foot soldiers to defend themselves, specifying the monthly taxes needed to pay them.[80] In view of their inability to provide Vavasour with the men and materials he required in 1643, the consternation provoked in the local gentry by these new demands may be imagined. Gerard at first found them 'very willing', but the deterioration in his relations with them is plain. The best evidence for the process is from Glamorganshire,[81] where the com-missioners, led by Sir Nicholas Kemeys, a local potentate and governor of Cardiff, wrote to Gerard protesting their inability to supply the men he demanded. Gerard's response was ruthless; he held Kemeys personally responsible for that inability, and replaced him as governor with an outsider, Sir Timothy Tyrrell. The recruits, and money, were subsequently produced in full.

In this manner Gerard filled every town and castle in Cardiganshire and Carmarthenshire with soldiers. Laugharne Castle alone was given 200 foot.[82] The major strongpoints, like Cardiff, were placed in the care of English veterans. A Colonel Lovelace was made governor of Carmarthen.[83] Aberystwyth Castle was entrusted to Roger Whitley, a captain in Gerard's horse regiment,[84] replacing Richard Herbert who was moved to a command in Monmouthshire, perhaps on the ancient Roman principle whereby men from one end of an empire were sent to hold down those at the opposite end. He accepted this posting without complaint, but Gerard was unable to win similar co-operation from the best resident local soldier, Herbert Price. Price was affronted by being placed beneath the authority of the stranger Gerard, and demanded at least the position of second-in-command. Gerard was unwilling to displace his existing officers, and begged Rupert to provide some other reward.[85] The Prince obliged, and Price became governor of Brecon. Between the network of Royalist fortresses and those of Laugharne Gerard created a zone of scorched earth, laying the countryside waste with a savagery which provoked horror in the Parliamentarian press.[86] One Royalist commissioner enriched himself by dealing in the plundered cattle brought back to Carmarthen.[87] At the end of the summer the work of fortification and consolidation was complete, and Gerard able to march his field troops back towards the King.

With Laugharne in full flight, and Charles Gerard embarked on his administrative overhaul, Rupert was free at last to take the field. His new army lay ready in two divisions, formed around the two existing forces of himself at Shrewsbury and Byron at Chester. Both had been recruiting hard for two months. In part their strength had been increased by the arrival of units from elsewhere. Rupert's own excellent foot regiment had come up from winter quarters at Bristol.[88] Agents had recruited a new foot regiment for Byron in Ireland, which had crossed to Chester before the Parliamentarian fleet arrived.[89] In addition, men were obtained by drawing them from existing garrisons, a policy with, as will be seen, fatal repercussions. The largest single detachment of garrison troops was the body of horse, a few hundred strong, which Leveson led to Rupert from Dudley Castle.[90] Finally, new recruits were obtained from North

Wales and its March. Some were certainly pressed, this work being undertaken alongside the pressing of men for the royal army ordered in March,[91] although the agents of individual regiments in that army were stopped.[92] Others may have joined voluntarily, and *Mercurius Aulicus*[93] boasted that many volunteers had come to the Prince since his victory at Newark, anxious to serve under a general who would win them booty. The news of Newark had certainly been carefully publicised by Rupert's governors with bonfires and other celebrations.[94] By 5th May Byron had 500 new-raised men in his force.[95] These recruits were apparently divided among existing regiments, as Brigadier Young's analysis of Rupert's army at Marston Moor[96] reveals no regiments raised since 1643. On the other hand, Capel's horse regiment under Mark Trevor, which had been 30 strong in February, now mustered 400 troopers.[97] These conclusions do much to weaken the thesis of Sir Charles Firth,[98] that the Royalists' failure was partly due to their practice of recruiting strength by commissioning new regiments rather than filling up those already in existence.

In mid May Rupert and Byron called their troops, dispersed to quarters, to their colours.[99] On the 16th Rupert's division left Shrewsbury. On the 18th Byron's division joined it at Whitchurch, the combined forces numbering 2 000 horse and more than 6 000 foot. They invaded Parliamentarian Cheshire, and detachments closed up the enemy garrisons while the rest of the army scattered to plunder, reuniting at prearranged places. On the 25th the whole force reached Stockport and stormed the town, pushing on into Lancashire.[100] The local Parliamentarians raised the siege of Lathom House and retreated to Bolton. On the 28th Rupert's army broke into this town and destroyed the forces inside. Two days later the horse from Newcastle's beleagured army, 5 000 strong, joined the Prince with 800 foot from northern garrisons. Thus greatly reinforced, Rupert turned west and took Liverpool to secure communications with Ireland.

As a result of these victories all west and central Lancashire fell into the hands of the Royalists, more territory than they had held in the county in 1643. The Prince spent a week settling its administration, in the same manner as he had that of his other territory. A committee of local gentry was set up at Liverpool to superintend the collection of money, but soldiers from outside the county were given its fortresses. Byron's brother Sir Robert was entrusted with Liverpool. The gentry who had defended Lathom House were displaced in favour of a stranger. The Earl of Derby himself, who had come with Rupert and expected to resume his former command, found himself ignored, and was forced to leave the county in an evil humour.[101]

On 24th June, Rupert and his army marched eastwards, on the road to York. Behind them they left a military empire covering all Wales, the Marches and western England, owing obedience to the Prince and his devoted brother. This huge area had been placed in the control of soldiers who might be considered both able and disinterested, aloof from local interests and local animosities. To prevent them succumbing to the vices of despots, and to prevent the alienation of the local leaders, the powers of the new commanders had been defined within a framework of rules which ensured the local gentry a share in government. This was a genuine revolution in wartime administration, and the most rational possible solution to the crisis in that administration which had been brewing in certain areas at the opening of the year. It remained now to see how it would stand the test of war.

PART FIVE

Warlords and civilians

The test was not long in coming. When it did, it precipitated a crisis in administration considerably worse than that which the Royalists had faced in early 1644. This crisis they countered and eventually overcame. The complexity of this story is so considerable that to tell it with greatest clarity I propose to subdivide the forthcoming section not by chronology nor by geography, but by theme. The first chapter will describe the military reverses suffered by the Royalist generals, the second will examine the civilian reactions provoked by those reverses and the third will analyse the response of the generals to the civilian initiatives.

CHAPTER FOURTEEN

After Marston Moor

On 2 July 1644, on a stormy evening at Marston Moor, Prince Rupert fought the combined armies of the Scots, Fairfax and Parliament's Eastern Association and almost won the Civil War for the King. Instead, by midnight, his army lay in heaps upon the moor, or fled terrified through the lanes beyond. With it perished the Royalist army of the North. The Royalist northern commander, Newcastle, fled overseas, York surrendered, and the Royalist presence in Yorkshire, Durham and Northumberland was reduced to a few beleaguered garrisons. For Rupert's own command the consequences were potentially as serious. To construct his army the Prince had drained Wales and the Marches of seasoned troops, new levies and money. If it had won the war this fact would not have mattered. With its defeat, the consequences became disastrous.

Rupert's departure from the Marches had coincided with a new series of Parliamentarian thrusts. With the coming of the new campaigning season its local generals were taking the offensive once more with new forces. The Earl of Denbigh[1]* had been immobilised at Coventry all winter by quarrels with the local leaders, who refused to allow him to denude Warwickshire of troops to make up a field army.[2] By spring, however, he had obtained the necessary powers, and raised a horse and a foot regiment, with which he plundered north-east Worcestershire when Rupert marched north from Shrewsbury.[3] Myddleton came up to join him with a fresh army recruited in the London area, and their troops were further reinforced with Staffordshire detachments.[4] With this composite force, 750 horse and 1 050 foot, the Earl determined to complete the con-

* Notes for this chapter are on p. 230.

quest of Staffordshire. On 29th May he bombarded Rushall Hall into surrender and then moved on to attack Dudley Castle, which had been weakened by the departure of Leveson and many of the garrison with Rupert.[5] Its remaining troops nevertheless resisted fiercely, and in June the siege was abandoned under pressure of external events. The royal army itself had suddenly arrived on the scene.

As Parliament's local adherents moved against their opponents, its field troops attacked the King. In May, after bitter quarrelling, the leading Parliamentarian generals, Essex and Waller, had been persuaded to use their armies in a pincer movement to crush the royal army at Oxford. Charles escaped the trap at the last instant and fled west with about 7 000 men. He entered Worcestershire on 5th June and hurried across it, smashing the bridges behind him and snatching Knotsford's garrison out of Evesham. On the 6th he reached Worcester and rested there in temporary safety.[6] Waller and Essex now divided forces. Essex marched to conquer the West, where Maurice's army had been worn down in the unsuccessful siege of Lyme. In the following weeks he relieved Lyme, Maurice retreating before him, took Weymouth and Taunton and moved into Devon. The country people did nothing to aid him but nor did they assist the Royalists.[7] Even in Cornwall, a county still entirely Royalist, efforts to collect subscriptions to a declaration against Essex aroused little response.[8] Meanwhile Waller pursued the King, and encamped for a week to the east of Worcester waiting for his opponent to emerge.

The King's secretary-at-war[9] maintained that during its rest at Worcester the royal army was well paid and fed, which indicates a colossal burden placed upon the city and its neighbourhood. Certainly £1,000 was demanded from the city[10] and supplies levied as far as Shropshire.[11] The eastern districts, which had recently been plundered by Denbigh and by Fox,[12] were forced to support the Parliamentarians. Charles exercised his horse by sending them to drive Denbigh from the siege of Dudley, only to see the Earl join his army to Waller's.[13] One of the strangest episodes of the war now occurred; Charles and his advisers, who had hitherto responded to the Parliamentarian offensive with no imagination or daring, suddenly began to display both. Deceiving their enemies with a feint, they dashed out of Worcester on 16th June, led the royal army back across the Avon valley and returned to Oxford to gather troops, leaving Waller and Denbigh far behind and bewildered. On his march the King broke the remaining bridges and exacted money and footwear from Evesham on the excuse that it had admitted Waller's army.[14] The campaign had resulted in an embarrassment for Parliament, but the true cost had been to the Worcestershire countryside.

Meanwhile, the ring of Royalist strongpoints constructed to contain Gloucester had been fractured. Massey had already struck at these in May, when he destroyed the small garrisons immediately to his west, at Westbury and Newham.[15] On his way north pursuing Charles, Waller had attacked Sudeley Castle. As the High Command had ordered, it had been garrisoned with local levies, and being inexperienced they surrendered at the first bombardment.[16] Massey came to meet him, storming Tewkesbury and destroying the remnants of what had been Beaumont's regiment.[17] The Gloucester garrison could now range unchecked, and while Waller and Denbigh oppressed eastern Worcestershire Massey plundered the south.

After Charles's escape Waller marched east after him. Denbigh turned back into Staffordshire. There he received an appeal from Mytton to assist an attack upon Oswestry. The town guarded the approaches to mid Wales, and much of its garrison had gone with Rupert. Moreover at that moment its governor, Shipman, was absent. Denbigh agreed, and on 23rd June they stormed the town. Denbigh left Mytton there as governor, and marched into Cheshire to rejoin Myddleton, who had been gathering the local Parliamentarian forces into a body capable of pursuing Rupert.[18] The loss of Oswestry not only exposed mid Wales but severed direct communications between Shrewsbury and Chester. The two veterans Rupert had left to guard these places, Hunckes and Marrow, determined to join forces and retake the town. This scheme was ruined by the ambition of Marrow, who attempted to win the sole glory, attacked Oswestry singlehanded, and was taken by surprise on 3rd July by Myddleton, racing to the town's aid before Hunckes could arrive. Marrow's force was routed, and Myddleton and Denbigh took advantage of this victory to conquer south-western Cheshire.[19] The Earl now left Myddleton at Nantwich to project an invasion of Wales, and retired to Stafford to await further employment. When this came, it consisted of a high civilian role, that of heading an embassy bearing terms to the King. His horse regiment, however, remained behind and joined the Warwickshire Parliamentarians in ravaging eastern Worcestershire again.[20]

Even in areas untouched by the enemy, this period witnessed problems in administration. In north-east Wales the newly levied soldiers in the local forces showed a natural tendency to slip away to their homes.[21] In the north west Sir John Mennes apparently regarded himself as an exile upon a barbarian shore, and the local people returned the compliment by proving 'lax and rotten' in his service. In particular, he was unable to persuade them to enlist as garrisons for the coastal castles, and eventually Ormonde had to send 300 foot under Colonel Thomas Trafford over from Ireland to perform the task. These – the last significant shipload of veteran troops – escaped the Parliamentarian fleet, but on their arrival Mennes, whose nerves were clearly frayed, promptly quarrelled with Trafford. He also lost patience with Archbishop Williams, whose usual desire to make himself indispensable inevitably involved meddling in everything Mennes did. Instead Sir John befriended a local gentleman of little prominence, Robert Jones, who benefited from his favour by imposing licences on coastal traffic from which Jones reaped a percentage of profit.[22]

On 25th July Rupert returned to Chester, bringing with him an unknown number of soldiers, the wreckage of his army.[23] He settled down to build a new army around them, proceeding with his usual thoroughness. An inquiry was ordered into financial problems in his command, and answers provided to the problems discovered.[24] All local officers were ordered to specify the quantities of money in their hands at that moment.[25] Those gentry who had not yet paid their 'privy seal letter' money were instructed to disgorge it. They included Bulkeley, who may have been starting to find his newly-won prominence a little inconvenient.[26] New levies of foot soldiers were ordered.[27] The Prince himself ensured that the Excise was imposed upon Chester, and pulled down many houses there to strengthen the fortifications.[28]

These efforts proved futile. The new levies showed no willingness to enlist under a defeated general, and deserted almost as fast as they arrived.[29] Rupert could in any case not find the arms and ammunition to equip them.[30] Some of his veteran officers demanded passes to find better employment abroad; one, like a true professional, sailed to London and joined Parliament.[31] These blows seem to have broken the Prince's spirit; on 20th August he abandoned the task, left Chester with his own regiments and marched into Wales. On the 25th he reached Monmouth, and the next day crossed to Bristol and settled there to recruit instead.[32]

His departure coincided with fresh disasters. Since June Massey had plundered almost at will in Gloucestershire but had been held off Herefordshire by the energy of Nicholas Mynne. On 4th August Mynne laid a trap for his enemy at Red Marley, by which he hoped to catch him between the Hereford forces and a Royalist detachment coming from Worcester. It was almost the end of Massey, but instead it was the end of Mynne, for Massey attacked him before the

Worcester force arrived, killed him and destroyed his regiment.[33] Herefordshire was now open to Massey's raids. Rupert's response was to send Vavasour back there as governor of Hereford[34] and request a report on the condition of the county.[35] As in the case of the financial report, its authors are unknown. It revealed a picture of unpaid soldiers living on free quarter because half of the local tax, instead of passing to the Treasurer, went direct to local leaders such as Pye and Croft, who presumably pocketed it as even their own regiments had dwindled to a few men. Vavasour never took up his governorship, presumably because of Lord Herbert's enmity, and instead on 10th September Rupert appointed Viscount Scudamore's younger brother Barnabas.[36] Although a local man, he was of no consequence in the community and doubtless earned the post by his service under Rupert in Staffordshire in 1643[37] and as Mynne's Major-General in the past months.[38] To Monmouth the Prince appointed a distinguished field army colonel from Somerset, Sir Thomas Lunsford.[39]

In the far north west at the same period the Royalist war effort expired. In August a detachment of the Parliamentarian forces which had defeated Rupert entered Lancashire, drove the King's adherents from the field, blocked up their garrisons and settled down to reduce Liverpool, the most important.[40] Cumberland and Westmoreland had hitherto seemed solidly Royalist counties. Only four gentry families had ever responded to Parliament's appeals, the strongpoints were held for the King by regular soldiers and the militia guarded the countryside. Yet when a force of Scots entered the area in September, the militia fled without offering battle and most of the garrisons surrendered immediately, leaving Carlisle, the only one in determined hands, to be beleaguered.[41] For Royalists elsewhere this complete collapse of a supposedly loyal area was an ominous sign. It may have been taken particularly to heart by the King's supporters in North Wales and its March, who seemed about to suffer the same fate.

In late June their greatest enemy, Brereton, had returned to Nantwich equipped with extensive new powers and £1,500,[42] and set to work strengthening his forces. The day after Rupert left Chester, the impulsive Marrow made a raid on Northwich, and was trapped and killed by Brereton together with his horse regiment.[43] That same night 2 000 more Royalist horse, under Sir Marmaduke Langdale, arrived in Cheshire. They represented the cavalry of the Royalist Northern Army, who after Marston Moor had attempted to patch together some local resistance to the victors, and failing in this had decided, rather than to surrender, to attempt an epic march to join the King. They crossed into Cheshire exhausted and badly shaken by the mauling they had just received from a Parliamentarian army in Lancashire.[44] They quartered for the night at Malpas, and when they had settled to sleep Brereton came upon them. Langdale was wounded, and his horse driven demoralised into North Wales.[45] At Chester Rupert's two protégés, Byron and Legge, quarrelled with each other,[46] the city Royalists resented the refugees from the county whom they were supporting[47] and the citizens demonstrated against the Excise.[48] Brereton was able to move his outposts up to Taruin, a few miles from the city.[49]

Under these circumstances Myddleton felt able to launch the invasion of mid Wales he had been planning since the fall of Oswestry. On 4th August he had joined Mytton to raid Welshpool and rout Rupert's horse regiment, which had been quartered there trying to gather cloth to re-equip the Prince's remaining foot soldiers.[50] This reconnaissance served to prepare the ground for the advance he commenced with his small army on 3rd September. On the 5th he captured a convoy of powder at Newtown sent north by Rupert to supply Chester, and advanced upon Montgomery Castle.[51] This fortress, reputedly impregnable, had been one of the few left in the hands of its owner, Lord Herbert of Chirbury,[52] who betrayed this trust by surrendering upon the first summons.[53] He was escorted happily into retirement at London, out of reach of the enraged Royalists, who included his son Richard.[54]

Richard and other local leaders reacted immediately, by uniting under two veterans from Ireland, Sir William Vaughan and the recently-exchanged Sir Michael Erneley, who were superintending the defence of Royalist Shropshire. They raised a force by detaching troops from garrisons, caught Myddleton's army at Montgomery and broke it, driving the foot into the castle and the horse, with Myddleton, to Oswestry. They then settled down to starve out the castle.[55] Myddleton sent an appeal to Brereton, and to the Parliamentarian army in Lancashire. These united to make up a force of 3 000 and arrived at Montgomery on the 18th, only to find that Byron had just arrived from Chester with more troops to swell the Royalist army to 2 000 foot and 1 500 horse. A pitched battle ensued. The Royalists seemed on the verge of victory when Ellis's inexperienced local foot regiment suddenly broke, spreading panic through their army. The result was catastrophic. Only a hundred Royalist foot escaped death or capture, and those last included most of the veterans from Ireland who had survived Marston Moor.[56]

Archbishop Williams considered the defeat worse than that at Marston Moor[57] and in strictly local terms he was correct. It reduced the Royalists to the condition of remaining in their fortresses awaiting siege. Brereton and the Lancashire army returned northward to reduce Liverpool, garrison the Wirral and tighten the pressure upon Chester.[58] Myddleton was joined at Montgomery by Sir John Price, who had already changed sides in 1642.[59] Together they paraded to Newtown and received the submission of the local gentry.[60] Myddleton next decided to secure his communications by taking the Red Castle, near Welshpool. Its owner, Lord Powys, unlike Lord Herbert of Chirbury, refused surrender, but his fortress was weaker than Montgomery and contained only sixty soldiers. On 2nd October Myddleton blew in the gates and stormed it.[61] All eastern Montgomeryshire was now his, and he proceeded to raid Denbighshire and Radnorshire, capturing Royalist gentry.[62]

Meanwhile the melancholy pilgrimage of the Northern Horse continued. Regrouping after their shock at Malpas, they were propelled south by Myddleton's advance. In early September they crossed Herefordshire, and then Worcestershire, hoping to reach Oxford on their march to the King. At Evesham, however, they found Massey's army in their path, determined to prevent them from reinforcing Charles. Demoralised, they retreated into Herefordshire.[63] Rupert conceived the plan of shipping them over the Severn, and sent a party to fortify Beachley as a bridgehead from which they could disembark. The Northern Horse accordingly streamed south. Their persecutor Massey arrived at Beachley first, driving them back into Monmouthshire.[64] He next turned north parallel to them, and on 23rd September appeared outside Monmouth. Lunsford had not yet arrived, the fortifications were neglected and one of the officers decided to profit from an unpromising situation by turning traitor. He let Massey's men into the town, and it fell. The Parliamentarians now held a crossing of the Wye, and began raiding Monmouthshire.[65] A full-scale invasion was only prevented by the appearance of Charles Gerard and his army, returning from southwest Wales. Massey retired to Gloucester, and Gerard and the Northern Horse were able to march to Worcester together, and from there to Oxford and the royal army. But Massey's garrisons remained in Monmouth and the Forest of Dean.[66]

The Royalists in Wales and the Marches may, or may not, have gained some comfort from the fact that by this time the fortunes of their monarch, and of their fellow partisans elsewhere in England, had begun to improve. In June the royal army, having obtained rein-

151

forcements, had crippled Waller's at Cropredy Bridge near Banbury. Then, continuing to display the strategic skill they had discovered at Worcester, Charles and his advisers led their army into the West and united with Maurice's forces. The rural population proved as unresponsive to appeals as they had been earlier, but the combined regular armies were sufficient to trap that of Essex in Cornwall in September and compel its surrender. Taunton and Weymouth remained in enemy hands, but the Royalists once again had command of the field. The King made a clear allocation of local resources to enable his partisans to block up the enemy garrisons, and placed the remaining strongholds in Dorset and Wiltshire under capable officers from his army with no local ties. Sir Richard Grenville, a local man but an impoverished younger son and a distinguished soldier, was left in charge of the blockade of Plymouth.[67] Charles now marched east with Maurice's troops and the small force gathered at Bristol by Rupert, and relieved his Hampshire and Berkshire fortresses before dispersing all these troops to quarters around Oxford for the winter. By these manoeuvres the King had prevented the total defeat of his cause. He had not, however, regained most of his losses and could do little to assist his followers in Wales and the Marches. His field troops badly needed rest. Their winter quarters had been impoverished by the long residence of troops in the area[68] and truncated by the loss of Abingdon and Reading. Within a few weeks many soldiers had deserted, running for the comfort of their homes.[69] The western Royalists were preoccupied by the new hostile garrisons in their midst. There was still a good chance that Parliament would effectively win the war that winter, by destroying the supply base of Wales and the Marches upon which the royal army depended to fit itself out for the next year.

This was precisely the hope that Parliament entertained. Its adherents had already fractured the defences of Royalist Wales at their north- and south-east corners. Now, if they could break through in the south-west, they could split the Royalist territory in the middle. In late summer 120 foot under a Colonel Beale had been despatched by sea from London. In October they landed at Pembroke, and emboldened Laugharne to take the field. He advanced on Laugharne Castle, and stormed it on 2nd November. The Royalists destroyed their other fortresses in south-west Carmarthenshire and concentrated in Carmarthen to hold the town.[70] Beale left Laugharne to recruit and marched across Cardiganshire to join Myddleton, who met him at Lampeter. The local Royalist commissioner Rowland Pugh raised a force of local people to attack them, but Myddleton and Beale easily dispersed these and burned Pugh's home. They went on to destroy Abbey Cwmhir, the principal Royalist strong-point in Radnorshire, on 4th December.[71] On the 24th Laugharne, ignoring Carmarthen, came up to attack Cardigan. The town fell, and an attempt to relieve it was defeated.[72] Myddleton took the opportunity to ravage northern Cardiganshire, burning the great houses.[73]

Any hope that Rupert might return to redeem the situation was destroyed on 30th November, when the Prince was promoted to command the royal army itself.[74] In his place, his brother Maurice was sent into the Marches. His commission has not survived, but it certainly included North Wales, Cheshire, Shropshire, Staffordshire, Herefordshire and Worcestershire. To underpin his authority in North Wales, Colonel John Owen, a local man but a fervent Royalist and proved soldier, was knighted and sent to Conway in December with a commission as governor of the town. His real mission, as the local gentry realised, was to represent the interests of the High Command in the area.[75]

Prince Maurice left Oxford on 14th January,[76] with a body of troops which included his own regiments of horse and foot. For a month he remained in Worcestershire and then marched north towards Cheshire, where the position of the Royalists had further deteriorated. In November Brereton had laid siege to Beeston Castle[77] and commenced a blockade of Chester. In January a sally by the garrison was heavily defeated.[78] The Denbighshire Royalists, fearing that their lines were over-extended, withdrew their garrisons from Bangor and other places on the Dee, and burned them.[79] This availed them little, as Brereton sent a strong party into the county which garrisoned Wrexham, sacked other towns and drove off cattle.[80]

At this moment Maurice arrived at Shrewsbury with a force swollen by the Worcestershire troops. He settled there to call in detachments from the main garrisons of Shropshire and Staffordshire, which when collected and combined with the best soldiers of the Shrewsbury garrison, increased his army to 2 000 men.[81] With these he entered Denbighshire in mid February, only to find that Brereton had also called in aid from neighbouring counties and was awaiting him with a larger army. The Prince outmanoeuvred his adversary, and entered Chester on the 20th. He strengthened the city's defences, only to have to retreat into Denbighshire again as Brereton came up.[82] He was in Denbighshire attempting to devise some plan of action when the appalling news reached him that Shrewsbury had

fallen. The Parliamentarians at Wem, learning that the garrison had
been depleted, had attacked the town before dawn on 22nd February,
and caught most of the defenders sleeping. The prisoners included
leaders of 1642 such as Sir John Weld and more recent commanders
such as Erneley. All the lesser Royalist garrisons in central Shropshire were hurriedly evacuated.[83]

The loss of Shrewsbury was the last of the succession of disasters
which had commenced with Marston Moor. Because of its completely unexpected occurrence, and the associations of the lost town
with the birth of the Royalist cause, it had an exceptionally severe
impact upon the spirits of the King's party. It demoralised his
negotiators at the Uxbridge peace talks, and depressed the monarch
himself.[84] Yet by this stage in time it is doubtful whether the military defeats, serious as they were, represented the principal anxiety of
the High Command. A crisis had arisen in territory yet within
Royalist hands, which threatened to destroy the royal cause from
inside.

The Marcher Association and the Clubmen

From the opening of the war Royalist commanders had, as illustrated, repeatedly complained of the indifference and hostility of local populations. In the late summer of 1644 these complaints took on a new urgency. One reason for this development lay in the pressure upon local resources produced by the troops which accompanied or followed Rupert from the North. The Prince scattered these to quarters in Wales and the Marches, while he gathered new recruits at Chester and Bristol. The inhabitants of the areas assigned for their support, who had been reluctant enough to sustain local garrisons, were openly hostile to these strangers. Gibson's foot regiment, sent to Conway in August, was shut out by the citizens. It quartered at Caernarvon instead, in an atmosphere of open animosity, until after a month it was recalled to Chester.[1][*] Some horse and foot under a John Van Bynissy were sent into eastern Shropshire. The horse were allotted quarters near Wenlock, where the countrymen refused to feed them, while the foot were sent to Bridgnorth, only to suffer the fate of Gibson's for, despite the orders of the governor, Kirke, the townsmen closed the gates to them.[2]

The greatest sufferings were those of the hapless Northern Horse, who drifted into one local administrative system after another. In Herefordshire they consumed the money and supplies needed by Scudamore for his local garrisons.[3] At Worcester Sir Gilbert Gerard apparently took steps to prevent this occurring, for the northerners complained of his meagre hospitality.[4] In Monmouthshire, where they lingered longest, their reception was proportionately worse; the countrymen in the areas assigned by the local leaders to support

* Notes for this chapter are on p. 232.

them rose up and attacked them when they requested supplies, and the gentry, including some Royalist commissioners, refused to punish the insurrectionaries.[5]

The impact of Rupert's defeated forces, however, merely served to worsen a situation already deteriorating. The Royalist defeats of the summer and autumn served to reproduce upon a grand scale the phenomenon already noted as operating upon the fortunes of local garrisons, the tendency of local people to withdraw support completely from defeated troops. This was a rational action, calculated to hasten the end of the war, and its destructive effects, in their locality. It ensured that the broken troops would be denied the resources to recover.

By the autumn of 1644 the Royalists in the Marches were caught in this downward spiral. In August Kirke sent out his garrison from Bridgnorth to demand the local tax, which had been unpaid since Denbigh's victorious invasion. The troops were overpowered at Shiffnal by countrymen led by a local gentleman, disarmed and sent back pelted with insults.[6] At Shrewsbury Hunckes had earned the enmity of the local gentry by 'being too much a soldier', and Rupert replaced him in August with his fellow officer Erneley, who found the population markedly hostile.[7] In Monmouthshire in early September a new drive to raise the local tax produced £30 out of the £1,000 due[8]. In late October Sir John Winter called a meeting of gentry at Chepstow to discuss defensive measures, but they would not consent to any scheme involving expenditure of money, so none was adopted.[9]

The great defeat of Montgomery had a particularly destructive effect upon local support. From Shrewsbury Erneley reported 'the edge of the gentry very much blunted'.[10] From Ludlow another officer commented that 'the malignancy which has lain in many men's hearts has now burst forward to a manifest expression'.[11] Woodhouse found his garrison there refused supplies by the neighbouring people.[12] In the cities of the Marches discontent also sharpened noticeably at this period, and the new Excise became a particular target for popular hatred. At Chester the Royalist candidate for the office of Mayor, Lieutenant-Governor Gamull, was heavily defeated to cries of 'No Gamull, No Excise', and an alderman elected who had opposed its introduction.[13] At Worcester the corporation defiantly elected as Mayor a man to whom the King himself objected, justifying their action on the grounds that nobody had complained against him locally.[14]

Against this background, the High Command had particular

reason to be wary of a movement which began with a meeting of the Shropshire Royalist gentry on 12th November. They resolved that, being weary of war, they would join with other counties in writing to Parliament demanding that it make peace with Charles.[15] At the same time Sir Gilbert Gerard and the Worcestershire commissioners decided to call a huge county meeting to discuss local problems, the qualification for attendance being that of the parliamentary franchise.[16] The meeting took place on 6th December, and produced a decision to join Shropshire in directing Parliament to make peace, and to enforce this demand by associating with Shropshire and other Royalist counties to produce a huge new force of local people capable of keeping order and warding off all Parliamentarian attacks.[17]

In this, as the Shropshire declaration acknowledged, they were following the example of the Royalist gentry of Somerset, who in turn were acting upon an idea of the King himself, calculated to utilise the growing desperation of the local population with the war's burdens. In April 1644 certain Royalist gentry had raised a petition in Hampshire, requesting Parliament to make peace with the King and threatening that henceforth the rural population would rise *en masse* to oppose any disturbers of the peace.[18] This probably inspired the King to issue his proclamation to 'One And All' at the opening of his eastward march in the autumn, calling on the populations of the counties in his path, which included Hampshire, to rise and assist him in forcing Parliament to come to terms. This appeal had no effect whatsoever on the countrymen to whom it was directed, but provoked some Somerset Royalist leaders to form the plan of joining the four western counties in a pledge to raise the population *en masse* to keep perfect local peace.[19] Such mass levies of local men, the *posse comitatus*, had been employed before in the course of the war. Leveson had tried to summon the *posse comitatus* of Staffordshire in January 1644.[20] The High Sheriff of Cornwall had successfully used that of his county to expel the local Parliamentarians after their indictment in 1642.[21] The Worcestershire *posse* had been called out against Waller in 1643.[22] In March 1644 the Royalist gentry of the Ludlow region had summoned the *posse* in order to select fifty men from it to form a permanent irregular defence force.[23] The proposed new Association armies would be a gigantic version of the county *posse*.

As it turned out, the plan for the Western Association aroused no interest among the bulk of the western gentry, and was eventually dropped.[24] The reason for this was probably that Charles's victory in September had restored Royalist military supremacy in the area, and his subsequent directions for the division of resources had resulted in the administration functioning with relative smoothness. The local Parliamentarians were blockaded in their fortresses, and the only pronounced ill-feeling in the winter was not between the military and the civilian population, but between the local-born military governors in Somerset and the strangers whom the High Command, in accordance with its now customary policy, was installing in charge of new garrisons erected in the county.[25] The proposed Association would not seem worth the effort.

In the fevered atmosphere of the Marches, however, where military and civilian leaders and the local population were riddled with mutual suspicion and united only in fear of an advancing enemy, the idea took root, as seen, with great strength. If feasible, it contained both a considerable advantage and a considerable danger to the King's cause. It offered an opportunity to turn war weariness into a lever to eject Parliamentarian troops from large areas of England. On the other hand, it also equipped local men with a powerful weapon which they could easily turn against the regular Royalist troops whom they so clearly regarded as a burden. The King's reply to the proposal made at Worcester was accordingly guarded.[26] He gave permission to associate and to form an army provided its chief officers were regular soldiers appointed by Prince Maurice. On receiving this reply, the Royalist JPs and the Grand Jury of Worcestershire wrote to the Shropshire commissioners in the name of their community proposing association.[27] By 11th January the Royalist gentry of the two counties had formally combined with those of Staffordshire and Herefordshire, and presented further requests to the King.[28] They asked that the new army elect its own officers, be subject to civil law and be supported by the proceeds of sequestered estates in their counties.

By this time the potential dangers of the Association had become very apparent to the Royalist officers. Its claim of sequestered estates represented a considerable blow to the regular garrisons, which certainly in north-west Wales,[29] Monmouthshire,[30] Shropshire[31] and Cheshire[32] and probably everywhere, had come to depend ever more heavily upon their proceeds as the yield of the local tax diminished. Moreover the relations between the local gentry and the military commanders had deteriorated further since the autumn, particularly in Shropshire. There Shipman had aroused the wrath of the gentry by imprisoning the servants of one of their number who had neglected to pay his 'Privy Seal letter' money.[33] Kirke called them 'rotten ashes'.[34] Dudley Wyatt called them 'mutinous spirits' and labelled the new Association an attempt 'to thrust out the soldier'.[35]

Erneley complained that the concern of the gentry for the new Association had removed any interest they might have had in his (Shrewsbury) garrison, so that no money was delivered to it at all.[36] Woodhouse noted that the project of the Association roused the countrymen around Ludlow to great excitement, much of it openly hostile to his troops.[37] In Herefordshire Barnabas Scudamore wanted to arrest the gentry and release them only when they paid their share of the local tax.[38] At Worcester Sir Gilbert Gerard, who had maintained excellent relations with the gentry since February 1644, died in mid January, leaving Maurice to find a successor.[39]

Nevertheless, on 15th February Charles gave the Association permission to proceed.[40] He may have considered the dangers of refusing it greater than those of permitting it. In addition he may have been reassured by the presence among the leaders of the Association of former Royalist heroes such as Ottley[41] and Russell.[42] The list of commissioners appointed to run it was headed by the Earls of Shrewsbury and Ardglass, noblemen who had hitherto played no part in the war but were unlikely to favour Parliament because both were Roman Catholics. At any rate the royal assent was qualified; Maurice was still to supply the commanders of the new army and vet all inferior officers proposed and one of the first tasks of the Association would be to impress 600 men for the field army. At a local level its powers were nevertheless enormous; it was granted the proceeds of sequestrations, could impose a local tax of its own and could call up any man aged sixteen to sixty. In Worcestershire at least the commissioners set to work immediately, sending out warrants to every village naming all able-bodied men in their parishes and to receive instructions to organise them.[43]

In setting to this work the local gentry had forgotten a lesson that they should have learned two winters before:[44] that the county was too wide a unit for the political horizon of the countryman. Then, elaborate schemes for the defence of counties had come to nothing, while men attended instead to the protection of their own settlements. This was to recur now, and the intensification of the local struggle was to ensure that it would take a dramatic form. The same months that witnessed the creation of the Association saw the appearance of militant neutralism for the first time since 1643, and with a difference. Then it had been a movement conceived and led by prominent gentry. Now it was a spontaneous outburst of peasants, led by men of no social significance, the so-called 'Clubmen'.

Clubman movements were to appear in many areas of southern England in the course of 1645, but the authorities upon them[45] all agree that those in the Marches were the earliest. The first notice of them appears in a report from Wem dated 18 December 1644, reprinted in a Parliamentarian newspaper.[46] It announced that the countrymen of the Shropshire hundreds of Clun and Purslow had risen 1 200 strong to resist the plundering of the Royalist colonel Vangeris. They were led by the parson of Bishop's Castle and some very minor gentry called Jeremy Powell, Richard Heath and Francis Harris, and demanded the re-posting of Vangeris, compensation for the goods taken and the evacuation of the local Royalist garrisons of Stokesay Castle and Lea Hall. Another group of local men had collected at nearby Leintwardine and was preparing to join them. Other notices of a rising in Shropshire appear in later Parliamentarian journals[47] but are considerably less precise and detailed than this. Part of it is authenticated by two letters from Woodhouse. The first,[48] dated 31st October, complains of the looting of the area by Vangeris, whom Rupert had sent with some horse to protect it, and announces the garrisoning of Lea Hall. The second,[49] dated 22nd February, refers to a 'rebellion' in his area in the recent past, while a letter from Erneley[50] on 3rd January speaks of 'seditious people in the county who have mustered three thousand' and whom the Parliamentarians hoped to assist. No sequel is recorded to the affairs; Vangeris was re-posted,[51] but the two garrisons remained.

The Worcestershire Clubmen are slightly better documented, as two of their own declarations were reprinted by a Parliamentarian newspaper, on 11th and 18th March.[52] The first is found also among Townshend's papers,[53] and in another journal.[54] The second is so circumstantial in its local detail that it also seems a genuine source.

The first is a declaration drawn up on Woodbury Hill on 5th March by men claiming to hail from 'North-West Worcestershire', presumably the area defined by the county boundary and the rivers Severn and Teme, with Woodbury rising in its centre. It was presented to the Royalist High Sheriff, Henry Bromley, by Charles Nott, the parson of Shelsley Beuchamp. It recognised the Sheriff and the Grand Jury as the only legal authority in the county. It declared to them that the countrymen of the region were forming a league to enforce the Worcestershire Royalists' own recent proclamation[55] for the discipline of their troops and the regulation of the county. Apart from this they stood to defend the Protestant religion, the known laws of the land and the honour of the King.

The second is also a declaration, this time undated. The newspaper claimed that it emanated from the same group as the first, described by it with sweeping vagueness as 'the Worcestershire Clubmen', but it obviously did not. It was produced at Malvern Link by the inhabitants of Great Malvern, Mathon, Cradley, Leigh Sinford, Suckley and Ponick (Powick?). These villages effectively define the area of the Malvern Hills, not far away from the Woodbury region but quite distinct from it. Like the former paper it proclaimed the establishment of a league for mutual defence, this time to enforce the orders for behaviour of troops laid down by the Royalist Parliament.

These two documents represent all the reliable evidence surviving upon the Worcestershire Clubmen. Parliamentarian journals[56] reported risings in other parts of the shire, but the details they give of these are vague and display an ignorance of local geography. There is no trace of such other movements in the relatively ample local Parliamentarian and Royalist records, and had they taken place in the more accessible parts of the shire it is difficult to account for this silence. In this context the two declarations present a paradox. They define a distinct topographical region, the hills of the west of the county, probably at that period the wildest and most remote part of Worcestershire and certainly the least exposed to the war. It lay off the main routes by which Royalist armies crossed the county, which insulated it from most of the extra levies noted earlier,[57] and from plunder. It was also the only part of the county which had escaped devastation by the Parliamentarians in 1644. Altogether the Clubman areas of 1645 must have represented a haven of peace compared with the rest of Worcestershire, and the defensive leagues appeared where they were apparently least needed.

This problem is intensified when it is observed that these leagues do not appear to have been provoked directly by military outrages of the sort that they were formed to counter. The Woodbury declaration certainly states that its association represented a formalisation of local informal self-defence measures undertaken at previous moments of emergency. However, it does not specify the date of those measures, and it is extremely unlikely that they needed to be enacted in the period immediately preceding the formation of the leagues in early March 1645. This was not, as one would expect, a time of unusually severe marauding by Royalist or any other soldiery. The Royalists were in possession of the whole shire, having defeated all enemy raiders the previous autumn.[58] Worcestershire was thus enjoying a period of relative calm, with the Royalists pressing no more heavily upon one part of it than another. In the month before the meeting at Woodbury there were in fact very few Royalist soldiers present in the shire to oppress it, because most of its troops were absent with Maurice. The permanent Royalist garrisons were at

Worcester, Evesham, Bewdley and Hartlebury Castle, none of which were in the Clubman areas. Nor would January seem to have been a month of exceptional outrages, for that had been the time of Maurice's arrival in the shire, and the Prince had carried out an energetic drive to discipline the soldiery.[59]

If the idea that these Clubman leagues were a mechanical reaction to increasing military depredations does not stand up, neither does the explanation for their inception offered by the Parliamentarian press. It claimed that the associations were provoked by new warrants for the county tax sent out by the Royalists at Worcester.[60] This is improbable because the Royalist documents prove that no alteration in the size or nature of the tax was made at the time and moreover the Royalists would have been unlikely to have attempted anything adventurous when Maurice had drained the county of troops and Worcester itself was cripplingly short of munitions.[61] The basic objection to this explanation, however, is that the actual Clubmen manifestos are concerned with the problem of order, not with taxation. They both appear to accept the principle and practice of the tax. The Royalist proclamation which the Woodbury league was committed to enforce laid down precise directives for its assessment and collection.

There does in fact seem to be only one explanation which can answer the objections raised to the others and also account for the location of the leagues in their particular part of the county. If correct, it is an extremely ironic one, for it suggests that the Worcestershire Clubmen were provoked into action not by the Royalist military establishment but by an organisation which ought to have represented an ally against it, namely the gentry Association. Its demands, promising universal enlistment and a second burden of taxation, must have been a particular shock to remoter areas which may not have fully understood its purpose.

In this context the Clubman declarations require a second scrutiny. The broad principles of the Woodbury league, to defend Protestantism, laws and King, are not very significant. They are lifted almost word for word from the Royalist declarations of the opening of the war, and may have served as a guarantee of the authors' continuing Royalist sympathies. More immediate to the local situation is the bitter hostility of both groups to soldiers of any kind and for any purpose. The Malvern league in particular refused membership not only to local men turned soldiers but to any who were marked for enlistment, which boded extremely ill for the Association. Both are equally bitter against Catholics, the traditional bogeys of the English populace. The extraordinary venom of the declarations against the Catholics, and their demands that local commissions be purged of them, seem at first sight puzzling, as Catholics were never prominent in the Royalist civil and military administration of the shire. The puzzle is resolved when it is realised that the name at the top of the signatures to the Association's warrants is that of the Catholic Earl of Shrewsbury. The gentry who elected him had apparently forgiven him his religion, but the back-woodsmen of the leagues did not. The mere existence of such local associations for self-defence in fact negated the very purpose of the Association.

Whatever their purpose, no evidence survives to show the Worcestershire leagues in action. In this they form a striking contrast to the Herefordshire Clubmen, the last and most aggressive of the Marcher risings. The best account of it is contained in John Corbet's history of his commander Massey's campaigns.[62] He relates that in March 1645 Massey advanced into Herefordshire and found 'multitudes of the country people appearing in arms'. He heard that Scudamore, 'sending for hay and contribution to his garrison, was so far denied by the country, that it came to blows'. His troops killed some local people and carried others to Hereford as prisoners. This provoked a mass rising of countrymen, who marched on Hereford and besieged it several days. They demanded the release of the prisoners and compensation for the slain, and an exodus of all regular Royalist soldiers from the county, leaving the local people to defend themselves against any invaders. Massey asked them to join forces with him, but they refused when he insisted they swear to serve Parliament and pay money to his troops, proclaiming their principal aim to be to 'secure the country from contribution and quarter' for any regular soldiers. Massey, unwilling to turn them against himself, retired to Ross-on-Wye. Scudamore came to terms with the Clubmen, and they dispersed.

This narrative is corroborated in every detail by other sources. Most of its information is found in a despatch from Massey himself, dated 22nd March.[63] He enclosed a list of the Clubmen's demands, dated the 19th, which accord with those cited by Corbet.[64] Among Scudamore's own papers is preserved a proclamation he issued against the Clubmen on the same date[65] offering mercy if they handed over their leaders, disbanded and paid the local tax in future. It names the seat of the rising as Broxash Hundred, at Marden and Cowarne, and the leaders as Thomas Careless, Thomas Wooten, two members of the Walwyn family of Cowarne and a Lawrence of the same village. All these names are obscure, none being of gentry. It is certain that in the previous month Scudamore, having driven Massey's outposts from the county,[66] was interested in a new effort to collect the tax.[67] By 3rd March the Clubmen were active, for Scudamore wrote to Rupert that day reporting that agitators were raising the countryside against his troops, inspired by the rising in Shropshire.[68] Finally, a letter survives from the King to Scudamore, dated 25th March, approving the terms the latter had made with the rebels.[69]

It is obvious, as Scudamore's letter illustrates, that all three Clubman movements cannot be divorced from their context among the general fever of anti-military feeling among the countrymen of the Marches at this period. Nevertheless it is equally clear that they differ too greatly from each other in their nature and aims to be regarded as a unified movement. Further, one of their main similarities is that each represented only a portion, and a similar portion, of their respective county communities. The Worcestershire Leagues, as shown, were formed in the western hills. The Shropshire Clubman hundreds comprised the south-western corner of that county, equally rugged country and empty of garrisons and moving soldiers until Myddleton's conquest of Montgomeryshire a few months before. Broxash Hundred is in the north-east of Herefordshire, also hill country and also empty of garrisons and hitherto sheltered from the war, which had affected the southern half of the county. Indeed Scudamore may have been concentrating upon it because the wealthier southern areas had become so exhausted. Hence the Clubman areas of the Marches were precisely the most socially and economically backward.

This conclusion is reinforced when an examination is made of certain developments in the more accessible areas. In north-west Wales tension between the unpaid soldiers and the civilian population became intense during the winter, and prompted the gentry, led by Archbishop Williams, to petition Rupert to permit the cattle trade with the Midlands to reopen, so that more money would enter the area.[70] In December the inhabitants of the Clwyd Valley of Denbighshire petitioned Byron for an end to free quarter and the supremacy of martial over civil law and for permission to raise a civilian force to repel Parliamentarian raids.[71] In March, emboldened by the Herefordshire rising, the gentry of the whole county repeated these requests, with the statement that the new force would also be used to discipline the regular soldiers.[72] In the same month one of Rupert's officers, attempting to escort a convoy of powder across

Monmouthshire, reported that the countrymen there, excited by the example of the Herefordshire Clubmen, were on the verge of rising against the Royalist soldiers. 'Here be two or three constables deserve hanging,' he snarled, 'and I had done it ere this, if I had but a party to defend me from their Welsh bills.'[73] Lord Herbert, however, prevented an outbreak by promising to present their grievances to the King in person, and did. They consisted of the usual demands for an end to free quarter and irregular exactions, which Herbert proposed could be achieved by concentrating all troops in two major garrisons, permitting a simplification of the system of supplies.[74]

The difference between these protests and those of the Clubmen is plain; the latter, in their poor and backward regions, lacked the gentry who could act as intermediaries between the countrymen and the High Command. They had no other means of stating their grievances than to enact the remedy, and thus their actions were notably more extreme although their basic sentiments rarely were. This conclusion parallels Professor Underdown's definition of the Somerset Clubmen as 'the Country, shorn of its upper echelon of politicised gentry'.[75]

The distinctions between the different Clubman groups and between the Clubmen and the rural population as a whole are certainly more apparent now than they were to both Royalist and Parliamentarian leaders in March 1645. The Parliamentarian press had obvious reason to present the Clubman risings as part of a general popular uprising against the iniquities of Royalist military rule, and did. But the Royalists were seriously frightened. Byron believed that the 'infestation' of Herefordshire would spread everywhere.[76] 'I fear all Wales will be in rebellion,' wrote Rupert himself, who, his nerves frayed by another winter of court politics, believed in a huge provincial conspiracy against his regular army, abetted by his civilian enemies at court.[77] In Monmouthshire Sir Trevor Williams, one of the original Royalist leaders, despaired sufficiently of his cause to write to Parliament offering to betray the county.[78] To many it must have seemed as though the whole structure of Royalist power in the region was about to crash in ruin.

CHAPTER SIXTEEN

The resurgence of the warlords

The preceding chapters have been concerned with the external and internal disasters to the Royalist war effort in the autumn and winter of 1644–5, and it was this negative aspect of the picture which, as shown, most impressed contemporaries. Yet parallel to this recession were positive omens, which indicated that some strength survived in that effort at a local level.

Most obviously, the Parliamentarian thrusts of the autumn were slowly halted and sometimes reversed. By early 1645 Myddleton's advance into mid Wales had stopped. To his west and south rose the barren Berwyn Mountains and Kerry Hills. To his north he had run into the ring of powerful castles constructed by Edward I to hold down North Wales, which now acted as a defence for the Royalist lands within it. He assaulted two of these, Chirk and Ruthin, and was beaten off.[1]* To his east Sir William Vaughan cut him off from his Shropshire colleagues by putting his horse regiment into Shrawardine Castle and the other fortresses of western Shropshire. From these Vaughan led his troopers against Parliamentarian quarters with such ferocity that he became known to his enemies as 'The Devil of Shrawardine'.[2] Within these limits Myddleton found the country too poor to support more than a tiny army, and his men grew idle, underpaid and demoralised.[3]

In Worcestershire and Monmouthshire the Royalists counter-attacked. In the former the local troops took the field in October, drove all enemy soldiers out of the county and plundered Warwickshire in vengeance.[4] At Monmouth the new Parliamentarian garrison became demoralised by the quarrels of its leaders and the hostility of

---

* Notes for this chapter are on p. 234.

the citizens, who preserved their loyalty for their Royalist master the Marquis of Worcester. When in November the governor drew out most of the garrison to attack Chepstow, a Royalist party from Raglan Castle attacked Monmouth and recaptured it with the citizens' aid.[5] In December the King sent his field army into the Cotswolds to live off the supplies upon which Massey's army at Gloucester depended. Within a month the latter's men began to mutiny and desert.[6] He retained his garrisons in Dean and kept the Royalist outpost at Lydney in check[7] but was incapable of taking the offensive. Any hope of relief from Warwick was ended when Rupert put three foot regiments under Sir Henry Bard, another of his protégés,[8] into Campden House on the Warwickshire border.[9]

Similarly not all Royalist administration showed only signs of lassitude and collapse. On leaving Worcester in June Charles, realising the exposed position of the county, had given Gerard the powers of a military despot to defend it, commanding the commissioners as he wished.[10] These were precisely the powers Sir Gilbert had longed for in January.[11] Rupert, however, had obviously taught him much, for what he proceeded to enact, on 22nd July, was another complete overhaul of the administration in partnership with the commissioners of the sort instituted by the Prince.[12] The county tax had now been reduced as Rupert promised to its former level, and the fixed number of troops was now reduced proportionately, to one foot regiment of 1 000 under Gerard and one horse regiment of 400 under Sandys. These were to be formed by an amalgamation of existing units, with a clear command structure established and the county divided into specific districts to support each company. Half the tax could be paid in kind. Gerard and the commissioners were to discuss current matters together on a fixed day each week.

It is unclear how far this local New Model Army was formed. Sandys, Knotsford and Gerard certainly pooled their various regiments, but Russell's horse and foot preserved their separate identity in the shire.[13] The reform certainly did cement good relations amongst the local leaders. In August Gerard wrote warmly to Rupert of the commissioners,[14] and the defeat of the Parliamentarians in October was achieved by the former rivals Sandys and Knotsford, working in partnership.

In Monmouthshire likewise schemes were enacted to solve administrative problems. After the recapture of Monmouth Charles Gerard returned to the shire with his army to stabilise the local government.[15] After an initial squabble over precedence with Sir John Winter,[16] the two settled down together to work with the commissioners upon a reform programme, which was duly published on 11th December.[17] Its novel feature was that all arrears upon the county tax would be commuted for a single payment of £1,000. Thereafter £1,600 per month was to be levied for four months, half to be paid in provisions. Free quarter and extra levies were to be ended. This arrangement must have been interrupted by the disturbances noted above, but progress was nonetheless made on the garrisons. Sir Thomas Lunsford arrived at Monmouth at the end of February and set 200 workmen to labour repairing the fortifications.[18] Lord Herbert used his influence to assist Sir Thomas in recruiting his garrison to 1,800 men.[19]

The task of Maurice was to follow the example of his brother Rupert, a year before, in making this process of military and administrative recovery general. The traditional reputation of this prince would make him seem a poor candidate for the task. All his life he was Rupert's understudy. Rupert went through every action miraculously unscathed, Maurice generally came out wounded. Rupert had an impregnable constitution, Maurice nearly died of camp fever. Rupert is remembered as a commander who stormed cities, Maurice is remembered as the commander who failed to take Lyme Regis. Clarendon portrayed him as a military boor with a notable capacity for alienating local populations. Rupert's most sycophantic biographer, Warburton, had nothing but contempt for Maurice.

The brief account given earlier of Prince Maurice's exploits in the West has suggested that this portrait is, even more than that of his brother, in need of reassessment. His behaviour in the Marches bears this opinion out. On entering into his new command he recognised the potential dangers of the Association to his regular army[20] and determined to reduce antagonism between soldiers and civilians. As early as January the Shropshire gentry noted his remarkable willingness to satisfy all local grievances[21] and on the 17th the Prince expressed to them his desire to 'ease and cherish' their county, doing justice to both soldier and civilian.[22] On his arrival at Worcester he enquired into all orders made for the regulation of the county hitherto. By 7th February he had read and assimilated them all. The level of the tax and the number of troops were left as fixed, but all disciplinary rules for the soldiers and all the tariffs for purchase of supplies were reissued as a comprehensive set. It added up, in fact, to a Charter of Rights, stating exactly what soldiers and civilians had a right to expect from each other in all matters. To enforce it the commissioners were to be equal partners with the army, sitting in all courts martial with equal votes and having equal power with the governor of Worcester over all civil matters. He provided for musters of the Association army, which were to be held before the heads of the military and civil machines, the governor and High Sheriff. Finally he asked the Grand Jury to approve the whole package and it did, making its own minor amendments.[23] In place of the deceased Gerard, he appointed Sandys governor, a proved soldier but a local man popular with the gentry.[24]

For all these efforts Maurice's work of restoration would not be significant unless he recreated confidence in the royal cause with a military victory, and this, as seen, he was unable to do in January and February. In an attempt to reverse the sequence of defeats, the King eventually reverted to his tactics of two years before, of sending detachments of the field army into the Marches to counter each enemy thrust. His response to the fall of Shrewsbury was to send Rupert himself to aid his brother. The Prince gathered most of the royal army, 2 000 foot and 1 000 horse, from its Cotswold quarters and united with Charles Gerard who marched his army from Monmouthshire. Their departure permitted Massey the sally into Herefordshire on which he met the Clubmen.[25] On 9th March Rupert and Gerard united at Bridgnorth with the 2 000 Northern Horse, who having recovered their morale in winter quarters at Oxford were just returning triumphant from a daring raid into Yorkshire.[26] Together they advanced across Shropshire, emboldening the local Royalists to reoccupy mansions a few miles from Shrewsbury, such as High Ercall.[27] During their advance Maurice had gained strength from other sources. He had called up the soldiers of north-west Wales under Sir John Owen, who had advanced to Wrexham and helped the Prince push Brereton's men out of Denbighshire.[28] Ormonde had managed to send a few more foot over to Chester.[29]

On 15th March the two princes united their composite armies near Ellesmere and advanced to the relief of Chester and Beeston Castle.[30] Brereton, as ever, knew when the time had come to run. He called off both sieges, pulled his men back into his strongholds in central Cheshire and bombarded Parliament with appeals for help.[31] The princes remained in western Cheshire about a week. They burned Brereton's evacuated outposts, demolished any potential strongpoints near Beeston and forced the locality to provide supplies and money for the castle, and for their army.[32] Owen's men returned to Caernarvonshire,[33] the detachments from the Marcher garrisons dispersed to their fortresses[34] and Gerard marched into mid Wales.[35] To replace them, new men were levied in Denbighshire to hold the crossings of the Dee[36] while to fill up their own army Rupert and Maurice drew all the surviving veterans from Ireland, 1 200 strong, out of Chester,[37] and recruited 1 000 more men from the local population.[38] The success of this recruiting testifies to the new repute of the royal cause. The next objective of the princes was clear. Having humiliated the external foe, the time had come to repress internal opposition. Their formidable army, containing at least 5 000 seasoned soldiers, turned south upon Herefordshire and the unsuspecting Clubmen.

There seems little doubt that Scudamore never intended to keep the terms he had made with the countrymen. The terms themselves only survive reprinted in Parliamentarian journals, which disagree upon the details.[39] They seem to have fallen short of the Clubmen's demands, promising only release of prisoners, compensation for those killed and remittance of a month's tax. Whatever they were, Scudamore made them to buy time, for the royal letter in reply to his despatch announcing the incident praises his 'discreet answers' and assures him Rupert will come to his aid.[40] Rupert and Maurice duly arrived at Bromyard at the end of March, and the Clubmen, emboldened by their success against Scudamore's soldiers, rose to fight them. The Royalist regulars made short work of their opponents.[41] Some of the Clubmen leaders fled to Massey,[42] others were captured and hanged.[43] The Royalists described this operation as 'freeing the people' from the grip of agitators.[44] Doubtless this echoes the tendency of ruling groups throughout history to ascribe all popular uprisings to the work of a few unrepresentative incendiaries, but the harshness of the treatment prescribed in the Worcestershire declarations for local men not wishing to join the Clubman leagues does lend some truth to the view. It reminds the historian that the Clubmen leaders, like the Royalist commissioners, seem to have been unusual individuals within their communities, and to identify the Clubmen with the entire rural population of their locality may be an error.

The princes' army settled down in Herefordshire to, as Rupert put it, 'refresh after the Dutch fashion', to levy money, supplies and men as it pleased, as if from a conquered territory.[45] The Royalist commanders had managed to overcome the humiliation of the dawn capture of Shrewsbury by believing that it had been betrayed by the citizens.[46] To prevent such a fate befalling Chester, Maurice imposed an oath upon all the inhabitants to oppose Parliament.[47] In April this oath was imposed upon Herefordshire, with the addition of a clause against Clubman leagues. It was to be administered by the Royalist commissioners to every man in the county, and any refusing it were to be enlised in Rupert's army.[48] In early May the same oath was extended to Worcestershire, Monmouthshire and south-east Wales.[49] Worcestershire like Herefordshire was ordered to provide the princes' army with money, food, horses and carts. The warrants for these commodities were issued by Maurice and the proceeds delivered to him directly, without passing through the civilian administration at all.[50] This does not imply that the princes had abolished the rule of law; on the contrary, Maurice's 'Charter' was still enforced in Worcestershire, and Rupert wrote to Owen ordering him to ensure that his troops behaved well towards the local people and collected no more money than those people had agreed to provide.[51] Herefordshire was being punished precisely because it had broken the law as the Royalist generals saw it.

This example worked powerfully. In March the Herefordshire rising had inspired other counties to revolt, in April its fate produced the opposite effect. The Worcestershire Clubmen submerged, and disturbances among countrymen in other counties ceased. So did any talk of the gentry Association in Shropshire, Herefordshire and Worcestershire. Only in Staffordshire in April did the new commissioners for the Association press ahead with their plans of the winter. They won the support of Bagot, but this was enough to alienate Leveson, who tore up their warrants. At this point a peremptory letter arrived from Rupert ordering them to proceed no further.[52] The position of the regular Royalist soldiers was now so strong that they no longer needed to tolerate potential rivals.

This sequence of events presents a curious semantic problem when one deals with the Marcher Clubmen. If one adopts a purely local viewpoint, then they represent an eminently sensible reaction to the war, to set up workable local mechanisms for the preservation of the countryside from plunder. Compared with them, the Association was a cumbersome and over-ambitious project. Moreover their broad principles, of opposition to Catholicising tendencies and to illegal and arbitrary acts, were only those of the national opposition to Charles I's regime before the war. On the other hand, if one adopts any wider view they represented all the shortsightedness and ignorance of truly backward people. They destroyed the chances of the only body potentially powerful enough to exert any proper control over an undisciplined regular soldiery and to preserve local order. Guided by intense localism and (in the case of the Worcestershire leagues) a religious prejudice which had in the circumstances of wartime both become outdated, they played into the hands of the regular military establishment.

The same course of events renders untenable the belief that the Royalist cause perished of 'financial thrombosis' because in early 1645 Charles signed away the financial resources of the provinces, which had supported his army, to the new gentry Associations.[53] This theory is fundamentally unsound, because the provinces studied had never contributed any money even in principle to the royal army except the donations of 1642, the 'Privy Seal Letter' money, the proceeds of Excise and sequestration and irregular levies on campaign. As shown earlier, the donations soon ceased, half the 'Privy Seal' money went to Rupert and the proceeds of sequestration frequently remained in the provinces. The final disproof of this view, however, is that during this critical period of 1645 the Association in fact never came into being, while the royal army was quartered in the provinces exacting resources more ruthlessly than ever before.

A final problem requires solution, whether the same period witnessed a genuine recovery of Royalist administration, or whether, as the Parliamentarian journalists insisted, the Royalist counties had become a wilderness in which soldiers fought countrymen for whatever they could seize. The answer is provided by some transcripts of lost documents preserved at Hereford.[54] The first set is particularly interesting, as it represents the warrants of the governor of Lea Hall, one of the garrisons which the Shropshire Clubmen had demanded be evacuated. As one would expect, in the winter the governor had great difficulty in having his warrants for money obeyed, and at one point threatened to 'burn all the books and make you pay all anew'. By April, however, all arrears had been paid, and the money was coming in regularly. The second set is the accounts of the Receiver of the county tax for Skenfrith Hundred, Monmouthshire. In the first three months of 1645 the hundred does not even seem to have been assessed for the tax, but by April it was being paid in full. These documents suggest that the local administration was probably working better after the crushing of the Herefordshire rising than even before.

It is possible, though less easy to demonstrate, that the same is true of the Royalist West. The crucial development in administration here occurred in March, when the Prince of Wales was sent to Bristol with a panel of privy councillors empowered to co-ordinate all aspects of the war effort in the four western counties. They set to work with energy, and although their efforts often fell short of their targets, the sheer range and dynamism of their work must have brought a greater pace and a tighter control to administration.[55] This was underpinned by an increase of military strength when a section of the royal army under its General of the Horse, George Goring, entered the area as the Prince and his councillors arrived at Bristol. Goring proceeded to prove his value immediately by out-manoeuvring and eventually repulsing a Parliamentarian invasion force which was sent against the West at the same time.[56] Its retreat enabled the Prince's Council to order the siege of Taunton and set about creating a new western field army in April.[57]

At the same time Rupert and Maurice were preparing the royal army for the coming campaigning season. A new press of men had been ordered from the Welsh shires,[58] and the recruits arrived in Herefordshire to be refreshed like the veterans at the expense of the hapless county. A very detailed Parliamentarian report speaks of 1 000 new-raised men quartered in the villages of Bodenham, Moreton-on-Lugg and Rosemaund, in the former Clubman area, in late April.[59] The new men seem, again, to have been added to existing regiments. They were exercised in some successful skirmishing with Massey in Dean. To strengthen Monmouthshire and shorten their lines, the Royalists withdrew their remaining troops in the Forest behind the Wye. Stoically, Sir John Winter burned his own mansion of Lydney to prevent his enemies garrisoning it. The whole Forest was plundered bare, money, food, cattle and iron being carried off to the army.[60]

By early May all was prepared. The princes' forces moved eastwards and the King westward from Oxford with more troops to meet them. They united at Stow-on-the-Wold on the 8th. Goring, who had now rejoined the King after his campaign in the West, was sent back to Somerset with the same soldiers and the rank of Commander-in-Chief of the western forces, which he was to weld together with his own men to prosecute the siege of Taunton. After his departure the King and the princes had 5 000 foot and 3 300 horse.[61] To these were immediately added Sir Henry Bard's 300 foot from Campden House, which Bard razed to prevent occupation by Parliamentarians, and most of the garrison of Evesham.[62] The first objective of the King was Chester, which the tireless Brereton, profiting from the princes' retirement, was again blockading. Legge had been promoted to the governorship of Oxford itself, and Byron at last confirmed as governor of Chester as well as Field-Marshal of North Wales. He now appealed to the King for relief, and the royal army moved north.[63]

Its progress was triumphant. It fanned out across eastern Worcestershire, and from Worcester Sandys's horse, 150 strong, and the foot regiment of the deceased Sir Gilbert Gerard came to swell it.[64] On the 11th a general rendezvous was held at Bromsgrove to attack a Parliamentarian garrison recently installed in north-east Worcestershire. It surrendered after two days. All the mansions of the region, potential garrisons, were destroyed.[65] The royal army entered Shropshire, and Vaughan's 400 horse poured out of their garrisons to join it.[66] On the 22nd it entered Staffordshire, and learned that its mere approach had achieved the relief of Chester. Brereton had called off his men for the third time and retired to his main garrisons.[67] From Montgomery came equally good news. Myddleton had committed the great castle to the renegade Sir John Price. This opportunist now regretted his defection and turned Royalist again, bringing the fortress with him. Thus the great defeat in September was bloodlessly reversed.[68] The Parliamentarians at Nantwich, Wem and Stafford cowered in their garrisons. Leveson and Bagot joined the royal army with 350 horse and some foot.[69] It moved eastwards, and on 31st May achieved a spectacular success by capturing Leicester.

Meanwhile Charles Gerard had been duplicating in Wales the achievements of Rupert and Maurice in the Marches. On leaving them in mid-March he had moved into Montgomeryshire, arresting Jeremy Powell, a leader of the Shropshire Clubman rising, on the way.[70] He settled at Newtown for a month to rest his army and levy supplies and recruits on what had become enemy territory.[71] One Parliamentarian newspaper[72] claimed that the local Royalist Richard Herbert had resigned his place in Gerard's army in protest at his commander's ruthless methods, and as Herbert did serve under Gerard and his own estates lay in the area, the report may be true. At any rate, these methods paid off. After a month Gerard was ready to strike and did so, with terrifying speed, towards Pembrokeshire. He crossed a hundred miles of mountains in a week, caught Laugharne's army by surprise outside Newcastle Emlyn on 23rd April, and tore it apart. The following day he pushed on to Haverfordwest, stormed the town and plundered it. This manoeuvre outflanked Laugharne's garrison at Cardigan, forcing it to evacuate by water to Pembroke.[73] The next day he stormed Picton Castle, and four days later Carew Castle.[74] These fortresses, and Haverfordwest, were strongly garrisoned. Gerard dared not attempt Pembroke and Tenby, but he did not need to, for with Haverfordwest and the two castles held against him Laugharne was now bottled up in his coastal towns like some maleficent djinn. Gerard settled down to recruit again, and by mid May was able to leave powerful garrisons in Pembrokeshire while retaining a field force of 20 000 foot and 700 horse.[75] This he led back across Wales, to rejoin the royal army and further reinforce it.

Contemplating his territory from his new acquisition of Leicester, Charles had good reason for satisfaction, and the highest hopes for the future. His great supply-base in Wales and the Marches had not been destroyed. Instead the entry-points, Monmouth, Montgomery and Haverfordwest, had been regained one by one. His supporters still dominated the West, where Goring was now besieging Taunton with a field army of 5 000 foot and 5 000 horse.[76] The Midlands were still littered with Royalist fortresses, and seven still held out in the six northern counties, and could be used as rallying-points for new forces if the enemy were driven from the field. A Royalist army had appeared in Scotland. Instead of holding his army on the defensive at Oxford as in 1643 and 1644 the King had been able to take the field with it before his opponents, and seize the initiative. If he and his advisers were to behave with the caution and dexterity they had displayed in the later summer of 1644, victory, or an honourable peace, was within their reach.

PART SIX

The failure of the Royalists

CHAPTER SEVENTEEN
After Naseby

On 14 June 1645 the Royalist cause committed suicide at Naseby. Intoxicated by their victories, the King and his advisers did not wait for Gerard's army to reinforce them, let alone Goring's, but decided to attack Parliament's field force, the so-called New Model Army, with their existing troops. They launched these uphill into an opposing force twice as numerous led by Parliament's two best generals. At Marston Moor the fall of night had permitted many Royalist foot soldiers to get away. At Naseby, in the brilliant noontide, they had no escape. Among the infantry killed or captured were the last who had followed the King since 1642 and the last of the veterans sent over by Ormonde.

The King, Rupert, Maurice and the horse got away, and fled west towards the Marches. In Staffordshire they returned Bagot's and Leveson's horse to their garrisons. The King noticed that Bagot was wounded in the arm[1]*: in reality he was dying. The situation which faced the refugees in the Marches was not inviting. As had happened the year before, the withdrawal of garrison troops into the field army for the campaign had greatly improved the position of the local Parliamentarians. The new weakness of the Evesham garrison had tempted Massey, and he stormed the town on 26th May, severing the Cavalier Corridor between Oxford and Wales.[2] The departure of Vaughan's horse had emboldened the Shropshire Clubmen to reappear in the south-west of the county, withholding the money owed to garrisons and opposing the soldiers sent to collect it.[3] This encouraged the Shropshire Parliamentarians in turn to take Stokesay Castle, an outpost of Woodhouse's garrison at Ludlow. Woodhouse

* Notes for this chapter are on p. 236.

summoned aid from Monmouth, Worcester and Hereford, but this composite army was defeated in a straight fight on 9th June. Among the slain was Croft, the local leader of 1642. The triumphant Parliamentarians rounded upon the western Shropshire castles of Caus and Shrawardine, and obtained the surrender of the few men Vaughan had left inside. They had gone on to besiege High Ercall.[4] At Montgomery Sir John Price, who had changed sides three times already, defected a fourth time on receiving news of Naseby, and returned the castle to Parliament.

Even in North Wales, shielded from attack, problems had appeared. Mennes had at last been released from his command there in May, and made Admiral of the non-existent Royalist navy, which effectively meant recall to court. It was intended to replace him with Sir Richard Cave, as a partial rehabilitation for this commander after his disgrace in 1643,[5] but Cave, ever the unlucky hero, perished at Naseby.[6] In the resulting vacuum a natural antipathy between Sir John Owen, a born fanatic, and Archbishop Williams, a self-seeking politician, grew unchecked. The former governed the town of Conway and the latter held the castle, so that friction was constant. At length the Archbishop's habit of cultivating every local gentleman, whatever his political record, became too much for Sir John. In April he tried to arrest Williams on a charge of corruption[7] and on 14th May seized Conway Castle and installed his own men. Williams complained to the King,[8] and Owen responded dramatically by charging his enemy with treason.[9] In Anglesey Viscount Bulkeley, whom the Archbishop had helped into office, was being taught more of the vicissitudes of leadership. In February he had received a furious letter from Maurice, who had been informed that Beaumaris Castle, lodged in Bulkeley's care in 1643, was still ruinous. The Viscount replied that the local gentry, who were supposed to pay for the repairs, had contributed nothing, and that he had been unwilling to coerce these men, his friends and neighbours. Maurice's response was to send Bulkeley's nephew, a hot-tempered man and a devoted Royalist who had already quarrelled with his uncle, to Beaumaris with orders to hang anybody who obstructed the refortification needed.[10] A parallel confrontation to that between Williams and Owen seemed probable.

In the West, likewise, the Royalists had begun to experience new difficulties. The long siege of Taunton took its toll both of the western army and the nerves of the Royalist leaders. Goring, the Prince of Wales's Council and the local military governors became thoroughly irritated with each other.[11] Moreover, as a result of the

new garrisons erected by both parties after the Parliamentarian seizure of Taunton and Weymouth, the fighting of the spring between
Goring and the Parliamentarian invaders, and the pressure upon the
region of the force besieging Taunton, the local warfare in Wiltshire,
Dorset and Somerset had now intensified to a point resembling the
situation in the Marches. The country people, as in the Marches,
began to take measures for their own protection, and in May and
June Clubman groups began to appear in these counties. Those of
the Wiltshire-Dorset border appear to have been the most sophisticated of all English Clubman associations, and are certainly now the
best-documented. They were the first Clubman groups to be subjected to a proper study[12] and have supplied most of the information
upon which recent general conclusions concerning Clubmen have
been based.[13] The problems of drawing such general conclusions
about such differing groups have been indicated already in this study.
They have also been emphasised by David Underdown,[14] who has
nevertheless given a possible explanation for the differences in terms
of a general hypothesis. This is based upon topographical factors,
maintaining that the Clubmen of the nucleated downland villages,
with their strong sense of a traditional hierarchy, were innately
Royalist in their sympathies, while those of the wood-and-pasture
areas, with their scattered settlements and looser traditional ties,
were naturally inclined towards Parliament. Like most work upon
Clubmen, this theory is based principally upon material from western and southern England, and even in this area, as Professor Underdown, with exemplary honesty, points out, certain Clubmen clearly
do not fit the pattern.

It is not within the scope of this book to analyse the western
Clubman groups in the same detail as those of the Marches.
Nevertheless, it may be useful to draw some comparisons between
the Clubmen of the two areas, and to state a few of the problems
involved in examining either. First, it must be said that the information upon most of the western associations is as sparse, or sparser,
than that for the Marches. A particular danger, which I have attempted to avoid in dealing with the Marcher Clubmen, lies in accepting
the statements made about such groups by the Parliamentarian press,
which would have the greatest interest in misrepresenting their
nature and intentions for the purposes of propaganda. This problem
is all the more serious in that our sole knowledge of some western
groups is based upon such reports. Second, as in the Marches, the
western associations represented limited areas with proportionately
limited concerns. The Wiltshire-Dorset groups in theory formed one

large association straddling the county border, but when they actually rose against troops they did so in small sets of villages, under different local leaders and with no common plan of action.[15] The Clubmen of the Langport area explicitly disassociated themselves from those around Shepton Mallet and Wells.[16] The Langport Clubmen, like those of Herefordshire, arose as a result of clashes with a garrison and set out to oppose, by force, soldiers who came to gather supplies.[17] The Wiltshire-Dorset Association more closely resembled, in its sophistication and moderation, the Worcestershire groups. Its primary purpose was to prevent plunder by the recently-established rival garrisons by ensuring that the local tax was properly collected, by its own officials, and delivered to the soldiers, a rational means of keeping them out of the countryside and a solution to the basic problem of military administration.[18] The reactions of these two groups were likewise very different when the New Model Army, after its victory at Naseby, marched into the West in early July 1645. The Langport Clubmen assisted it, the Wiltshire-Dorset groups attacked it. This is the distinction which Professor Underdown would explain in terms of topography. My principal objection to his theory is that it ignores the factor of experience. The troops with whom the Langport Clubmen had consistently come into contact were the underpaid and unruly Royalists, to whom the uniquely well-paid and well-disciplined New Model Army would have presented a great contrast. The Dorset-Wiltshire borderlands had been occupied not merely by Royalists but by the defeated and demoralised Parliamentarian invaders of the spring, and may have acquired a jaundiced view of all armies. In addition, the Langport Clubmen possessed a leader, Humphrey Willis, of unusual shrewdness and breadth of vision. Before he came to terms with the New Model Army his group seems to have been negotiating a deal with Goring.[19]

Having said all this, there remains one important point at which Professor Underdown's ideas hold good for all Clubmen, including those of the Marches; that they tended to appear in areas with few important gentry and many smallholders. This is strikingly true of the Wiltshire-Dorset borderland, where the community had a tradition of communal action to resist attack which extended backwards to the anti-enclosure riots of 1629–31 and was to persist until the Captain Swing risings of 1830–2. Professor Underdown's researches seem to show that this pattern holds good for all the southern and western Clubman risings. The great contrast visible in the Clubman associations is not so much between the Clubman groups as between these groups and the rural population which did not form Clubman associations. This is certainly a problem demanding some detailed topographical study.

Whatever their nature, the presence and activity of the Clubmen, and the already considerable pressure of Royalist troops upon resources made the West seem even less attractive than Wales and the Marches as a haven for the broken troops fleeing from Naseby. The latter area, for all its problems, still possessed formidable resources. The Marches were still full of Royalist strongholds held by men of the calibre of Byron and Scudamore. After three years of repeated fortification their defences were very strong. Few vantage points remained to an attacking enemy. The suburbs of Worcester and Chester had been razed in 1643 and 1644, and in May 1645 Scudamore demolished those of Hereford[20] while Kirke immolated the principal buildings of Bridgnorth to strengthen the castle.[21] To the burning mansions left in the wake of the royal army in May, Woodhouse added those of the Ludlow area. Even the home of the Royalist Croft family was fired.[22] Each Marcher garrison stood within a widening circle of ashes. Behind this grim barrier, as far as Haverfordwest, stretched South Wales, the richest part of the Principality, wholly Royalist and barely touched by the war. Charles determined to settle there and attempt to repeat his success at Shrewsbury in 1642.

On 19th June the King and his exhausted cavalry reached Hereford, and rested there ten days, in which Charles Gerard's army came up. Maurice and his regiments were sent to hold Worcester. He had an immediate quarrel with the bellicose governor Sandys[23] but managed to settle this and to begin raising men and money.[24] Vaughan was sent to restore the situation in Shropshire. 'The Devil of Shrawardine' struck the county with the impact of a hurricane. His horsemen found the local Parliamentarian army besieging High Ercall and destroyed it. Its recent conquests were recaptured or evacuated and the prisoners helped ransom some of the Royalist foot captured at Naseby.[25] In Herefordshire Charles knighted the local leader Lingen and appealed to the gentry for donations of money. Even now personal loyalty to the monarch was so strong that he received many,[26] even though at the same moment the horses of his soldiers were eating up the growing grass upon which much of the local economy depended.[27] Some gentry were commissioned to raise new regiments to defend the county.[28] On 23rd June a Council of War at Hereford decided to raise 10 300 new foot to replace those lost at Naseby. Of these 800 were to come from North Wales and the rest from South Wales and its March.[29] Three days later Rupert departed with a detachment of troops to govern Bristol.[30] On 3rd July Charles himself moved to Raglan Castle to be entertained by the Marquis of Worcester until his new army was ready.[31]

In early July the recruits began to come in. They never arrived in the numbers requested, and those who came deserted as soon as an opportunity occurred.[32] Money to pay them proved as difficult to find as ever.[33] Nevertheless many new soldiers were raised, and dispersed into the garrisons of South Wales to await the summons to muster in the field.[34] The gloomy files of pressed men, hurried along under guard, became a folk memory in Herefordshire.[35] In Worcestershire the Foley forges turned out arms for them.[36] 'We shall have an army fit to fight for a kingdom,' wrote Digby on 10th July.[37]

A week later the mood of the Royalists had already started to darken. After Naseby, as said above, the New Model Army marched into the West. Goring's army had been reinforced by most of the troops of Gerard, shipped across the Bristol Channel. Nevertheless, the New Model Army still outnumbered it, and, on the day that Digby made his boast, shattered it at Langport.[38] The broken Royalists fled into Devon, leaving the field clear for the New Model Army to commence the reduction of the principal fortresses of Somerset and Dorset. While it did so, Parliament decided to destroy the embryo royal army in South Wales by calling against it the army of its Scottish allies, which had been reducing Carlisle. The Scots arrived at Alcester on the 7th, and pushed west to attack Hereford.[39] Scudamore destroyed all the remaining defensible mansions near the town, pulled back his outposts and prepared for the siege.[40] By the 25th it had begun.[41]

While Scudamore bought him time, Charles attempted to strengthen the defences of the counties in which his new army was taking shape. On the 17th he and Gerard met the Glamorganshire commissioners at Cardiff and instructed them to raise 1 000 men in a week, gather the arrears upon the county tax and increase the level of that tax to an unprecedented £1,250 per month.[42] The following day he returned to Raglan and issued parallel orders to the Monmouthshire commissioners, which differed only in that the new tax was to be £1,200 per month.[43] On the 25th he met the Monmouthshire commissioners at Usk to review the men he had ordered raised. They presented him with a proposal to raise the entire male population of the county in irregular regiments, one to be stationed in each hundred under an individual commissioner. If the Scots invaded Monmouthshire, these irregulars would harass them and destroy their foraging parties, operating a guerilla warfare to wear the enemy down. It was to represent a defence in depth.[44]

Charles approved the scheme. In doing so he created precisely the phenomenon which he and his officers had feared in the spring, at the inception of the Marcher Association: an irregular local army capable of imposing its will upon his regular troops. Perhaps he believed that his own presence at the head of the regulars, and the fact that the enemy were foreigners, would guarantee local loyalty. Perhaps the proximity of the Scots, and the need to protect his new army, forced his hand. Whatever the reason for his disregarding his former fears, they were about to be realised.

On the 29th he proceeded to Cardiff to review the 1 000 men he had ordered from Glamorganshire. He found not 1 000 but about 4 000, drawn up under the local gentry in an atmosphere of barely-concealed menace. They requested the replacement of Gerard's governor of Cardiff, Tyrrell, with a local man. Charles agreed. The gentry and their irregular soldiers withdrew four miles from Cardiff and encamped. On the 30th they requested official recognition for their troops and on the 31st recognition of the right of these troops to elect their own officers. These points were conceded. On 1st August they took the ominous name, 'the Peaceable Army', implying their separation from the Royalist cause, and requested that all remaining commanders in the county be replaced with local gentry, that arrears upon the tax be remitted and that the tax be reduced to a level suitable to the wealth of the county rather than the needs of the regular soldiers.[45]

Charles and his cortège were amazed by this reaction, having expected loyalty and obedience.[46] The reasons for it are still disputable. The most interesting explanation is that put forward by a Parliamentarian newspaper.[47] It claimed that the Glamorganshire commissioners had raised the new soldiers ordered by Charles on the 17th, whereupon the recruits had mutinied and demanded the removal of the foreigner Tyrrell, whose troops had plundered their farms to enforce the tax. The gentry, fearing a popular uprising, agreed and raised more men to put pressure on the King.

If this report is true, it represents a decisive intervention by the common people in the Great Rebellion. There are, however, grounds for doubting it. Firstly, one of Charles's officers noted that the gentry made popular unrest their reason for disaffection, with the comment that the excuse was palpably untrue.[48] Secondly, the circumstantial evidence is hostile. The Parliamentarian press had as said before every reason for reporting spontaneous popular revolts against Royalist atrocities. When the same 'Peaceable Army' rose against Parliament in 1646[49] the same press ascribed this event to the machinations of a few gentry. Furthermore the gentry had, as shown earlier, their own quarrel with Gerard and Tyrrell. They had found the comparatively modest demands of Vavasour and Gerard difficult to meet, and could hardly have reacted cheerfully to the unprecedented burden imposed by Charles. At the same time the credit of Charles's cause was evaporating. He had lost Bridgewater and was clearly incapable of relieving Hereford, and immediately after the 'Peaceable Army' first appeared bad news arrived from Pembrokeshire. The djinn had escaped his bottle.

In mid July Gerard's officers at Haverfordwest had sent out men to destroy the growing corn around Pembroke. Laugharne had to fight or starve, and on 1st August attacked his enemies on Colby Moor and broke them after a hard battle. He took Haverfordwest and began to reduce the remaining Royalist garrisons in Pembrokeshire.[50] Charles could spare no men to stop him.

At Cardiff the hapless monarch conceded most of the gentry's demands.[51] He replaced Tyrrell with the local Sir Richard Bassett, whom he had knighted at the siege of Gloucester. He replaced Gerard as commander in South Wales, although not with a local man but with Lord Astley, the tough old veteran who had commanded the foot in the royal army. Gerard was richly compensated with a peerage, Astley's former post and permission to berate the local gentry in public for their disloyalty. The tax was not reduced, nor its arrears remitted, but Charles agreed not to press for its collection.

This done, the King left the area. He had lost faith in the project of completing a new army. Instead he seemed likely to be caught between the Scots and Laugharne, amid a population already wavering in its loyalty. He determined to join his only undefeated army, in Scotland, and on 5th August gathered his remaining field troops and marched to Brecon. The governor there was his old supporter Herbert Price, a local gentleman but unpopular because he had gathered money efficiently to pay his garrison. The townspeople requested his removal and Charles, now ready to concede anything, took Price back into his army.[52] He continued through Radnor, Ludlow and Bridgnorth to Staffordshire. There he drew more troops out of the garrisons[53] and completed his sequence of surrenders to local demands by agreeing to let the Marcher Association be put into action as soon as possible.[54] By 13th August he had left the region.

Within three weeks he had returned, the Scottish project having proved as much a mirage as the new army. In his absence, however, the military situation had slightly improved. Astley had found the South Welsh gentry, indeed, as unhelpful as expected. Not only had they made no effort to assist Hereford but those of Glamorganshire, finding that Bassett took his duties as governor of Cardiff seriously, forced him to deliver the town to the 'Peaceable Army'. Some began to correspond with Parliament.[55] On the other hand Laugharne was held up outside the Pembrokeshire castles, the New Model Army was tied up in the siege of Bristol, which was believed very strong and defended by Rupert himself, and the Scottish army outside Hereford was disintegrating. Much of it had gone home to counter the Scottish Royalists and the remainder were demoralised by Scudamore's desperate resistance. Charles saw his opportunity; having returned from the North to Oxford he gathered all his available horse, 3 000 strong, and advanced upon Hereford. The Scots did not await him, but raised the siege and fled on 2nd September.[56]

Their departure made possible a more ruthless policy towards South Wales, the destruction of dissent and the enforced completion of the new army abandoned a month before. Charles entered Hereford in triumph on the 4th, knighted Scudamore and his Lieutenant-Governor and ordered the confiscation of the estates of gentry who had co-operated with the Scots. A new press of men commenced in the county.[57] The King despatched Gerard to Shropshire and Langdale to Glamorganshire with cavalry to brow-beat the gentry, while he himself entered Monmouthshire on the 7th to deal with the men Astley had marked down as disaffected. Five were arrested, the most prominent being Sir Trevor Williams, who had contacted Parliament as early as March.[58] The lesser gentry were imprisoned, but Williams was bailed at the plea of the Marquis of Worcester's family. At Cardiff Langdale faced the 'Peaceable Army' and forced it to agree to disband, and to provide 1 000 recruits and money for the regular army.[59] The royal cortège were beginning to celebrate when news arrived of the worst disaster since Naseby. Rupert had surrendered Bristol.

The blow was threefold. Firstly, it cost Charles the second city of his realm and exposed the whole West Country. Secondly, his rage was so great that he dismissed Rupert, whereupon Maurice and Gerard resigned in sympathy. Thirdly, the news impelled Charles to recall Langdale and move northward to Hereford, whereupon the 'Peaceable Army' and Sir Trevor Williams immediately declared for Parliament. Parliamentarian troops crossed from Bristol to Cardiff, Williams raised his own force in Monmouthshire, based upon the irregular regiment he had commanded since the July agreement, and a new Parliamentarian army under Sydenham Poyntz arrived in Herefordshire, ordered to pursue and capture Charles himself.[60] Charles revived his scheme of fleeing to Scotland. *En route*, he determined to repeat his success before Hereford by relieving his principal stronghold at the other end of the Marches, Chester.

In May Byron had warned the King that Brereton would soon attack the city again, and he devoted the summer to strengthening its resources. Finding Chester itself incapable of providing money for fresh fortification, he met the commissioners of North Wales at Denbigh in June and persuaded them to provide a monthly levy of cash to the city, on condition that free quarter be ended. Charles almost wrecked this scheme in July by sending Langdale's Northern Horse to live off free quarter in the north-west while he raised his new foot soldiers in the south. Byron made a journey to Raglan to obtain their recall and by August the new money was coming in. Bulkeley's nephew had left Anglesey, his work complete. The feud between Owen and the Archbishop was cooled by a message from Charles ordering them both to behave. When Parliamentarians from Montgomery invaded Merionethshire in August, Owen gathered the local troops and chased them out. Byron returned to Chester in early September with the money he needed and the local troops of north-east Wales, leaving the area relatively united behind him.[61]

This labour was needed, for Brereton had been equally busy. He had spent the summer amassing units from several neighbouring counties to combine with his original army into a force big enough to defeat any local Royalists. By early September, after much wrangling, this was ready, and opened a full-scale siege of Chester. This had been in progress two weeks when Charles appeared from the south with his cavalry. Brereton drew off his troops onto Rowton Heath, and the royal army attacked him there on the 23rd. It had, however, discounted the army of Poyntz, who came up on its heels and joined Brereton. Charles's men were routed and driven into Wales.[62]

For four days the King rested in Denbighshire to gather stragglers and review his situation. There was no longer any prospect of rebuilding a field force anywhere in Wales or the Marches. Nor was the situation in the West any more attractive. Since July Goring's broken forces had been resting in Devon. The New Model Army, busy with its sieges, had left them in peace and they were numerous enough to impose their will on the local community. Thus, although the gentry of Devon had discussed raising an irregular force like the 'Peaceable Army' this project had been suppressed,[63] and although risings did occur against Royalist rule in Cornwall they were ruth-lessly put down.[64] Nevertheless, far from reinforcing and supplying his army, he could not pay his existing soldiers enough to stop them from deserting. Devon and Cornwall were now too exhausted to provide the resources needed to enable him to launch any offensive against the New Model. Thus he remained paralysed, quarrelling bit-terly with the Prince of Wales's Council, while the New Model Army reduced Bristol.[65] Having accomplished this task, the Par-liamentarian army divided. A detachment went to destroy the last Royalist garrisons in Wiltshire and Hampshire while the main body moved upon Goring and began the slow work of pushing his troops further and further down the south-western peninsula, so that their resources, and numbers, diminished even more. The King had no alternative but to turn his back upon both his principal surviving areas of territory. On the 27th September he marched east towards Newark and never returned to either the Marches or the West.

With his departure, and the risings in Glamorganshire and Mon-mouthshire, his supporters in South Wales began to collapse county by county, like dominoes. Massey had at last left Gloucester, pro-moted to command a field army, and been replaced by another capa-ble soldier, Thomas Morgan. Hearing of Williams's rebellion in Mon-mouthshire, Morgan marched west to capture the Royalist garrisons caught between himself and the rebels. On 10th October he joined forces with Williams and bombarded Chepstow Castle into surren-der.[66] They then attacked Monmouth, which surrendered on the 24th. There followed a crisis when Williams's irregulars marched home, proclaiming that they 'did not come to keep garrisons', leav-ing their leader and Morgan to hold the town with the latter's few regulars. Reinforcements, however, arrived from Gloucester, all known Royalists in the town were expelled and only Raglan Castle was left Royalist in the county.[67]

Meanwhile Laugharne was advancing eastwards. In September he reduced the last Pembrokeshire strongholds. In the same month ris-ings in Cardiganshire occurred against the Royalist troops,[68] who abandoned Cardigan. With Glamorganshire now Parliamentarian, Carmarthenshire was in a vice. Carmarthen itself was undermanned and the garrison lacked arms because the weapons destined for it had been seized at Cardiff. The gentry petitioned Charles for aid without success,[69] and when Laugharne advanced in early October they decided that resistance was pointless. They dismissed the officers Gerard had left to hold Carmarthen and handed town and county over to Laugharne on the 12th.[70]

Breconshire and Radnorshire now stood alone. The most prominent Royalist left in these counties was Howell Gwynn, who had
been Lord Herbert's Lieutenant-Colonel. He is reputed to have
commented 'Heigh God, Heigh Devil, I will be for the stronger
side'.[71] The citizens of Brecon demolished their own fortifications[72]
and on 23rd November the gentry of the county formally declared
for Parliament.[73] The Radnorshire gentry followed suit.[74] Only
Aberystwyth Castle held out for the King in all South or mid-Wales
now, and Laugharne laid siege to it.

The last of the shock waves of despair broke in southern Worcestershire. There the countrymen met on Breedon Hill on 11th November for a conference with the Parliamentarians from Evesham.
They agreed to pay no more money to the doomed Royalists at
Worcester and to form an irregular army in imitation of that of Williams to help finish them off. They elected as their commander
Edward Dingley, who had been an active Royalist Commissioner of
Safety. Larger meetings were held in subsequent weeks and the army
took shape.[75]

In the public and private writings of the war all irregular troops,
whether employed privately or by the opposed factions, are referred
to indiscriminately as 'clubmen', a testimony to their primitive
equipment. This usage, together with a superficial similarity, has led
historians[76] to class the 'Peaceable Army' and those of Williams and
Dingley with the Marcher peasant risings of early 1645 for which the
term Clubmen is generally adopted. The difference however is clear.
The earlier risings were directed against soldiers in general, without
reference to the overall military situation. The later were directed
against Royalist soldiers, in partnership with Parliament, and
inspired directly by Royalist defeats and loss of credit. The earlier
were characterised by their lack of powerful gentry leadership. The
later occurred in precisely the areas which had remained quiet earlier,
led by the same prominent gentry who had kept them quiet. They
acted as individuals, to salvage their fortunes from the collapse of the
royal cause. But they also acted as leaders, to protect their communities from the demands of men who would waste their resources
in prolonging a fruitless war and from the destruction consequent
upon a hopeless resistance.

This was not, of course, appreciated by the dedicated Royalists,
those few men to whom the general cause outweighed the local
interest and the greatest sacrifices were well spent. To them, the
decision of these defectors represented the vilest treachery. The reaction of the diehards is best captured in a declaration of Sir Henry

Bard, issued at Worcester on 1st November, reprinted in a Parliamentarian newspaper[77] and often quoted out of context. It was directed to the countrymen of south Worcestershire, whom Bard had governed in his period at Camden House and who were now making the overtures to the garrison of Evesham which were to culminate in the pact on Breedon Hill. He declared that when at Campden he had regarded arrears upon the local tax as inevitable. Now, however, he believed them to be the product of disaffection, so he ordered them to bring six months' tax to Worcester in a week, failing which he told them 'you are to expect an unsanctified body of horse among you, from which if you hide yourselves (as I believe each of you hath his hole) they shall fire your houses without mercy, hang up your bodies wherever they find them and scare your ghosts into your drabbling garrison'.

Five months before, Charles had set out to raise a new army in the parts of his territory which had been most protected from the war and which could therefore be expected to respond most fulsomely to his demands. Now only his peripheral fortresses were left to him. He had made the mistake, to be repeated by later, greater monarchs in 1918, of forgetting that revolution usually begins among the reserves, while the front-line troops remain loyal longest.

CHAPTER EIGHTEEN

The last stand

By December 1645 it had become obvious to most observers that the King was losing the war in England. In Scotland too his adherents were now defeated. There remained Ireland, the one kingdom where Parliament and its allies had made little progress. The Royalist Ormonde held Leinster, while the interior was controlled by the Catholic rebels, officially neutral in the struggle between King and Parliament. If Charles could persuade them to enter the war on his behalf, their thousands of experienced, fanatical warriors could reverse the decision in England. To this end he had appointed their co-religionist Lord Herbert a special emissary to them in March 1645. By the end of the year these negotiations seemed about to succeed and an Irish army was reported ready to cross to Chester and North Wales.[1]* To receive it, Charles needed to maintain his existing garrisons there, and in the West-Midlands, to provide the bridgehead for its campaign.

The man selected for this task was Lord Astley. On 6th December he was commissioned as Lieutenant-General of Worcestershire, Staffordshire, Herefordshire and Shropshire. His orders were to strengthen the garrisons in those counties and to work with neighbouring generals such as Henry Hastings to relieve Chester. In addition he was to raise 2 000 new foot by 1st April and march them to Oxford, to be combined with troops withdrawn from garrisons to make up a new English field army.[2] He was instructed to collect arrears of taxation, eliminate free quarter, prevent countrymen from forming irregular armies for any purpose, discipline the soldiers and work with and honour the civilian commissioners. The military governors

* Notes for this chapter are on p. 238.

and the commissioners were encouraged to take an active and creative role in assisting him.[3]

The task appeared even more daunting than Astley's summer command over the wavering Welsh gentry. Chester itself had been closely besieged since Rowton Heath. Attempts to storm it had failed, but food was running low in the city. Its great outpost at Beeston Castle had been starved out in November. From North Wales Byron's brother Sir Gilbert and a mercenary from Lorraine, Vicomte St Paul, made attempts to harry the besiegers, but the city could clearly not hold out much longer.[4]

In other Royalist garrisons serious quarrels had broken out. At Bridgnorth the remaining Royalist Shropshire gentry, including Ottley, had taken refuge, and were soon at odds with the hot-tempered governor Kirke.[5] At Worcester the equally irascible Sandys had quarrelled with the commissioners over the demands he made for his garrison.[6] At Dudley, Leveson had renewed his vendetta against the commissioners for the gentry Association.[7] At Lichfield Henry Hastings had taken advantage of Bagot's death to reassert his authority in Staffordshire, which had waned in the past year. When Rupert appointed a field army veteran as the new governor, Hastings persuaded Charles to put pressure on the Prince to withdraw him.[8] Hastings's own candidate, Bagot's younger brother Henry, was duly installed, and ruled Lichfield under Hastings's tutelage until December.[9] Then they quarrelled, and Henry and the local gentry ejected Hastings from the town.[10] He retired to his family castle at Ashby, and after a month made peace with Parliament.[11]

If the garrisons were in turmoil, the countryside was in chaos. In October, from Newark, Charles had despatched Sir William Vaughan to Denbighshire with the title of General of Horse for North Wales and its March, equipped with all the remaining cavalry from the old field army except the Northern Horse. 'The Devil's' mission was to harass the outposts and foraging parties of the besiegers of Chester until they abandoned the siege for lack of supplies Vaughan arrived at Chirk on 26th October and by calling in garrison troops increased his force to 800 horse and 280 foot. Brereton, however, hearing of this muster, despatched Mytton to attack him with a much larger force. He caught Vaughan's army at Denbigh on the 31st and shattered it.[12]

The broken horse scattered over Shropshire, Herefordshire and Worcestershire. Vaughan spent two months trying to weld them together with more garrison troops for a fresh attempt, but both the available men and his reputation had perished at Denbigh.[13] In this period the troops wandered at will, harassed by parties from local enemy garrisons. The greatest casualty of these episodes was the man who had raised Cheshire for the King in 1642, Sir Thomas Aston, who took his death wound in a skirmish near Bridgnorth.[14] The local Royalist soldiers made the field troops unwelcome, for they consumed local supplies.[15] No commander remained in the area capable of allocating quarters to them. Maurice had kept it in relative order until September, and earned great popularity among the local people,[16] but then he had resigned. Inevitably, Vaughan's men misbehaved. They took free quarter by force. They held local gentry to ransom, including the commissioner Sir Ralph Clare and the ironmaster Foley. They insulted local soldiers and civilian officers who attempted to control them.[17]

Equally naturally, the plundered countrymen reacted violently. The former Clubmen of south-western Shropshire, learning from the example of the South Welsh irregular armies, made common cause with the Shropshire Parliamentarians to destroy Royalist raiders.[18] On 6th December the Clubman league of north-west Worcestershire resurrected in its original, neutral, form. It declared against all plundering soldiers and against Catholics and established an elaborate warning system.[19]

As if this situation were not enough, Astley's assumption of his command coincided with another major disaster. Among the mansions Scudamore had destroyed in the summer had been that of Sir James Bridges. Bridges took the loss of his home so badly that he went to Parliament and offered to arrange the betrayal of Hereford. Parliament approved, detached 1 000 foot from its New Model Army under Colonel John Birch, and sent them to Gloucester to reinforce Morgan. Bridges meanwhile suborned two discontented officers in the Hereford garrison. On 16th December Morgan and Birch sallied out from Gloucester, announcing that they were taking up winter quarters in Herefordshire. They camped, and then after nightfall moved on Hereford. Bridges's contacts opened a gate, and the town fell. Scudamore escaped with a few soldiers to Worcester, where he was court-marshalled for negligence. He was sentenced to death, although the penalty was suspended. Birch was made governor of Hereford and the whole county, save Goodrich Castle, passed to Parliament.[20]

Astley arrived at Worcester on Christmas Day[21] and spent the next month touring his command. He gathered Vaughan's horse into a body and kept them with him.[22] At Worcester he asked the Grand Jury to reissue Maurice's 'Charter', gave the commissioners equal power in military as well as civil matters and recognised the right of countrymen to resist plundering soldiers. This pleased the civilians but plainly infuriated Sandys, who resigned his governorship and retired to the lesser garrison of Hartlebury Castle, kept by his uncle. Astley then ordered the collection of £2,000 of arrears upon the local tax and offered to withdraw all troops from the countryside if the gentry would guarantee the tax. They refused, and free quarter remained.[23] In Sandys's place the Lieutenant-General left the distinguished field officer Henry Washington. At Bridgnorth the quarrel was decided for him, as Kirke was captured by an enemy party.[24] Astley replaced him with Sir Robert Howard, a local gentleman who had commanded a field regiment. At Lichfield he recognised neither Hastings nor Henry Bagot as commander, but installed another celebrated field army colonel, Sir Thomas Tildesley, with Bagot as his deputy. Sir William Blakiston, of the Northern Horse, was put in charge of Tutbury Castle.[25]

As he settled each garrison, he detached troops for the relief of Chester. By late January he had prepared about 2 000 horse and 1 500 foot, too small a force to relieve the city by itself but formidable in co-operation with the army expected from Ireland.[26] Then the bombshell broke. The Irish army was not coming, because Ormonde and the Protestant Irish would not accept the terms the Catholics demanded in return for it.[27] Byron gave up hope. His soldiers were dying of hunger and the citizens beginning to rebel. On 2nd February he surrendered Chester to Brereton.[28]

None the less the Royalists did not despair. In October Charles had ordered and empowered Byron to retire to Caernarvonshire if he surrendered Chester. There he could make a stand protected by the great castles of Edward I, and await the Irish.[29] This Byron now did. There was a chance that Ormonde and the Catholics would reach an agreement. Astley returned to his alternative project of raising a new field army in his command. Both gained strength from a phenomenon resulting from the very shrinkage of Royalist territory. As a fortress surrendered, its troops were usually permitted to march away to join a friendly garrison. Thus Byron and Astley received a steady stream of hardbitten veterans from lost strongholds eager for employment.[30] Furthermore both must have been encouraged by developments in Glamorganshire. The gentry who had defected in the summer seemed to be reversing their decision.

Parliament had received these new adherents with official warmth but little trust. It had recognised the 'Peaceable Army' and commissioned a local gentleman, Bussy Mansell, as its commander, but the key fortresses of Cardiff and Swansea were garrisoned by English regulars with English governors.[31] Administration of the county was vested in a committee from which the leading gentry were deliberately excluded. A heavy local tax was imposed and the traditional Prayer Book outlawed in accordance with Parliament's religious reforms. By December the local leaders were seriously discontented. Charles had threatened the local economy and offended localist sentiment. Parliament did both these things and menaced the social and religious order as well.[32]

The spark to ignite this situation fell from Monmouthshire. In December Charles commissioned Lord Herbert's youngest brother, Lord Charles Somerset, as his general in Monmouthshire.[33] Lord Charles commenced his military career by leading the garrison of Raglan in a series of savage raids, in which he levied money and men and punished anybody who had aided the Parliamentarians.[34] In mid January he launched a full-scale campaign and destroyed the new Parliamentarian garrisons of western Monmouthshire. Many formerly Royalist gentry who had defected with Williams turned Royalist again or let Lord Charles's troops pass unopposed. Some attempted to betray Monmouth. Williams himself retreated, appealing for aid.[35] By early February Lord Charles had reached the borders of Glamorganshire.

On 6th February Bussy Mansell mustered the 'Peaceable Army' to fight Lord Charles in Parliament's name. To his surprise it mutinied and arrested him and the other gentry who still favoured Parliament. In his place it elected Edward Carne, a former Royalist officer whom Parliament had appointed High Sheriff. It then declared that it would ally with the Royalists to expel the Parliamentarians, after which the Royalists, like all 'foreign forces', would depart. These aims were entirely compatible with its declarations to Charles. It occupied Cardiff and besieged the castle, from which the Parliamentarian governor sent for help, commenting that the real aim of the Glamorganshire gentry was that 'this county should be independent from England, both King and Parliament'.[36] Militant neutralism had reappeared with vehemence.

Parliament could not afford to ignore this challenge, which might inspire the bulk of the population of South Wales, if not England, to a similar rising. Laugharne marched from Aberystwyth and Williams, reinforced by some of Morgan's soldiers, from Chepstow. Williams broke through the Raglan Royalists and united with Laugharne to make a force of 1 400 men. On the 18th they attacked Carne's larger army outside Cardiff. The battle illustrated again the impotence of irregulars faced with regulars. The 'Peaceable Army' had won its previous victories by menaces, and faced with a determined enemy it fired one volley and then fled. The Parliamentarians bombarded Cardiff town into surrender and relieved the castle. They then set about hunting down Carne. He attempted to muster his troops once more, but his enemies caught him in the process and finally dispersed them. Carne himself surrendered soon after. Laugharne granted generous terms to the rebels to encourage their continued submission, promising the use of the old Prayer Book and demanding merely that they promise to muster again only if ordered by Mansell.[37] He returned to besiege Aberystwyth Castle and eventually reduced it.[38] Morgan and Williams pushed Lord Charles Somerset back to Raglan. The last Royalist offensive of the war and the last assertion of militant neutralism had both ended.

Astley set to work all the harder to raise his new regulars, while securing the surviving Royalist territory in his command. He raided Parliamentarian territory to obtain money.[39] He caught the irregular army of south Worcestershire besieging Madresfield Court, a new Royalist garrison in the Malvern Hills, and dispersed it.[40] He dealt with complaints of maladministration, in at least one case deciding for the plaintiff.[41] He seems to have called in garrisons of isolated fortresses such as Chirk Castle to swell his army.[42] By mid March that army was ready, about 3 000 strong. His territory, which he had inherited in chaos, was restored to some sort of responsible government, an achievement marked shortly after his departure by a council of war at Worcester. It was held by governor Washington and his principal officers to try a local gentleman who had killed a fellow officer who had attempted to rob him during the period of disorder. Despite its military complexion, the court decided unanimously for acquittal.[43]

The last act of the Royalist tragedy opened in mid March, when Astley entered hostile territory with his vital army on its march to Oxford. This was a moment the Parliamentarians had been dreading, and awaiting. Instantly Morgan and Birch left their respective garrisons, united their troops and followed him. Hunter and hunted crossed the Vale of Evesham and entered the Cotswolds, the two Parliamentarians harrying the Royalist and attempting to slow him up until reinforcements arrived. They succeeded, for Brereton hurried down from the north and joined them. Together, they overwhelmed Astley's army at Stow-on-the-Wold on 21st March and captured Astley himself.[44] The last battle of the war had been fought.

Few doubted that it was the *coup de grâce*. A week before, the last remnants of the Royalist western army had surrendered to the New Model Army in Cornwall, so that the King no longer had any troops in the field. Six weeks later the hapless monarch surrendered his person to his enemies. Nothing remained for Parliament's soldiers to do but to reduce the surviving Royalist fortresses. Each army was allotted particular garrisons to destroy. The Shropshire forces were left to take Bridgnorth. Their former colleague Thomas Mytton, who had quarrelled violently with them,[45] was sent into North Wales to attack Byron and reduce the castles. Brereton was sent against Lichfield, Dudley Castle and Tutbury Castle. Birch was ordered to take Ludlow and Goodrich Castle. Morgan was left to tackle Raglan Castle, Hartlebury Castle and Worcester. The Scots besieged Newark. The New Model Army left detachments outside the few surviving western Royalist garrisons and marched against the Royalist capital, Oxford.

Mytton's task was the most important, as while Byron held north-west Wales a bridgehead for Irish Royalist troops still existed. Byron himself had been working hard to preserve it. On his arrival in Caernarvonshire on 5th February he paused at Conway and wrote ahead to the gentry, courteously requesting quarters for the troops he had brought from Chester.[46] These agreed, he contacted the governors of the local fortresses to arrange deployment of their troops with his to construct a local army.[47] He also wrote to Ormonde urging him to hasten the Irish.[48] His prospects of success were enhanced by the strength of the medieval fortresses ringing his territory. Mytton, despite great efforts, spent three months reducing the most easterly, Ruthin and Hawarden, which were by no means the most formidable.[49]

Yet Byron's efforts were paralysed almost immediately by the hostility of the local community. For all his tact he was inevitably resented as a foreigner.[50] Furthermore, they could not share his hopes, for the prospect of having to support an army of savage Irishmen filled them with horror. While Byron begged Ormonde to send troops, they begged the Marquis to withhold them.[51] Some began to incline towards the solution of their brethren in the south, of making their own terms with Parliament. Immediately after his arrival Byron uncovered a plot to betray Caernarvon.[52] In October the Anglesey gentry had forced Viscount Bulkeley to accept one of their number, David Lloyd, as governor of Beaumaris Castle. Byron attempted to replace him with Bulkeley's son Richard, who had served ably in the field army, but the gentry refused to accept Richard. Lloyd wrote secretly to Parliament requesting negotiation.[53] Parliament sent a former Royalist commissioner, Sir Robert Eyton, to the area to nurture the growing opposition to Byron.[54]

By March the rupture between the Anglesey gentry and the Field-Marshal was obvious. They intercepted his letters to Ormonde[55] and when the Marquis did send a few soldiers to Anglesey these men were disarmed and expelled. Byron had himself rowed over Menai Strait to protest, and was almost assassinated by unknown gunmen on the shore.[56] Bulkeley proved a man of feeble character, neither encouraging nor reproving his neighbours, and Byron described him as 'the drunken Lord'. His ally Archbishop Williams appeared by contrast 'a mixture of a madman and a knave'.[57] The Archbishop was in fact adhering consistently to his single political and moral principle of self-advancement. He cultivated Byron and wrote to Ormode about him in terms of worried concern.[58] He wrote to Bulkeley advising him to keep independent of both Byron and the gentry.[59] And, of course, he wrote to Parliament offering his services[60] and to Royalist military governors encouraging them to defect.[61]

In mid April Mytton, having reduced Ruthin Castle, decided to put the secret promises of the gentry to the test, and advanced directly upon Byron, ignoring the intervening fortresses. Byron, unable to raise a field force capable of meeting him, supplied the local garrisons, particularly that of Sir John Owen at Conway, and shut himself up in Caernarvon.[62] Archbishop Williams wrote Owen a sugary letter promising assistance[63] and then went to Mytton's camp and joined him, followed by the other Caernarvonshire gentry.[64] Owen reacted by leading his men in a last furious sally to devastate their lands.[65] Mytton ignored him and struck at his main opponent, Byron. By early May Caernarvon was closely besieged. Byron's spirit was broken. He had no wish to withstand another terrible and hopeless ordeal such as he had endured at Chester. He gave Ormonde a month to send an army, and then surrendered and passed overseas.[66] His war was at last over.

During the siege of Caernarvon, Mytton opened negotiations with the Anglesey gentry. They were protracted only by that gentry's desire to obtain the best possible terms. A moment of drama occurred when young Richard Bulkeley seized Beaumaris Castle from his rival Lloyd, but it soon became apparent that he had done so simply to strengthen the position of his family in winning pardon from Parliament. On 14th June, ten days after Byron's departure, the whole island formally surrendered to Mytton.[67] The last compact bloc of Royalist territory had been shattered. Its individual fortresses could be reduced at leisure.

In the Midlands and Marches the remaining Royalist governors displayed a mixture of reactions to their predicament. Leveson at Dudley Castle, Blakiston at Tutbury Castle, Woodhouse at Ludlow and Sandys at Hartlebury Castle decided rationally that further resistance was pointless. They surrendered immediately, or after a short siege, on good terms.[68] Leveson's easy escape produced fury among the local people, who having been forced to serve him for three years were deprived even of the satisfaction of seeing him endure the rigours of a siege. He galloped away amid 'many thousand curses', with a Parliamentarian escort to protect him from being lynched.[69] He was never forgotten nor forgiven, and his malevolent ghost is still believed to haunt the now ruined castle.

At Bridgnorth Sir Robert Howard, Ottley and the other Shropshire gentry behaved with something approaching hysteria. On 29th March their enemies attacked the town and stormed it, penning them into the castle. From there they issued warrants to the townspeople demanding money. The townspeople, not surprisingly, replied that with Parliamentarian troops among them they could not provide it. The Royalists' answer was to fire grenades into the town, which being built of wood was soon an ocean of flame.[70] Yet only three weeks after this atrocity they made terms.[71]

The remaining governors settled down grimly to fight. To spare them further suffering the captive Charles issued a general order to them on 10th June,[72] directing them to surrender. Only the governor of Oxford obeyed. In at least one case, that of Lichfield, the garrison seems to have doubted the authenticity of the document and cherished a pathetic belief that it would be relieved.[73] But elsewhere the Royalists seem to have possessed no illusions concerning their isolation. Indeed, the note sounded in their replies to their besiegers is of lonely and defiant pride. The very defection and submission of most of their comrades seemed to strengthen their own determination to testify to the intrinsic worth of their cause. They required an act of expiation, and chose the most primitive and vital of such acts, the shedding of blood.[74]

The last Royalist warlords behaved like madmen, or heroes. At Goodrich Castle, Lingen fought until the walls were beaten into rubble about his ears, only capitulating in July when they completely collapsed.[75] Tildesley gave up Lichfield the same month, after three months under attack.[76] The weight of the New Model Army itself was required before the Marquis of Worcester surrendered Raglan

Castle[77] or Washington accepted terms at Worcester.[78] A few days before Raglan capitulated in August, Pendennis Castle, the single western fortress to hold out after the spring, surrendered, and the Royalists no longer possessed a base in England. It remained to starve out the impregnable Welsh fortresses. Roger Mostyn gave up Flint Castle two weeks after Raglan fell.[79] William Salusbury, nick-named 'Old Blue Stockings', held Denbigh Castle until the King sent him a personal message to desist in October.[80] Owen at Conway ignored alike the cannon of Mytton and the entreaties of Archbishop Williams until November.[81] Sir Richard Lloyd, who had first raised the Denbighshire gentry for the King, withstood a year's siege at Holt Castle, surrendering in January 1647.[82] Last of all, Owen's brother William gave up Harlech, 'the castle of lost causes', on 15th March 1647.[83]

Most of the civilian Royalist commissioners made their peace with Parliament, usually upon payment of a fine, and retired to their manor-houses. Fourteen years of political impotence and humiliation awaited them until with the Restoration those who survived were restored to something like their pre-war position and saw the triumph of the ideals for which they claimed to have fought. Most of the military leaders went abroad, to serve other monarchs or follow an impoverished court in exile. Few returned. Vavasour and Vaughan fell in battle. Maurice drowned at sea. Astley, Byron and Leveson died in foreign beds. Only Rupert, Gerard, Langdale and Owen returned to honours at the Restoration and none became a statesman of the first rank. Yet they achieved their own immortality, on the canvases of Victorian artists, in the weekend recreations of modern brigadiers and in the memories of the country people. Other ghosts than Leveson's stalk their battered fortresses. Across Shropshire hill-sides the phantoms of Vaughan's horsemen are still reputed to canter. The reputation of Scudamore's soldiers, the Red Men of the Dusk, is only now dying in rural Herefordshire. It is hard to say who have been the ultimate victors.

Conclusion

In what were to become the Royalist areas of England and Wales, the Civil War did not arise, inevitably, from any fundamental social, economic, religious or even political cleavage within local society. It was an artificial insemination of violence into the local community. The traditional rulers of England, King, Lords and Commons, betrayed the first duty of government, to promote the order and security of the governed. Instead they set leading men of each county against each other to the ruin of themselves and their communities.

From the beginning some communities recognised and resisted this process. When the King and Parliament initially appealed to the provinces to support their respective claims they evoked a positive response in certain places. In Herefordshire, Cumberland, Westmoreland and most of Wales the majority of the community displayed loyalty to the King, while Birmingham strongly supported Parliament. On the other hand, in most of the English counties upon which the Royalist war effort was later to be based attempts to evoke general enthusiasm for either cause met with indifference or hostility. Hence the Royalist armies began virtually as private enterprises, like joint-stock companies, the money donated by individual partisans being used to attract recruits into regiments led by prominent Royalists.

It is difficult to determine any single motive behind the decision of Royalist activists to commit themselves to their cause. They varied in status from powerful nobles to middle-rank gentry, and the degree and duration of their enthusiasm also varied greatly between individuals. As far as can be ascertained their commitment to Royalism was a personal decision, made in response to the King's declarations.

The failure of Charles's army to win a decisive victory in the autumn of 1642 resulted in attempts by the Royalists to harness the resources of the territory they controlled by laying general impositions upon the communities within it. This process escalated with the continuation of the war until by early 1644 every county held by Royalists was expected to contribute large quantities of men, money and supplies to their cause. To encourage local men in this effort, the King was initially careful to leave the region in the hands of local gentry, with overall command invested in generals appointed for their social prestige rather than their military experience. By early 1644 this policy had proved a disaster. Not only did the inexperienced generals suffer defeat and the gentry quarrel amongst themselves but the provinces consistently failed to provide the support needed. This was partly the result of the unprecedented weight of the burdens imposed in relation to the limited resources of the communities, which were further decreased by the number of Parliamentarian enclaves in Royalist territory which ensured that the richer Royalist counties suffered the destructive effects of continual warfare. It may also, however, be attributed to the reluctance of most men to make personal sacrifices to promote this war.

The King's reaction was to invest local power in men selected for their military ability and their lack of any previous contact with the areas they commanded. They could be expected to be aloof both from local hatreds and from any loyalty to the communities they had to exploit. This policy was generally successful. The new commanders regained much of the ground their predecessors had lost and the most important, Rupert, displayed a considerable talent for administration. In the process he raised and equipped an army which may have come near to winning the war at Marston Moor.

During the following winter the new military men met with a considerable hostile reaction from the communities they governed, resulting not merely from growing war weariness but from recent Royalist defeats which produced administrative chaos and a loss of faith in the King's cause. Some gentry sought to raise an army capable of controlling the regular troops, while countrymen in the remoter areas staged armed uprisings. The King's generals eventually overcame this challenge, repressing the uprisings and the schemes of the gentry, and utilising their victory to exploit certain areas more successfully than ever before. By the summer of 1645 they had restored confidence in their cause and put a formidable army into the field.

The events of the spring made clear the lesson that ultimately it did not matter if the local population were alienated from the royal cause, as long as the King possessed an army with which to terrorise the provinces into providing him with the materials of war. At Naseby, however, that army was destroyed. This forced the King to appeal for fresh sacrifices from the wealthiest remaining communities in his territory while depriving him of the means to coerce them into making the sacrifices. The communities concerned chose instead to ally with Parliament in evicting the King's forces. This subtraction of support ensured that the Royalists were incapable of resisting their enemies and were overwhelmed.

The military history of the Great Civil War retains its value in the sequence of events described above, as battles did decisively affect the course of these events. Yet their significance is lost without an understanding of the other war, fought between the partisans of both causes and the bulk of the population, which they attempted to press into service. In the last analysis it was the local community, not Parliament, which defeated Charles I, not from hatred of his cause but from hatred of the war itself.

APPENDIX
Royalist civilian commissioners

The names of Royalist civilian commissioners in Wales and the West Midlands can be located in the following sources:

Northamptonshire RO Finch-Hatton MS 133

Brit. L. Harl. MSS 6804 f 107; 6852 f 10

Bod. L. Dugdale MS 19; Carte MSS 8 f 155; 10 ff 22, 439

NLW Wynn MS 1712; L1/MB/17 ff 23, 48, 81, Llanfair-Brynodol MS 51; Crosse Of Shawe Hill MS 1112

Worcestershire RO 1714/899/192 ff 329–32

Birmingham RL 351507

UCNW Baron Hill MSS 5364, 5369

TSANHS 1898, pp. 158–9

M. Mahler, *A History Of Chirk Castle And Chirkland*, pp. 164–5

Put together, these provide the following sample of names:

Cheshire	23	Anglesey	8
Herefordshire	22	Caernarvonshire	13
Monmouthshire	31	Denbighshire	34
Shropshire	41	Flintshire	21
Staffordshire	26	Glamorganshire	34
Warwickshire	23	Merionethshire	18
Worcestershire	35	Montgomeryshire	15
		Radnorshire	14

The following number of these names can be located in the works of biography, topography and genealogy listed in the secondary sources in the Bibliography (pp. 259–64):

Cheshire	19	Anglesey	4
Herefordshire	21	Caernarvonshire	7
Monmouthshire	15	Denbighshire	26
Shropshire	30	Flintshire	12
Staffordshire	26	Glamorganshire	29
Warwickshire	23	Merionethshire	7
Worcestershire	35	Montgomeryshire	9
		Radnorshire	8

Wherever a Commissioner of Array, 'for the guarding the county' Impressment or for Taking Accounts can be identified by this process he is a prominent gentleman or the heir of one. Where a name cannot be located in the works of topography or genealogy used it seems invariably to result from the lack of a detailed work to cover the home area of the individual concerned, so that I have had to remain content with national sources in which only the greatest gentry would appear. The Commissioners of the Excise, by contrast, seem to have been genuinely obscure individuals. This is hardly an unexpected discovery, as the King would hardly have been likely to entrust the tasks of the Commissions of Array, Safety or Impressment to men without power in their communities.

The secondary works in the Bibliography used to identify activists were those by Cockayne, Dugdale, Duncumb, Earwaker, Keeler, Nash, Ormerod, S. Shaw, W.A. Shaw and Tucker, together with the Victoria County Histories and the DNB and DWB.

Notes

PART ONE: THE ACHIEVEMENT OF CIVIL WAR

Chapter 1

1. Brit. L. 669 f 4 81.
2. LJ Vol. 5, p. 10.
3. E. 147.17.
4. E. 146.16.
5. Brit. L. 669 f 5 17.
6. J. Rushworth, *Historical Collections*, Part 3, Vol. 1, pp. 635–7, 653–4.
7. NLW Llanfair-Brynodol MS 34, MS 1546E (iii).
8. Camden Society 1853, *Letters Of Brilliana Harley*, No. 143–158; HMC 14th Report, Appendix 2, pp. 86–92.
9. Gloucester Common Council Minute Book ff 205, 207.
10. H. Owen and J.B. Blakeway, *A History Of Shrewsbury*, Vol. 1, pp. 415–16.
11. L. Fox, *The Borough Town Of Stratford-Upon-Avon,* p. 23.
12. E. 149.15.
13. E.149.25.
14. HMC 13th Report, Portland MSS 1, p. 35.
15. PRO SP 16/488/100, Certificate 31 Jan. 1642.
16. E.146.1, 20; 147.5; 150.29; 152.2.
17. Neatly (and sarcastically) summarised in E.292.27.
18. Mainly in transcript, Northamptonshire RO Finch-Hatton MS 133. For a well-preserved original, see Birmingham RL 351507.
19. Finch-Hatton 133.
20. *Archaeologia Cambrensis*, 1875, p. 203.
21. For example HMC 14th Report, Appendix 2, pp. 90–1.
22. Northamptonshire RO Finch-Hatton MS 133.
23. Worcestershire RO 1714/899/192 ff 203–27.
24. Brit. L. Add. MS 11332 f 122.
25. J. Rushworth, op. cit., Part 3, Vol. 1, pp. 674–5.
26. Bod. L. Tanner MS 63 f 84.

27. HMC 5th Report, Appendix, p. 175.
28. See J.S. Morrill, *Cheshire*, pp. 16–17.
29. ibid. pp. 49–51.
30. Chetham Society 1844, G. Ormerod (ed.), Lancashire Civil War Tracts, pp. 18–20.
31. Brit. L. Add. MS 36913 ff 90–4.
32. HMC 13th Report, Portland MSS 1, pp. 43–5; LJ Vol. 5, p. 200.
33. E. 149.30.
34. Brit. L. Harl. MS 2135 f 65.
35. HMC 13th Report, Portland MSS 1, pp. 51–2; Malbon's Diary, ed. by Lancashire and Cheshire Record Society 1889, pp. 23–5.
36. Bod. L. Ashmole MS 830 ff 282–4.
37. Brit. L. Harl. MS 2107.
38. Morrill, op. cit., pp. 58–9.
39. Brit. L. Harl. MS 2135 f 100.
40. E. 118.10.
41. Brit. L. 669 f 6 55.
42. Brit. L. Harl. MS 2155 f 108.
43. Chester RO A/B/2 f 56.
44. LJ Vol. 5, p. 115.
45. See above, p. 6.
46. CJ Vol. 2, pp. 657, 661.
47. E. 107.32.
48. Worcestershire RO 1714/899/192 ff 235–6.
49. CJ Vol. 2, p. 684.
50. Worcestershire RO 1714/899/192 ff 237–9, 705/24/873.
51. Brit. L. 669 f 5 65.
52. Birmingham RL 351507.
53. Birmingham RL 351505; T.R. Nash, *Collections For The History Of Worcestershire*, Vol. 1, p. 499.
54. Worcestershire RO 1714/899/192 ff 237–9, 251–2.
55. ibid. f 253.
56. ibid. f 262; LJ Vol. 5, pp. 335–6.
57. Worcestershire RO 1714/899/192 ff 257–9, 271–2.
58. ibid. f 262.
59. ibid. ff 278–92.
60. E. 240.2.
61. CJ Vol. 2, pp. 761, 764.
62. Staffordshire RO D593/P/8/1.
63. LJ Vol. 5, pp. 269–70.
64. Brit. L. 669 f 6 69, E. 114.36.
65. Owen and Blakeway, op cit., p. 430.
66. TSANHS 1894, pp. 34–7.
67. ibid., esp. Fowler to Ottley, Weld to Ottley.
68. HMC 13th Report, Portland MSS 1, p. 53.
69. HMC 5th Report, Appendix, p. 145.
70. Owen and Blakeway, op. cit., p. 46ln.
71. Earl of Clarendon, *History Of The Rebellion*, V. 339.
72. See above, p. 3.
73. E. 150.28.

74. Brit. L. 669 f 6 75; HMC 5th Report, Appendix, p. 141.
75. HMC 5th Report, Appendix, p. 141.
76. CJ Vol. 2, p. 661.
77. Bod. L. Ashmole MS H. 23.25.
78. HMC 14th Report, Appendix 2, pp. 89–94.
79. Brit. L. 669 f 6 64.
80. Bod. L. Tanner MS 303 f 113.
81. Camden Society, *Letters of Brilliana Harley*, No. 165–177; HMC 14th Report, Appendix 2, pp. 87–9.
82. HMC 14th Report, Appendix 2, p. 94; Appendix 8, p. 203.
83. R. Baxter, *Reliquiae Baxterianae*, Part 1, Section 57.
84. HMC 14th Report, Appendix 8, p. 203; PRO SP 16/492/28, Nehemiah Wharton 30-9-42.
85. TSANHS 1895, pp. 244–5.
86. CJ Vol. 2, p. 673.
87. E. 113.6.
88. CJ Vol. 2, pp. 503, 527, 545, 548–9, 575; LJ Vol. 5, pp. 57–8.
89. HMC 13th Report, Portland MSS 1, pp. 62–3; H. Dircks, *Life . . . Of The Second Marquis Of Worcester*, pp. 330–1.
90. Dircks, op. cit., pp. 41–2, 44–6, 330–1.
91. Northamptonshire RO Finch-Hatton MS 133.
92. E. 109.27.
93. *Archaeologia Cambrensis* 1846, pp. 33, 327; Rushworth, op. cit., pp. 643–4.
94. HMC 14th Report, Appendix 2, p. 94.
95. NLW MS 5390D.
96. CJ Vol. 2, p. 701; PRO SP 16/491/131, Thomas Niccolls 26-8-42.
97. CJ Vol. 2, p. 762; M.R. Keeler, *The Long Parliament*, p. 314.
98. Bod. L Tanner MS 59 f 332; *Trans. Caernarvonshire Historical Society* 1953, pp. 1–34; PRO SP 19/22 f 75.
99. *Archaeologia Cambrensis* 1917, Supplement pp. 295–6; NLW Clennenau Letters, Appendix 2.
100. CJ Vol. 2, pp. 372–623, *passim.*
101. ibid. p. 701.
102. E. 150.28.
103. A.H. Dodd, 'The Pattern Of Politics In Stuart Wales', pp. 20–56.
104. Dodd, 'Wales In The Parliaments Of Charles 1. Part Two', pp. 59–73.
105. ibid. Part One, pp. 47–8.
106. C.B. Phillips, 'The Royalist North', pp. 170–1.
107. Sir Charles Firth (ed.), *The Life Of William Cavendish, Duke Of Newcastle*, pp. 10–11; Roger Howell Jr, *Newcastle-Upon-Tyne And The Puritan Revolution*, pp. 144–6.
108. For the details of this, see my article, 'The Failure Of The Lancashire Cavaliers'.
109. The best account of this treaty is in Manning's thesis, *Neutrals and Neutralism*, pp. 26–32.
110. A.C. Wood, *Nottinghamshire In The Civil War*, p. 17.
111. LJ Vol. 5, pp. 133–4.
112. For the details of this, see my article, 'Clarendon's "History Of The Rebellion"'.

113. CJ Vol. 2, pp. 676, 701, 783.
114. ibid. p. 864; *A Declaration By The Hon, The Earl Of Bath* . . . (26 Sept. 1642).
115. Somerset Record Society 1902, C.E.H. Chadwyck-Healey (ed.), *Bellum Civile*, pp. 1–2.
116. LJ Vol. 5, pp. 314–15.
117. See above, p. 10
118. LJ Vol. 5, pp. 164–5.
119. ibid. pp. 165–6.
120. For example E. 92.18.
121. LJ Vol. 5, p. 195; E. 109.3.
122. Brit. L. Add. MS 11364 ff 14–15.
123. CSPD 1641–3, p. 361.
124. Sir R. Bulstrode, *Memoirs and Reflections*, p. 72; E. 110. 8, 669 f 6 58.
125. HMC 12th Report, Appendix 2, p. 320.
126. Worcestershire RO 1714/899/192 ff 72–5.
127. HMC 2nd Report, Appendix, p. 36; Clarendon, op. cit., V. 446n.
128. CJ Vol. 2, p. 685.
129. Brit. L. 669 f 6 58; Clarendon V. 441n; PRO SP 16/491/105, Sir John Danvers 9-8-42.
130. E. 114.25; PRO SP 16/491/133, Nehemiah Wharton, 26-8-42.
131. Clarendon V. 446n.
132. Bulstrode, op. cit., p. 72.
133. Brit. L. Add. MS 11364 f 15.
134. E. 109.3.
135. CJ Vol. 2, p. 731.
136. For example E. 96.22.
137. Most recently restated in B.S. Manning, *The English People And The English Revolution*.
138. E. 115.2.
139. Bod. L. MS Eng Hist c 53 f 33; E. Warburton, *Memoirs Of Prince Rupert*, Vol. 2, p. 162.
140. E. 100.8, 96.22.
141. PRO SP 16/491/133, Nehemiah Wharton 26-8-42; LJ Vol. 5, p. 321.

Chapter 2

1. For a Parliamentarian view of this process, see J. Malcolm's 'A King in Search of Soldiers' and *The English People And The Crown's Cause*. Much of the present section consists of an alternative presentation of the events of 1642 to Dr Malcolm's, using less partisan sources.
2. Brit. L. 669 f 6 75; Rev. S. Shaw, *History And Antiquities Of Staffordshire*, Vol. 1, p. 362.
3. HMC 5th Report, Appendix, p. 141.
4. J. Rushworth, *Historical Collections*, Part 2, Vol. 2, p. 1243.
5. HMC 13th Report, Portland MSS 1, p. 63.
6. Like Richard Bagot, of whom more below.
7. NLW Bettisfield MS 468.
8. P. Young, *Edgehill*, pp. 212–13.
9. ibid. pp. 22–3, 232.

10. ibid. pp. 227–8; NLW Wynn MS 1711.
11. NLW Clennenau Letter 531.
12. HMC 10th Report, Appendix 4, p. 399.
13. Young, op. cit., pp. 223–4; NLW Tredegar MS 911.
14. NLW Bettisfield MS 111.
15. PRO SP 16/492/13, 14 Sir Edward Nicholas 13/15-9-42.
16. ibid.
17. Clarendon, *The History Of The Rebellion*, VI. 62n.
18. Staffordshire RO D593/P/8/1/3.
19. E. 118.28.
20. WSL Salt MS 496; Warburton, *Memoirs of Prince Rupert*, Vol. 1, p. 396.
21. *Archaeologia Cambrensis* 1846, pp. 33–4.
22. HMC 13th Report, Portland MSS 1, p. 51.
23. HMC 5th Report, Appendix, p. 141.
24. Brit. L. Harl. MS 2173 ff 8–9.
25. TSANHS 1894, pp. 41–3.
26. ibid. 1900, pp. 4–5.
27. Clarendon, VI. 62n.
28. Owen and Blakeway, *A History of Shrewsbury*, p. 418.
29. Shropshire RO Box 586.
30. TSANHS 1894, pp. 41–3.
31. Clarendon, VI, 62n.
32. Rushworth, Part 3, Vol. 2, pp. 20–1.
33. HMC 10th Report, Appendix 6, p. 86.
34. W.A. Shaw, *The Knights Of England*, Vol. 2, p. 214.
35. Staffordshire RO D593/P/8/1/4.
36. Shropshire RO Box 298.
37. CJ Vol. 2, p. 742.
38. HMC 5th Report, Appendix, p. 344.
39. E. 119.25; Chester RO A/B/2 f 57.
40. Rushworth, op. cit., Part 3, Vol. 2, pp. 5–11.
41. Chetham Society 65 (1909), pp. 71–2.
42. Brit. L. Add. MS 36913 f 103.
43. W.A. Shaw, op. cit., Vol. 2, p. 214.
44. E. 119.25.
45. Brit. L. Add. MS 36913 f 103; HMC 5th Report, Appendix, p. 344.
46. E. 119.3; Brit. L. Harl. MS 2135 f 22.
47. E. 119.3; 119.25.
48. E.119.25; *Archaeologia Cambrensis* 1846, p. 33.
49. E. 200.61; Clarendon, VI. 67.
50. CJ Vol. 2, p. 763.
51. Dircks, *The Life ... Of The Second Marquis Of Worcester*, p. 331.
52. NLW Tredegar MS 911; CJ Vol. 2, p. 785.
53. CJ Vol. 2, p. 793.
54. E.122.14.
55. HMC 13th Report, Portland MSS 1, pp. 61–2.
56. Somers Tracts Vol. 5, p. 302, J. Corbet, *History Of The Military Government Of Gloucester*.
57. ibid. p. 306.

58. Warburton, op. cit. Vol. 1, pp. 396–8; Bod. L. Firth MS C6 f 20; E. 240.9.
59. PRO SP 16/492/21, 32 Nehemiah Wharton 26/30-9-42.
60. Bod. L. Tanner MS 303 f 113; Worcestershire RO 1714/899/192 ff 239–41.
61. LJ Vol. 5, p. 413.
62. Brit. L. Harl. MS 6851 f 211; Somers Tracts Vol. 5, p. 263, *Iter Carolinum*; A. Collins (ed.), *Letters And Memorials*, Vol. 2, p. 667; Clarendon VI. 71.
63. Young, *Edgehill*, pp. 55, 219, 225.
64. ibid. p. 217.
65. R. Gough, *Human Nature Displayed In The History Of Myddle*, p. 31.
66. ibid. p. 15.
67. DWB 'Herbert Of Montgomery', 'Owen'; HMC 14th Report, Appendix 2, p. 94; Young, op. cit., pp. 223–4, 227–8.
68. Chester RO CR 63/2/6.
69. PRO SP 16/488/100, Certificate 31-1-42.
70. NLW Crosse Of Shawe Hill MS 1118; E.122.14; Clarendon VI. 73.
71. E.119.3, 121.3.
72. Shropshire RO Box 298.
73. HMC 5th Report, Appendix, p. 142.
74. For example TSANHS 1905, p. 315.
75. Bulstrode, *Memoirs And Reflections*, pp. 75, 86.
76. Brit. L. Add. MS 36913 f 101; NLW Llanfair-Brynodol MS 39, Wynn MS 1711, Crosse Of Shawe Hill MS 1094, 1116.
77. WSL Salt MS 402 f 204.
78. Clarendon VI. 65–6.
79. For example Staffordshire RO D593/P/8/1.
80. For example E.122.14.
81. Rushworth, op. cit., Part 3, Vol. 2, p. 23.
82. For example TSANHS 1905, p. 314.
83. Clarendon VI. 64, 72.
84. ibid. VI. 72.
85. HMC 2nd Report, Appendix, p. 48.
86. TSANHS 1895, p. 249.
87. Shropshire RO Box 298.
88. E. 242.2.
89. 1 000 from Denbighshire alone – NLW Crosse Of Shawe Hill MS 1118.
90. TSANHS 1894, pp. 45–6.
91. HMC 10th Report, Appendix 4, p. 399.
92. W.A. Shaw, op. cit., p. 214.
93. Chester RO Cowper MSS 2 ff 21–2.
94. E.121.36; PRO SP 16/491/131, Niccolls, 26-8-42.
95. See above, p. 18.
96. Somerset Record Society, *Bellum Civile*, pp. 19–23; R.N. Worth, *The Buller Papers*, pp. 60–84.
97. Somers Tracts, *Iter Carolinum*.
98. T. Harwood, *History Of The Church And City Of Lichfield* pp. 19–20.
99. WSL Salt MS 562/1.

100. E. 242.2.
101. Young, op. cit., pp. 86–91, 174.
102. ibid. p. 76.

Chapter 3

1. Brit. L. Harl. MS 6804 f 197.
2. NLW Llanfair-Brynodol MS 41; UCNW Baron Hill MS 5362.
3. NLW Clennenau Letters, Appendix 2.
4. PRO WO 55/425 ff 164–6.
5. Dugdale's Diary, ed. W. Hamper, p. 46; Clarendon, *History Of The Rebellion*, VI. 237.
6. Rushworth, *Historical Collections*, Part 3, Vol. 1, pp. 672–4. The commission was not actually signed until after Hertford's departure.
7. E.121.9; Somerset Record Society, *Bellum Civile*, pp. 17–18.
8. T. Carte (ed.), *Original Letters*, pp. 14–15.
9. PRO SP 19/21 f 161, 19/126 ff 105–8.
10. LJ Vol. 5, pp. 440–1.
11. E.127.28, 128.4.
12. Though the Rev. J. Webb, writing before Phillips, did not.
13. LJ Vol. 5, pp. 415, 425–6, 440–1, 444, 453, 475, 511.
14. Bod. L. Tanner MS 303 f 113.
15. Dugdale's Diary, p. 46.
16. Dircks, *The Life Of The Second Marquis Of Worcester*, pp. 331–3.
17. CJ Vol. 2, p. 800.
18. LJ Vol. 5, pp. 425–6.
19. NLW LI/MB/17 f 2.
20. TSANHS 1894, pp. 48, 59.
21. NLW Crosse Of Shawe Hill MS 1123.
22. ibid. 1093.
23. I. Roy, *The Royalist Army In The First Civil War*, p. 168.
24. Clarendon VI. 238.
25. Firth (ed.), *Life Of ... Newcastle*, pp. 24–33, 332–7.
26. Clarendon VI. 275; A.C. Wood, *Nottinghamshire*, pp. 28–30.
27. F. Madan, *Oxford Books*, Vol. 2, No. 1134, 1187.
28. Firth op. cit., p. 28.
29. Victoria and Albert Museum, Forster Bequest, Sir Bevil Grenville To His Wife, 6-1-1642/3: *Bellum Civile*, p. 35.
30. CSPD 1641–3, pp. 442–3.
31. Bod. L. Tanner MS 303 ff 113–15.
32. Hereford RL 3668 f 587.
33. J.R. Burton, *A History Of Bewdley*, Appendix xxxi.
34. Brit. L. Add. MS 18980 ff 8–9, 20.
35. ibid.
36. Worcestershire RO 1714/899/192 f 309.
37. ibid. f 295.
38. ibid. ff 299–304.
39. See below, p. 87.
40. Worcester Corporation Order Book 2 ff 210–11; Rev. J. and Rev.

T.W. Webb, *Memorials Of The Civil War* ... [in] *Herefordshire*, Vol. 2, pp. 354–5; PRO SP 16/492/21, Nehemiah Wharton 26-9-42.
41. Webbs, op. cit., pp. 354–5; E.121.34; PRO SP 16/492/21, 32 Wharton 26/30-9-42.
42. Shropshire RO Box 298.
43. E.130.22.
44. Brit. L. Harl. MS 6852 f 1.
45. HMC 10th Report, Appendix 4, pp. 403–4.
46. Brit. L. Add. MS 36913 f 116.
47. TSANHS 1894, p. 64; 1895, pp. 264–5.
.48. ibid. 1895, pp. 256–7.
49. HMC 10th Report, Appendix 4, p. 403.
50. TSANHS 1894, pp. 74–5.
51. Owen and Blakeway, *A History Of Shrewsbury*, p. 431.
52. TSANHS 1894, pp. 55–6, 57, 71–2.
53. ibid. 1895, p. 250.
54. E.246.16; NLW Crosse Of Shawe Hill MS 1095.
55. NLW Crosse Of Shawe Hill MS 1118.
56. E.246.16; Brit. L. Harl. MS 6852 f 1.
57. Cheshire RO DCC/47/[42]fi See pp. 41–2.
58. Brit. L. Add. MS 36913 f 122.
59. See above, p. 25.
60. A.M. Johnson, 'Politics In Chester ...', pp. 206–10.
61. Chester RO A/B/2 f 60.
62. Brit. L. Add. MS 36913 ff 122–3.
63. Lancashire and Cheshire Record Society, Malbon's Diary, p. 29.
64. ibid. p. 30; NLW Crosse Of Shawe Hill MS 1114.
65. Brit. L. Add. MS 36913 ff 122–3.
66. Cheshire RO DCH/X/15/14.
67. TSANHS 1894, pp. 60–2.
68. E.84.37.
69. CJ Vol. 2, pp. 916–17.
70. Carte, *Letters*, pp. 14–15.
71. ibid.
72. Staffordshire RO D593/P/8/1/6, D260/M/F/6/1 f 1.
73. E.127.3; 126.23 (Misc. Parl. Newsp. 1642)
74. Staffordshire RO QS/R, Special Sessions 1642, f 10.
75. WSL Salt MS 342/1.
76. S. Shaw, 'The History And Antiquities Of Staffordshire', Vol. 1, p. 434; Brit. L. Add. MS 18980 f 20; Bod. L. Clarendon MS 23 f 120.
77. WSL Salt MS 402 ff 205–6.
78. ibid.; HMC 2nd Report, Appendix, p. 48; Staffordshire RO QS/R Epiphany 1643.
79. CJ Vol. 2, p. 862; E.242.27.
80. WSL Salt MS 402 f 205; HMC Hastings MSS 2, pp. 90–1 nl.
81. E.89.17.
82. ibid.; E.90.11; HMC Hastings MSS 2, pp. 90–1.
83. Brit. L. Add. MS 36913 ff 122–6; Burghall's Diary, p. 159.
84. E.86.22.
85. WSL Salt MS 550.

86. For a parallel interpretation of these events, see J.T. Pickles, *Studies in Royalism In The English Civil War*, pp. 51–84. I endorse, and develop, Mr Pickles's explanation for the Moorlander rising but differ from him in believing that the gentry had divided before that rising.

87. See p. 10.

88. G.A. Harrison, *Royalist Organisation In Wiltshire*, pp. 125–6.

89. Manning, *Neutrals And Neutralism*, pp. 26–32; Firth, op. cit., pp. 332–3.

90. See my article, 'The Failure Of The Lancashire Cavaliers'.

91. Somerset Record Society, *Bellum Civile*, pp. 23–36; Corpus Christi Library, *Mercurius Aulicus*, 8th Week 1643; CJ Vol. 2 pp. 987, 998–1000.

92. A.C. Wood, op. cit., pp. 29–30.

93. HMC Hastings MSS 2, pp. 87–8.

94. TSANHS 1894, pp. 55–7.

95. HMC 5th Report, Appendix, p. 142.

96. Worcestershire RO 1714/899/192 ff 309–10.

97. Bod. L. Wentworth Proclamation 16.

98. ibid. 4.

99. TSANHS 1894, pp. 64, 68–9; 1895, pp. 267–73.

100. PRO SP 16/497/3.

101. Bod. L. Tanner MS 62 f 541.

102. TSANHS 1894, p. 73; Brit. L. Harl. MS 2155 f 109.

103. Brit. L. Harl. MS 6851 ff 79–94.

104. LJ Vol. 5, pp. 535, 538–41.

105. Bod. L. MS Eng. Hist. c 53 f 6.

106. TSANHS 1894, pp. 60–2.

107. ibid. pp. 64–5; NLW Crosse Of Shawe Hill MS 1095; Llanfair-Brynodol MS 45.

108. Brit. L. Add. MS 36913 ff 105–14.

109. ibid. f. 123.

110. Bod. L. Tanner MS 62 f 537.

111. ibid.; HMC 13th Report, Portland MSS 1, p. 94; Burghall's Diary, p. 159.

112. CJ Vol. 3, p. 484.

113. For a discussion of the motives, other than expediency, behind this alliance, see Morrill, *Cheshire*, pp. 65–6. I agree completely with Dr Morrill's analysis of the neutralist movement, differing only over the date of its collapse.

114. HMC 13th Report, Portland MSS 1, pp. 95–6.

115. E.90.11.

116. HMC 13th Report, Portland MSS 1, pp. 95–6.

117. Brit. L. Harl. MS 2128 f 54, Add. MS 36913 ff 123–4.

118. Brit. L. Harl. MS 36913 ff 123–4.

119. Lancashire and Cheshire Record Society, Malbon's Diary, pp. 38–9.

120. Brit. L. Harl. MS 2135 f 103; Add. MS 34253 f 23; Burghall's Diary, p. 160; DWB 'Ellis'.

121. LJ Vol. 5, pp. 520–2.

122. E.91.5.

123. Dugdale's Diary, p. 47.

124. WSL Salt MS 571; HMC Hastings MSS 2, pp. 94–5.
125. E.91.19; 86.41.
126. Dugdale's Diary, p. 48.
127. Bod. L. Firth MS C6 f 12.
128. HMC Hastings MSS 2, pp. 94–5; TSANHS 1894, pp. 74–5; E.86.41.
129. Brit. L. Add. MSS 18980 f 23.
130. E.86.41; 246.37.
131. HMC 10th Report, Appendix 6, p. 95; Bod. L. MS Eng. Hist. c. 53 f 21.
132. S. Shaw, op. cit., p. 52; E.91.8, 94.11.
133. E.247.20, 26.
134. S. Shaw, op. cit., p. 54; Bod. L. Firth MS C6 f 159; WSL Salt MS 568; E.99.18.
135. Clarendon, VII. 31; Bod. L. Clarendon MS 28 f 129; PRO WO/55/ 1661/18.
136. Clarendon, VII. 31; HMC Hastings MSS 2, pp. 97–8; Bod. L. Firth MS C6 f 159; Warburton, *Memoirs Of Prince Rupert*, Vol. 2, pp. 155–6.
137. E.100.8; Bod. L. MS Eng. Hist. c. 53 f 31.
138. E.99.30.
139. E.99.28.
140. PRO WO/55/423 f 15.
141. Brit. L. Add. MS 18980 ff 46–52.
142. Morrill, *The Revolt of the Provinces*, p. 37.

PART TWO: THE GRANDEES

Introduction

1. I. Roy, 'The Royalist Council Of War'.
2. Newcastle's army has been thoroughly studied by P.R. Newman in his 'The Royalist Armies'. Some of his conclusions have been published in his two articles on Catholic Royalists.
3. See my 'Lancashire Cavaliers'.
4. Bod. L. Dugdale MS 19 ff 11–12, 13.

Chapter 4

1. Dircks, *The Life ... Of The Second Marquis of Worcester*, pp. 44–6.
2. HMC 3rd Report, Appendix, p. 420.
3. Warburton, *Memoirs Of Prince Rupert*, p. 92.
4. Brit. L. Harl. MS 6804 f 133.
5. J. Duncumb, *Collections Towards The History And Antiquities Of The County Of Hereford*, Vol. 1, pp. 245–6; Bod. L. Tanner MS 303 ff 116–20.

6. Duncumb, ibid.; Young, *Edgehill*, pp. 223–4.
7. D.J. Davies, *The Economic History Of South Wales Prior To 1800*, pp. 75–6; A.H. Dodd, *Studies in Stuart Wales*, pp. 25–7.
8. Bod. L. MS Eng. Hist. c 53 f 30, Tanner MS 303 f 115.
9. Bod. L. Clarendon MS 21 f 202; Northamptonshire RO Finch-Hatton MS 133; Sir Edward Walker, *Historical Discourses*, p. 130.
10. Tanner MS 303 ff 114–15.
11. Bod. L. MS Eng. Hist. c 53 f 12.
12. Camden Society, *Letters Of Brilliana Harley*, No. 185.
13. ibid. No. 187.
14. ibid. No. 185.
15. Somers Tracts, Corbet, *A History Of The Military Government of Gloucester*, pp. 310–11; Gloucester Council Minute Book ff 239–40.
16. Corbet, ibid.
17. Bod. L. Firth MS C6 f 9.
18. Bod. L. Tanner MS 303 f 115.
19. ibid.
20. Clarendon, *History Of The Rebellion*, V. 291.
21. Rushworth, *Historical Collections*, Part 2, Vol. 2, p. 1243.
22. Corbet, p. 312.
23. Clarendon V. 291.
24. Bod. L. MS Eng. Hist. c 53 ff 27–8; LJ, Vol. 6, pp. 4–5; Brit. L. Add. MS 18980 f 30; HMC Hastings MSS 2, pp. 96–7; Corbet, pp. 313–14.
25. LJ Vol. 5, pp. 602–3.
26. HMC 13th Report, Portland MSS 1, pp. 703–4; L.W. Dillwyn, *Contributions Towards A History Of Swansea*, p. 27.
27. Corbet, p. 314; Bod. L. MS Eng. Hist. c 53 f 29.
28. HMC 14th Report, Appendix 2, pp. 104–6.
29. Bod. L. MS Eng. Hist. c 53 f 30.
30. E.247.25.
31. Corbet, p. 314.
32. LJ Vol. 6, pp. 4–5.
33. ibid; Duncumb, op. cit., pp. 245–6; Corbet, p. 315.
34. ibid; WSL Salt MS 600; Corbet, p. 315.
35. Corbet, p. 315.
36. Duncumb, op. cit., pp. 245–58.
37. Bod. L. Tanner MS 303 ff 113–20.
38. E.101.2.
39. Webb and Webb, *Memorials Of The Civil War*, pp. 288–9.
40. Hereford RL 3668.
41. TSANHS 1895, pp. 316–17.
42. HMC 13th Report, Portland MSS 1, pp. 709–10; Worcestershire RO 1714/899/192 ff 313–16.
43. Corbet, p. 317.

Chapter 5

1. D. Lloyd, *State Worthies*, pp. 344–6; DNB.
2. Brit. L. 669 f 6 64.

3. Brit. L. Add. MS 18980 ff 8–9.
4. TSANHS 1895, p. 278.
5. HMC Hastings MSS 2, p. 96.
6. TSANHS 1895, pp. 300–1.
7. Dodd, *Studies In Stuart Wales*, pp. 14, 23.
8. NLW Llanfair-Brynodol MSS 43, 45.
9. Bishop J. Hacket, *Scrinia Reserata*, p. 187.
10. *Trans. Anglesey Antiquarian Society and Field Club* 1945, pp. 25–37.
11. W.H.B. Court, *The Rise Of The Midland Industries*, pp. 78–82, 175.
12. TSANHS 1894, pp. 71–2; 1895, pp. 288–90.
13. PRO WO 55/1661/18; Brit. L. Add. MS 34325 f 32; HMC Hastings MSS 2, pp. 95–6; TSANHS 1895, pp. 290–1.
14. NLW Llanfair-Brynodol MS 58.
15. PRO SP 16/498/8 ff 21–2, 36–7; Brit. L. Harl. MS 6802 f 72.
16. Brit. L. Add. MS 18980 f 44, 21506 f 80; Bod. L. Firth MS C8 f 120.
17. NLW Crosse Of Shawe Hill MS 1097.
18. WSL Salt MS 487.
19. TSANHS 1895, pp. 303–4.
20. Brit. L. 669 f 7 1.
21. NLW Llanfair-Brynodol MSS 48–50.
22. WSL Salt MS 487.
23. Warburton, *Memoirs Of Prince Rupert*, Vol. 1, p. 495.
24. Brit. L. 18980 ff 34, 37.
25. ibid. f 44; Bod. L. Firth MS C6 f 162; TSANHS 1895, pp. 311–12; Burghall's Diary, p. 162; E.99.15.
26. HMC Hastings MSS 2, p. 99.
27. NLW Llanfair-Brynodol MSS Appendix, Crosse Of Shawe Hill MSS 1098–9.
28. NLW Crosse Of Shawe Hill MSS 1098–9; Llanfair-Brynodol MS 57.
29. Bod. L. Dugdale MS 19 f 14; NLW Crosse Of Shawe Hill MS 1123.
30. Owen and Blakeway, *A History of Shrewsbury*, p. 434; Gough, *Human Nature Displayed*, p. 74.
31. TSANHS 1895, p. 311.
32. UCNW MS 1921 f 35.
33. ibid; UCNW Baron Hill MSS 5364–5.
34. Hacket, op. cit., p. 210.
35. *Archaeologia Cambrensis* 1917, Supplement, p. 296.
36. Bod. L. Dugdale MS 19 f 48.
37. Burghall's Diary, p. 164; E. 103.10.
38. S. Shaw, *The History ... Of Staffordshire*, p. 55; Burghall's Diary, p. 163; E.103.8, 104.16.
39. Dugdale's Diary, p. 52; WSL Salt MS 402 f 206.
40. Burghall's Diary, p. 166.
41. ibid. p. 164; E.105.8, 55.4; TSANHS 1895, pp. 325–6.
42. E.104.16.
43. WSL Salt MS 488.
44. E.249.3, 56.2.
45. TSANHS 1895, pp. 324–5.
46. LJ Vol. 6, pp. 90–2.
47. ibid. p. 102.

48. ibid. p. 80; Dodd, op. cit., pp. 29, 46–7.
49. DNB 'Mennes'; TSANHS 1895, pp. 321–3.
50. TSANHS 1895, p. 329.
51. ibid. pp. 332–3.
52. NLW Crosse Of Shawe Hill MS 1102.
53. NLW Llanfair-Brynodol MSS 51–4.
54. E.60.17.
55. Chester RO ML/2.
56. NLW Llanfair-Brynodol MSS 55–6.
57. NLW Crosse Of Shawe Hill MS 1123.
58. HMC 4th Report, Appendix, p. 263.
59. NLW Crosse Of Shawe Hill MSS 1105, 1123; M. Mahler, *A History Of Chirk Castle And Chirkland*, pp. 164–5.
60. HMC 5th Report, Appendix, p. 420.
61. HMC 4th Report, Appendix, p. 263.
62. NLW Crosse Of Shawe Hill MS 1108.
63. HMC 2nd Report, Appendix, p. 61.
64. TSANHS 1895, pp. 344–5.
65. Brit. L. Add. MS 33374 ff 10–11.
66. TSANHS 1895, pp. 347–8.
67. ibid. pp. 349–50.
68. E.59.8; Burghall's Diary, p. 165.
69. Burghall's Diary, p. 166; TSANHS 1895, pp. 343–6; V. Vicars, *God's Ark*, p. 18.
70. Burghall's Diary, p. 167; CJ Vol. 3, p. 123.
71. NLW Crosse Of Shawe Hill MSS 1109, 1111, 1113.
72. PRO SP 23/195 f 144; Crosse Of Shawe Hill MSS 1109, 111, 1113.
73. Lancashire and Cheshire Record Society, Malbon's Diary, pp. 67–70.
74. NLW Crosse Of Shawe Hill MS 1112.
75. E.67.7, B. Lib. 669 f 7 35.
76. Burghall's Diary, p. 167.
77. ibid; Bod. L. Firth MS C7 ff 296–7.
78. M. Mahler, op. cit., pp. 165–6.
79. Rushworth, *Historical Collections*, Part 2, Vol. 2, p. 1243.
80. NLW Add. MS 320D.
81. CJ Vol. 3, p. 155; E.250.5.
82. Burghall's Diary, pp. 168–9.
83. W.A. Day (ed.), *The Pythouse Papers*, p. 17.
84. Shaw, op. cit., p. 216.
85. Bod. L. Dugdale MS 19 f 30.
86. PRO WO/55/459 ff 477–82.
87. HMC Hastings MSS 2, pp. 104–6.
88. E.71.1, 71.16; HMC 13th Report, Portland MSS 1, pp. 141–3.
89. ibid. pp. 134–5, 141–3.
90. DWB 'Trevor'.
91. *Archaeologia Cambrensis* 1846, p. 35.
92. E.77.33.
93. HMC 13th Report, Portland MSS 1, pp. 151–3; E.77.27, 77.10; NLW Clennenau Letter 538; *Archaeologia Cambrensis* 1846, p. 35; Bod. L. Carte MS 7 ff 434, 523.

94. E.77.2.
95. Bod. L. Carte MS 7 f 424.
96. ibid. f 523. ,
97. Burghall's Diary, p. 164.

Chapter 6

1. See p. 35.
2. W.A. Shaw, p. 215.
3. ibid; DWB.
4. Bod. L. Dugdale MS 19 f 11. The most prominent of those expelled were Sir Hugh Owen and Griffith White, of whom more below.
5. Brit. L. Harl. MS 6852 ff 63–4.
6. *Archaeologia Cambrensis* 1915, pp. 3–4.
7. CJ Vol. 3, p. 109.
8. For example Brit. L. Add. MS 18980 f 91.
9. ibid. f 94.
10. E.65.29.
11. *Archaeologia Cambrensis* 1915, p. 4.
12. Bod. L. Tanner MS 61 f 315.
13. H.A. Lloyd, *The Gentry Of South-West Wales 1540–1640*, pp. 18–19.
14. PRO SP 16/497/148.
15. Bod. L. Z1.17.16.
16. PRO SP 19/¹²⁶ fifi ¹⁰⁵₋8.
17. *Archaeologia Cambrensis* 1915, pp. 4–6; NLW Haverfordwest Borough Records No. 709, 1–2.
18. E.75.13.
19. Corpus Christi Library, *Mercurius Aulicus*, First Week 1644.
20. E.32.17.
21. CSPD 1641–3, p. 499.
22. PRO SP 19/126 ff 105–8.
23. Bod. L. Ashmole MS 832 ff 194–5.
24. See p. 34.
25. PRO SP 19/21 f 98.
26. A. Leach, *The History Of The Civil War In Pembrokeshire* . . . , pp. 44–5.
27. E. 436.7.
28. E.42.13, 14, 19.
29. PRO SP 19/126 ff 105–8.
30. PRO SP 16/498 f 38.
31. NLW Add. MS 4849D; Bod. L. Firth MS C7 f 14.
32. Dodd, *Studies In Stuart Wales*, p. 37.
33. Bod. L. Firth MS C8 ff 340–1.
34. ibid. f 342.
35. ibid; NLW Add. MS 4849D; Brit. L. Harl. MS 6802 f 129.
36. PRO SP 19/126 ff 105–8.
37. Brit. L. Add. MS 18981 ff 123, 145, 149; Bod. L. Firth MS C7 ff 46, 100.

Notes

Chapter 7

1. Court, *The Rise Of The Midland Industries*, pp. 24–5.
2. E.115.2.
3. S. Shaw, *The History And Antiquities Of Staffordshire*, p. 55.
4. Brit. L. Harl. MS 6802 f 114.
5. Brit. L. Add. MS 34325 ff 12–13, 20, 30, 45; PRO WO 55/459 ff 263, 659; See I. Roy's introduction to 'The Royalist Ordnance Papers'.
6. Townshend ff 344–5.
7. Worcestershire RO 1714/899/192.
8. ibid. ff 733–4.
9. R.H. Silcock, *County Government In Worcestershire 1603–1660*.
10. Worcestershire RO 1714/899/192, ff 375–6; Worcestershire Historical Society, Russell MSS reprinted in J.W. Willis-Bund's edition of Townshend, Vol. 1, pp. xxx–xxxi.
11. ibid, xxx–xxxv.
12. PRO SP 16/493/9.
13. Worcestershire Historical Society, Russell MSS, pp. xxx–xxxv; HMC 14th Report, Appendix 8, p. 203.
14. See p. 37.
15. Worcester Corporation Order Book 2 f 214.
16. Bod. L. Rawlinson MS D924 ff 153–4.
17. ibid. ff 150–4; Worcestershire RO 174/899/192 f 344.
18. Bod. L. Rawlinson MS D924 f 152.
19. Camden Society 1859, Richard Symonds's Diary, pp. 11–13.
20. ibid; Worcestershire RO 174/899/192 ff 379–80; Bod. L. Dugdale MS 19 f 16.
21. Camden Society, Symonds's Diary, pp. 11–13.
22. Worcester Corporation Order Book f 215.
23. Worcestershire Historical Society, Russell MSS p. xxxii.
24. Worcestershire RO/1714/899/192 ff 344, 349–51.
25. ibid. ff 313–15.
26. ibid. f 316.
27. Worcestershire RO 3762/8 f 185; Birmingham RL 398329–30.
28. Worcestershire RO/1714/899/192 ff 334–5.
29. PRO WO 55/1661 f 19, 55/459 f 400.
30. Worcestershire RO 1714/899/192 ff 317–18; Birmingham RL 398331.
31. Bod. L. MS Eng. Hist. c 53 f 71.
32. Worcestershire RO 1714/899/192 ff 320–2.
33. Worcester Corporation Order Book f 217.
34. See pp. 127–8.
35. Worcestershire RO 1714/899/192 ff 349–51.
36. ibid. ff 353–8.
37. Brit. L. Harl. MS 6851 f 135.
38. Bod. L. Rawlinson MS D918 f 145.
39. PRO SP 16/325/5.
40. Worcestershire RO 1714/899/192 ff 342, 365–73.

Conclusions

1. See my 'Lancashire Cavaliers'.

2. The best Royalist accounts of these campaigns are in Somerset Record Society's '*Bellum Civile*', pp. 35–58, and Richard Atkyns's *Vindication*, ed. by Peter Young.
3. Bod. L. Firth MS C6 f 206.
4. Clarendon, *Life*, Vol. 1, p. 195n.
5. Bod. L. Clarendon MSS 23 f 10, 26 f 163.
6. Camden Society, 1872, Trevelyan Papers pp. 239, 241–2.
7. The Firth (ed.) *Life* was largely written to answer these charges in Newcastle's lifetime. The most recent modern works to consider his campaigns, C.V. Wedgwood, *The King's War*, and P. Young, *Marston Moor*, both pay tribute to Newcastle's virtues but do not acquit him of the faults traditionally associated with his leadership.

PART THREE: THE ROYALIST WAR EFFORT

Chapter 8

1. Bod. L. Dugdale MS 19.
2. Bod. L. Rawlinson MSS D918, D924.
3. NLW L1/MB/17.
4. Bod. L. Dugdale MS 19 f 74.
5. See p. 37.
6. Bod. L. Dugdale MS 19 ff 6–7.
7. ibid. Worcestershire RO 1714/899/192.
8. Bod. L. Dugdale MS 19 f 8.
9. ibid. f 14.
10. ibid. ff 19–21.
11. Brit. L. Add. MS 18981 f 222.
12. NLW Crosse Of Shawe Hill MS 1103.
13. Bod. L. Firth MS C6 f 122.
14. UCNW Baron Hill MSS 5362, 5364.
15. Worcestershire RO 1714/899/192 ff 299–307.
16. ibid. ff 433–42.
17. Birmingham RL 398279.
18. Bod. L. Rawlinson MS D924 ff 152–4.
19. NLW L1/MB/17 ff 76–8.
20. HMC 7th Report, Appendix, p. 689.
21. Worcestershire RO 1714/899/192, ff 344–7.
22. Cornwall RO, Bassett MS 2 ff 42–4.
23. Camden Society, *Letters Of Brilliana Harley*, No. 174.
24. *Archaeologia Cambrensis* 1846, p. 34.
25. Bod. L. Tanner MS 62 f 541.
26. CJ Vol. 2, pp. 966–7.
27. LJ Vol. 5, p. 669.
28. See p. 61.
29. NLW L1/MB/17 ff 17–23.
30. Bod. L. Dugdale MS 19 ff 23–4, 27–8.

31. ibid. ff 27–9, 32–3, 41, 48.
32. ibid. f 50.
33. ibid. f 62.
34. Worcestershire RO 1714/899/192 ff 654–5.
35. Brit. L. Harl. MS 2135 ff 9–10.
36. Bod. L. Dugdale MS 19 ff 50–1, 89.
37. NLW/L1/MB/17 f 9.
38. Worcestershire RO 1714/899/192 f 358.
39. Brit. L. Harl. MS 2135 ff 9–10.
40. Worcestershire RO 1714/899/192 ff 649–50.
41. NLW/L1/MB/17 f 66.
42. Camden Society, *Letters Of Brilliana Harley*, Appendix 3.4.
43. M. Prestwich, *Cranfield*, p. 573.
44. Worcestershire RO 1714/899/192 ff 346, 368.
45. M. Coate, *Cornwall In The Great Civil War*, p. 104.
46. Brit. L. Harl. MS 2002 ff 68–70.
47. J. and T.W. Webb, *Memorials Of The Civil War*, Vol. 1, p. 352.
48. ibid. Vol. 2, pp. 411–13.
49. NLW/L1/MB/17 f 73.
50. C.M. Thomas, *The First Civil War* . . . .
51. NLW L1/MB/17 f 73.
52. See pp. 13–14.
53. NLW L1/MB/17 f 73.
54. ibid. ff 46, 73.
55. R. Baxter, *Reliquae Baxterianae*, Part 64.
56. Clarendon, *History Of The Rebellion*, V11. 394–5; Rushworth, *Historical Collections*, Part 3, Vol. 2, pp. 580–1.
57. Bod. L. Dugdale MS 19 ff 69, 71; Camden Society, Trevelyan Papers, p. 243.
58. TS ANHS 1896, pp. 258–60.
59. I.Roy, *The Royalist Army*, pp. 185–7.
60. Bod. L. Dugdale MS 19 f 16.
61. Coate, op. cit., pp. 65–6.
62. See p. 63.
63. NLW L1/MB/17 f 27.
64. Brit. L. Harl. MS 6852 f 193.
65. Bod. L. Dugdale MS 19 ff 37, 42–3, 46, 50, 52.
66. NLW Add. MS 320D f 37.
67. Brit. L. Add. MS 18981 f 73.
68. Bod. L. Dugdale MS 19 ff 63–5; Brit. L. Harl. MS 6804 f 142.
69. Bod. L. Dugdale MS 19 f 77.
70. Madan, *Oxford Books*, No. 1638–9.
71. Bod. L. Dugdale MS 19 ff 74, 79–84, 91, 101.
72. Bod. L. Firth MS C7 f 209.
73. ibid. C8 f 334.
74. Underdown, *Somerset In The Civil War*, p. 81.
75. Bod. L. Clarendon MS 23 f 8.
76. Bod. L. Dugdale MS 19 ff 86–7, 89, 91.
77. Bod. L. Firth MS C8 f 334; See p. 00.
78. NLW L1/MB/17 f 61.
79. See Appendix.

Chapter 9

1. Clive Holmes, *The Eastern Association In The English Civil War*.
2. Alan Everitt, *The Community Of Kent And The Great Rebellion*. See above, p. 1.
3. Worcestershire RO 1714/899/192.
4. Birmingham RL 398331.
5. See p. 30.
6. Collins, *Letters And Memorials*, Vol. 2, p. 667.
7. Bod. L. Rawlinson MS D924 f 149.
8. S. Shaw, *History And Antiquities Of Staffordshire*, Vol. 2, p. 144.
9. Dircks, *The Life . . . Of The Second Marquis Of Worcester*, pp. 329–30.
10. See pp. 132–3.
11. Shropshire RO Box 298.
12. Brit. L. Harl. MS 2135 ff 40–3.
13. *Chester And North Wales Historical And Archaeological Society Transactions* 1914, p. 151.
14. WSL Salt MS 402 f 204.
15. PRO 55/457/60 f 1.
16. Staffordshire RO Q SIR Epiphany 1643 ff 11–12.
17. Brit. L. Add. MS 36913 f 112.
18. Worcestershire RO 1714/899/192 f 333.
19. WSL Salt MS 479.
20. HMC Hastings MSS 2, pp. 109–10.
21. Shropshire RO Box 298.
22. TSANHS 1896, pp. 223–4.
23. J. and T.W. Webb, *Memorials Of The Civil War*, Vol. 2, p.169.
24. Brit. L. Harl. MS 2135 ff 54–8.
25. Shropshire RO Box 298.
26. Staffordshire RO D260/M/PVI/1.
27. Birmingham RL 398331.
28. G.P. Mander, *A History of Wolverhampton*, p. 78.
29. Worcestershire RO 1714/899/192 f 325.
30. ibid. f 346; HMC 15th Report, Appendix 2, pp. 99–106, provides a very good picture of the number of irregular burdens imposed by the royal army when on campaign in the West in 1644.
31. Worcestershire RO 3762/8 f 185.
32. Christ Church MS 164 f 25.
33. Worchestershire RO 1714/899/192 f 316.
34. Brit. L. Harl. MS 6804 ff 139–40.
35. Bod. L. Wentworth Proclamation 66; TSANHS 1895, pp. 324–5.
36. Rushworth, *Historical Collections*, Part 3, Vol. 2, pp. 365–7.
37. For example Staffordshire RO QS/R M. 1647 f 11; Bod. L. MS Eng. Hist. c 53 f 36.
38. Bod. L. MS Eng. Hist. c 53 ff 72–3; see I. Roy, 'England Turned Germany?', for a study of the impact of war upon the Severn Valley.
39. Brit. L. Harl. MS 6851 ff 140, 155.
40. Shaw, op. cit., p. 145.
41. HMC Hastings MSS 2, p. 104.
42. Shaw, op. cit., p. 168.
43. HMC 13th Report Portland MSS 1, p. 700.

44. LJ Vol. 5, p. 469.
45. Shaw, op. cit., pp. 144–5.
46. HMC Hastings MSS 2, pp. 106–16.
47. ibid. pp. 106–22; Shaw, op. cit., pp. 145–6; WSL Salt MSS 545,550.
48. NLW Bettisfield MS 113.
49. WSL Salt MS 551.
50. Brit. L. Harl. MS 6802 f 55.
51. WSL Salt MS 556. All these quarrels are more fully described by J.T. Pickles in *Studies In Royalism*, pp. 119–31. Unlike myself, Mr Pickles regards them as an unqualified disaster for the Royalists.
52. Lichfield CL, 'Original Documents Relating to the Siege of the Close', ff 78–80, 83–4, 171; HMC Hastings MSS 2, pp. 115–16.
53. T. Harwood, *History Of The Church And City Of Lichfield*, pp. 40–47.
54. HMC Hastings MSS 2, pp. 115–16.
55. ibid. pp. 111–12.
56. E. 77.33, 81.19, 285.25; Shaw op. cit., p. 145.
57. For example ibid. Vol. 1, General History, pp. 60–1.
58. E. 46.10.
59. E. 75.13.
60. E. 6.12.
61. E. 269.5.
62. HMC 4th Report Appendix, p. 275.

Chapter 10

1. Notably Everitt, *The Community Of Kent*, section v; Morrill, *Cheshire*, ch. 3; Holmes, *The Eastern Association*, chs. 3–10; Fletcher, *A County Community In Peace And War: Sussex*, chs. 15–16; D.H. Pennington and I.A. Roots, *The Committee At Stafford*; C.B. Phillips, 'County Committees And Local Government In Cumberland And Westmoreland'. All these studies, together with several unpublished theses and much additional research, have been synthesised in Morrill, *The Revolt Of The Provinces*, pp. 52–80. Dr Morrill also makes some tentative comparisons between Royalist and Parliamentarian administration, which on the whole are confirmed by the present study.

PART FOUR: THE WARLORDS

Chapter 11

1. P. Young and M. Toynbee, *Strangers in Oxford*, p. 197.
2. E.99.22.
3. Bod. L. Dugdale MS 19 ff 20, 26.
4. NLW Add. MS 4849D.
5. Bod. L. Dugdale MS 19 ff 19, 20, 23.
6. HMC 14th Report, Appendix 2, p. 111.

7. Brit. L. Add. MS 18980 f 90.
8. Camden Society, *Letters of Brilliana Harley*, No. 201.
9. Camden Society Add. MS 18980 f 91; Hereford RL 3668 f 607.
10. NLW L1/MB/17 ff 3–17.
11. Brit. L. Add. MS 18980 ff 95, 97; HMC Marquis of Bath MSS, pp. 1–7.
12. Somers Tracts, Corbet, p. 319.
13. Bod. L. Tanner MS 61 f 197.
14. Brit. L. Add. MS 18980 ff 99, 101.
15. NLW L1/MB/17 ff 25, 29.
16. See above, p. 88.
17. NLW L1/MB/17 ff 25–45.
18. Dircks, *The Life ... Of The Second Marquis Of Worcester*, pp. 328–30.
19. HMC Marquis of Bath MSS, pp. 1–22.
20. ibid., pp. 26–7.
21. PRO WO 55/459 ff 464–5.
22. NLW L1/MB/17 f 42.
23. ibid, ff 50, 51, 61.
24. LJ Vol. 6, pp. 218–19.
25. CJ Vol. 3, p. 392.
26. HMC 13th Report, Portland MSS 1, pp. 133–4; NLW L1/MB/17 f 48.
27. NLW, L1/MB/17 f 56; Brit. L. Add. MS 18981 f 4.
28. NLW L1/MB/17 ff 57, 59, 63.
29. E.45.12.
30. HMC 14th Report, Appendix 2, p. 117.
31. HMC 13th Report, Portland MSS 1, pp. 133–4.
32. HMC 13th Report, Vol. 2, p. 489.
32. CJ Vol. 2, p. 489.
33. Bod. L. Dugdale MS 19 f 30.
34. Brit. L. Harl. MS 6852 f 222; Corbet, pp. 331–2.
35. Corbet, ibid.
36. See p. 92.
37. Corbet, p. 333; Rushworth, *Historical Collections*, Part 2, Vol. 2, p. 1242; W.A. Day, *Pythouse Papers*, p. 16.
38. Corbet, p. 333–5; Bod. L. Clarendon MS 27 f 73; Brit. L. Add. MS 18981 ff 29, 45; Bod. L. Rawlinson MS D395 f 17.
39. Brit. L. Harl. MS 6852 ff 54–62.
40. Brit. L. Harl. MS 6802 ff 69–114.
41. Bod. L. Rawlinson MS D395 ff 172–3, Firth MS C7 f 13; Brit. L. Add. MS 18981 f 76.
42. Brit. L. Add. MS 18981 ff 76, 144; Brit. L. Harl. MS 6802 f 62; Bod. L. Firth MS C7 f 13.
43. Corbet, pp. 344–5; Bod L. Clarendon MS 27 ff 74–5; Brit. L. Add. MS 18981 f 144.
44. Brit. L. Add. MS 18981 f 156.
45. *Pythouse Papers*, p. 16; Brit. L. Add. MS 18981 f 134.
46. Bod. L. Clarendon MS 27 ff 73–5.
47. Brit. L. Add. MS 18981 f 16.
48. ibid. ff 16, 112.
49. Bod. L. Firth MS C8 f 337.

50. Brit. L. Harl. MS 6802 f 111.
51. LJ Vol. 6, pp. 518, 578–9.

Chapter 12

1. Clarendon, *Life*, Vol. 1, p. 195n.
2. The best Royalist sources for these campaigns are J. Bamfield, *An Apologie*, pp. 6–7; Brit. L. Add. MS 18980 ff 110, 125, 142, *Mercurius Aulicus*, 31st–40th Weeks 1643. The account in Clarendon is wholly misleading – see my 'Clarendon's "History Of The Rebellion"'.
3. Somerset Record Society, *Bellum Civile*, pp. 61–73; Bamfield, *An Apologie*, pp. 7–10.
4. Like Sir John Berkeley, at Exeter.
5. W.D. Christie, *A Life Of Anthony Ashley Cooper*, pp. 45–6.
6. DNB 'Byron'; J.P. Earwaker, *East Cheshire*, Vol. 2, p. 567; Rushworth, *Historical Collections*, Part 2, Vol. 2, p. 1243.
7. Bod. L. Ashmole MS 832 ff 191–4.
8. Young, *Edgehill*, pp. 214–15.
9. Brit. L. Add. MS 18980 ff 147, 154.
10. W.A. Day, *The Pythouse Papers*, p. 2; Brit. L. Add. MS 18980 ff 144, 145, 147.
11. Warburton, *Memoirs of Prince Rupert*, Vol. 2, pp. 329–30; Brit. L. Harl. MS 6852 f 217.
12. PRO WO 55/459 ff 621, 625; Bod. L. Rawlinson MS 395 f 3, MS Film 191 f 100.
13. TSANHS 1896, p. 205; Bod. L. Carte MS 7 f 555.
14. Brit. L. Harl. MS 2135 f 16.
15. Bod. L. Carte MS 7 f 192.
16. ibid. ff 389, 409–10, 412.
17. Bod. L. Wentworth Proclamation 43.
18. Bod. L. Rawlinson MS D924 ff 145–6; NLW Clennenau Letter 539.
19. Bod. L. Carte MS 7 ff 393, 409–10.
20. ibid. ff 14, 192, 255–6, 424, 462, 564.
21. ibid. ff 533, 647.
22. ibid. 8 ff 91–2.
23. ibid. 7 f 624.
24. ibid. 8 ff 112, 482–90.
25. ibid. 7 ff 637–8.
26. ibid. f 529.
27. Bod. L. Dugdale MS 19 f 44.
28. Bod. L. MS Eng. Hist. c 53 f 106.
29. Bod. L. Carte MS 7 ff 637–8.
30. Brit. L. Harl. MS 2135 f 18; Bod. L. Carte MS 7 ff 637–8, 8 ff 3, 7.
31. Bod. L. Carte MS 8 ff 211–12.
32. ibid. 7 ff 637–8.
33. Chester RO AF/26/4; HMC 3rd Report, Appendix, p. 259.
34. UCNW Baron Hill MS 5367.
35. NLW MS 1546E (iii); Bod. L. Carte MS 8 ff 211–12.
36. ibid. 8 f 137.

37. E.30.7.
38. Bod. L. Carte MS 8 ff 211–12, 464–5; Burghall's Diary, p. 172; E.81.19, 30.7. These events and those preceding and succeeding them are described in detail and with verve by J. Lowe, in 'The Campaign Of The Irish Royalist Army', pp. 47–76. I differ from Dr. Lowe on several small points, mainly resulting from my use of the original Carte MSS where he has confined himself to the selection in publication.
39. NLW Add. MS 320D f 37; TSANHS 1896, pp. 206–7; see above, p. 61.
40. HMC 3rd Report, Appendix, p. 259.
41. Bod. L. Dugdale MS 19 f 43; Brit. L. Add. MS 18981 f 2.
42. E.33.20; Carte, *Letters*, pp. 40–2.
43. Carte, *Letters*, pp. 36–40; HMC 10th Report, Appendix 4, pp. 68–9; Somers Tracts Vol. 5, pp. 387–8; Brit. L. Add. MS 18981 f 8.
44. Brit. L. Add. MS 18981 f 2.
45. See, for example, Bod. L. Carte MS 7 ff 637–8.
46. ibid. 8 f 444.
47. Brit. L. Harl. MS 6988 ff 166–7.
48. *Trans. Lancashire and Cheshire Historical Society* 1961, pp. 97–124.
49. Burghall's Diary, pp. 177–8; E.33.33.
50. Bod. L. Carte MS 9 f 81; Carte, *Letters*, pp. 39–40; Brit. L. Harl. MS 2135 ff 40–3, 54–8.
51. TSANHS 1896, p. 209.
52. Bod. L. Firth MS C6 f 52.
53. ibid. f 279; Somers Tracts, Corbet, p. 334; E.45.12.
54. Bod. L. MS Film 191 f 101; PRO WO 55/459 ff 643–5.
55. Camden Society 1859, Symonds's Diary, pp. 12–13.
56. Brit. L. Add. MS 18980 f 165.
57. Worcestershire Corporation Order Book 2 f 219.
58. PRO WO 55/459 f 659; Bod. L. Rawlinson MS D395 ff 98–9.
59. Dugdale's Diary, pp. 55–6.
60. ibid. p. 57; E.37.1.
61. Brit. L. Add. MS 18980 f 165; Bod. L. Firth MS C6 f 58.
62. Bod. L. Firth MS C6 f 52.
63. Dugdale's Diary, p. 59.
64. Bod. L. Firth MS C6 f52.
65. ibid.

Chapter 13

1. Bod. L. Dugdale MS19 f 48.
2. See my article 'The Structure Of The Royalist Party'.
3. Bod. L. Dugdale MS 19 f 55.
4. Bod. L. Clarendon MS 28 f 129.
5. WSL Salt MS 551.
6. Owen and Blakeway, *A History Of Shrewsbury*, Vol. 1, p. 439.
7. Bod. L. Carte MS 9 f 123; Brit. L. Add. MS 18981 f 8.
8. Brit. L. Add. MS 18981 ff 25, 27, 28; Bod. L. Firth MS C6 f 71.
9. Bod. L. Clarendon MS 28 f 129.

10. Worcestershire RO 705/24/876.
11. Worcestershire Corporation Order Book 2 f 220.
12. Camden Society 1859, Symonds's Diary, pp. 11–12.
13. Brit. L. Add. MS 18981 f 85.
14. ibid. ff 68, 85; Worcestershire Corporation Order Book 2 ff 220–1.
15. WSL Salt MS 518.
16. Bod. L. MS Eng. Hist. c 309.
17. W.A. Shaw, *The Knights Of England*, p. 215; Bod. L. Clarendon MS 28 f 129.
18. Bod. L. Clarendon MS 28 f 129.
19. Bod. L. Firth MS C6 f 80.
20. Bod. L. MS Eng. Hist. c 53 f 122.
21. TSANHS 1896, p. 240.
22. HMC 6th Report, Appendix, p. 472.
23. TSANHS 1898, pp. 158–60.
24. ibid. 1896, pp. 223–4.
25. PRO SP 23/2 f 86.
26. TSANHS 1896, pp. 223–4.
27. HMC 6th Report, Appendix, p. 472
28. Brit. L. Add. MS 18981 f 53; Bod. L. Firth MS C6 f 81, Clarendon MS 28 f 129; Warburton, *Memoirs Of Prince Rupert*, Vol. 2, pp. 375–6.
29. N.A. Day, *The Pythouse Papers*, p. 52; Bod. L. Rawlinson MS D395; PRO WO 55/459.
30. Bod. L. Carte MS 9 f 254.
31. Warburton, op. cit., p. 382.
32. Brit. L. Add. MS 18981 ff 19, 44.
33. Warburton, op. cit., pp. 384–5; Bod. L. Carte MS 10 f 263.
34. Brit. L. Add. MS 18981 f 95; *Pythouse Papers*, p. 52.
35. Bod. L. Carte MS 8 ff 555–6, 9 ff 87–8, 215, Clarendon MS 28 f 129; Firth MS C6 f 11; Warburton, op. cit., Vol. 1, p. 494.
36. *Pythouse Papers*, p. 5.
37. Bod. L. Clarendon MS 28 f 129.
38. ibid; E.39.3, 42.26, 43.18; Brit. L. Add. MS 18981 f 62; Bod. L. Firth MS C7 f 91; HMC Earl of Denbigh MSS Vol. 1, pp. 77–8.
39. E.42.26; WSL Salt MS 518.
40. Burghall's Diary, p. 178; *Archaeologia Cambrensis* 1846, p. 36; Brit. L. Add. MS 18981 f 118.
41. HMC Marquis of Bath MSS, pp. 28–38.
42. Bod. L. Dugdale MS 19 f 69; Brit. L. Add. MS 18981 ff 107–8, 113–14.
43. Brit. L. Add. MS 18981 f 86.
44. PRO WO 55/459 ff 52–3; *Pythouse Papers*, p. 53.
45. *Pythouse Papers*, p. 16; Brit. L. Add. MS 18981 f 130.
46. Bod. L. Carte MS 10 f 263.
47. *Pythouse Papers*, pp. 8–9; Dugdale's Diary, p. 65; HMC 9th Report, Appendix 2, p. 434; Brit. L. Add. MS 18981 f 136; Bod. L. Firth MS C7 ff 77, 103, C8 ff 261–3, Carte MS 9 ff 464–5.
48. Bod. L. Clarendon MS 28 ff 129.
49. Worcestershire RO 1714/899/192.
50. TSANHS 1896, p. 242.

51. Brit. L. Harl. MS 2135 ff 22, 30, 31, 62–3, 108.
52. HMC 10th Report, Appendix 4, p. 399; Brit. L. Add. MS 18981 f 67.
53. HMC 6th Report, Appendix, p. 472.
54. J. and T.W. Webb, *Memorials Of The Civil War*, Vol. 2, p. 410.
55. Bod. L. Carte MS 11 f 16; UCNW Baron Hill MS 5368. No such invasion occurred; reports on Parliamentarian pamphlets of a capture of Caernarvon in April 1644, which Phillips took literally, are certainly a mistake for Carmarthen.
56. Brit. L. Add. MS 18981 f 77.
57. NLW Llanfair-Brynodol MS 62.
58. Brit. L. Add. MS 18981 f 97.
59. Bod. L. Clarendon MS 23 ff 122–3.
60. Bod. L. Carte MS 10 f 439.
61. NLW Clennenau Letters 537, 542. See above, ch. 2.
62. Bod. L. Carte MS 10 f 601.
63. Gough, *Human Nature Displayed*, p. 32.
64. Worcestershire RO 1714/899/192 ff 551–3, 649–50, 679.
65. NLW Wynn MSS 1728–36.
66. For example HMC 14th Report, Appendix 8, p. 203.
67. NLW Wynn MS 1733, and see NLW Rhual MS 177.
68. See the accounts of the Dartmouth garrison, Devon RO Seymour Papers 1392.
69. Somerset RO Phelips MS 75.
70. Bod. L. Wood 376.55.
71. Camden Society 1872, *Trevelyan Papers*, pp. 249–50.
72. A.R. Bayley, *The Great Civil War In Dorset*, p. 138.
73. Somerset Record Society, *Bellum Civile*, p. 62; E.44.6.
74. For reasons I am unable to discover, Warburton, Gardiner and Dame Veronica Wedgwood consistently refer to him as 'Sir Charles'. I have copied this error in my article on the Lancashire Cavaliers.
75. W. Dugdale, *The Baronage Of England*, Vol. 2, p. 418; *Pythouse Papers*, p. 8.
76. Phillips's belief that Cardiff had also fallen, based on E.4.12, is disproved by WSL Salt MS 517. See also E.51.7.
77. Dugdale's Diary, p. 67.
78. WSL Salt MS 517.
79. NLW L1/MB/17 ff 44.
80. ibid. f 72; Bod. L. Dugdale MS 19 f 77.
81. NLW L1/MB/17 ff 81–5.
82. E.256.44.
83. E.4.12.
84. John Rylands Library, Mainwaring MSS, Letter A.10.
85. WSL Salt MS 517.
86. E.13.19, 16.8.
87. PRO SP 23/109 ff 10–12.
88. Brit. L. Add. MS 18981 f 62.
89. Bod. L. Carte MS 9 f 544.
90. P. Young, *Marston Moor*, pp. 54–6, 94–7.
91. *Archaeologia Cambrensis* 1846, p. 37; Brit. L. Add. MS 18981 f 62. See above, ch. 8.

92. Brit. L. Add. MS 18981 f 77.
93. E.43.18.
94. Add. MS 18981 f 103.
95. Bod. L. Firth MS C7 f 103.
96. Young, op. cit., pp. 54–6, 94–7.
97. ibid.
98. C. Firth, *Cromwell's Army*, pp. 25–8.
99. HMC 4th Report, Appendix, p. 265.
100. Bod. L. Clarendon MS 28 f 129; Carte MS 10 f 664; Brit. L. Egerton MS 785 f 102; Chester RO CR 63/2/19.
101. See my article 'The Failure Of The Lancashire Cavaliers'.

PART FIVE: WARLORDS AND CIVILIANS

Chapter 14

1. See p. 63.
2. For example Bod. L. Tanner MS 62 f 422; HMC 4th Report, Appendix, pp. 262–4.
3. CSPD 1644, pp. 111–12, 124, 161–2; E.46.10.
4. CSPD 1644, pp. 161–2; E.46.25.
5. CSPD 1644, pp. 177–9, 193–4; E.46.28.
6. Christ Church MS 164 ff 1–22.
7. LJ Vol. 6, pp. 607–8.
8. Bod. L. Clarendon MS 26 f 165.
9. Worcestershire Christ Church MS 164 f 22.
10. Worcestershire Corporation Order Book 2 f 222.
11. TSANHS 1896, p. 247.
12. E.46.10.
13. CSPD 1644, pp. 235–7.
14. ibid., p. 247; Christ Church, MS 164 ff 24–5.
15. E.46.19.
16. Corpus Christi Library, *Mercurius Aulicus*, 24th Week 1644.
17. Somers Tracts, Corbet, p. 349.
18. E.53.3; HMC 4th Report, Appendix, p. 267; CSPD 1644, pp. 284, 286, 331.
19. E.54.16; PRO SP 16/502/51; CSPD 1644, pp. 337–9.
20. Brit. L. Add. MS 1891 f 222; HMC 4th Report, Appendix, p. 270.
21. ibid. p. 268.
22. Bod. L. Carte MSS 10 ff 294, 462, 601, 11 ff 46, 246, 12 f 519; Carte, *Letters*, pp. 52–4.
23. Bod. L. Carendon MS 28 f 129.
24. Bod. L. Firth MS C8 f 334.
25. HMC 2nd Report, Appendix, p. 86.
26. UCNW Baron Hill MS 5372, Bangor MS 1921 f 36.
27. Brit. L. Add. MS 18981 f 223; CSPD 1644, p. 392.

28. CSPD 1644 p. 394.
29. ibid.
30. ibid; Bod. L. Carte MS 12 f 140.
31. Bod. L. Rawlinson MS A147; the officer, Sir John Hurry, had defected to Rupert's army from Parliament in 1643, and was to change sides again.
32. Bod. L. Carendon MS 28 f 129.
33. Corbet, pp. 352–3; CSPD 1644, pp. 396–8; Bod. L. Tanner MS 61 f 106.
34. Brit. L. Add. MS 18981 f 235.
35. Bod. L. Firth MS C8 f 328.
36. J. and T.W. Webb, *Memorials Of The Civil War*, Vol. 2, p. 80.
37. TSANHS 1895 ff 291–3, 315.
38. Corpus Christi Library, *Mercurius Aulicus*, 21st Week, 1644.
39. Brit. L. Add. MS 18981 f 231.
40. See my 'Lancashire Cavaliers'.
41. C.B. Phillips, 'County Committees And Local Government In Cumberland And Westmoreland', pp. 37–8, and 'The Royalist North', pp. 170–4.
42. L.J. Vol. 6, pp. 449, 479, 486–8.
43. Burghall's Diary, p. 180; Warburton, *Memoirs Of Prince Rupert*, Vol. 3, pp. 21–2.
44. Warburton, ibid; Brit. L. Add. MS 18981 ff 227–8; Bod. L. Firth MS C7 f 146.
45. WSL Salt MS 486.
46. Bod. L. Carte MS 12 f 519.
47. Chester RO A/B/2 f 68.
48. Brit. L. Stowe MS 190 f 18.
49. Lancashire and Cheshire Record Society, Malbon's Diary, p. 145.
50. E.6.23; CSPD 1644, pp. 405–6.
51. CSPD 1644, p. 538; E.256.2; Brit. L. Add. MS 18981 ff 245, 253.
52. See p. 136.
53. NLW Herbert MSS, Series 2, No. 9 f 3.
54. ibid. f 4; Bod. L. Firth MS C7 f 167.
55. *Archaeologia Cambrensis* 1846, pp. 37–8; Brit. L. Add. MS 18981 ff 245, 253.
56. L.J. Vol. 6, pp. 713–15; Bod. L. Carte MS 12 ff 185, 360–1.
57. Bod. L. Carte MS 12 f 519.
58. CSPD 1644, p. 524, 1644–5, pp. 6–7.
59. See p. 31.
60. CSPD 1644, p. 534.
61. ibid. 1644–5, pp. 3–4.
62. ibid. p. 34; E.12.8, 14.6
63. Brit. L. Add. MS 18981 f 285; WSL Salt MS 518; E.9.4; CSPD 1644, pp. 512–13.
64. CSPD 1644, pp. 512–13; Corbet, pp. 356–7; Bod. L. Firth MS C7 ff 178–9; Brit. L. Add. MS 18981 f 261.
65. Corbet, p. 357; Brit. L. Add. MS 18981 f 237; CSPD 1644–5, p. 31.
66. CSPD 1644–5, pp. 42, 52–4; Bod. L. Firth MS C7 f 209.
67. An excellent narrative of this campaign is found in Christ Church,

MS 164, written by Sir Edward Walker with amendments by Charles himself. This was published, concealing the amendments, in Walker's *Historical Discourses*. The details of the allocation of local resources may be found in House of Lords RO, Hist. Coll. 65.

68. Bod. L. Firth MS C7 ff 241–5, 248, 251–3.
69. ibid. f 237.
70. E.256.44.
71. E.21.26, 258.6; CSPD 1644–5, pp. 181–2.
72. E.25.1, 258.22.
73. *Cambrian Quarterly Magazine* 1829, p. 61.
74. Bod. L. Dugdale MS 19 f 96.
75. HMC 2nd Report, Appendix, p. 86; NLW Wynn MS 1746; W.A. Shaw, *The Knights Of England*, p. 219.
76. Dugdale's Diary, p. 77.
77. Lancashire and Cheshire Record Society, Malbon's Diary, p. 152.
78. E.26.9; CSPD 1644–5, pp. 255, 257–60.
79. *Archaeologia Cambrensis* 1846, p. 38.
80. Malbon's Diary, pp. 159–60.
81. E.258.22.
82. Malbon's Diary, pp. 161–2; E.258.25; Bod. L. Carte MS 14 f 102.
83. E.271.2, 270.33; Burghall's Diary, p. 184.
84. Clarendon, History Of The Rebellion, VIII. 239, 253.

Chapter 15

1. Bod. L. Fairfax MS 32 f 85; NLW Wynn MS 1740; Brit. L. Add. MS 18981 f 296.
2. ibid. Brit. L. Add. MS 18981 f 216.
3. Herefordshire RO LC Deeds 325.
4. Brit. L. Add. MS 18981 f 265.
5. ibid. ff 268, 294; Bod. L. Firth MS C7 ff 183, 215.
6. Brit. L. Add. MS 18981 f 225.
7. Baxter, *Reliquiae Baxterianae*, Part 1, Section 67; Bod. L. Carte MS 12 f 140; Brit. L. Add. MS 18981 f 233.
8. ibid. Brit. L. Add. MS 18981 f 251.
9. ibid. ff 308–9.
10. ibid. f 299.
11. Warburton, *Memoirs Of Prince Rupert*, Vol. 1, p. 530.
12. ibid. p. 526.
13. Brit. L. Stowe MS 190 f 18; Chester RO AF 27/2–4.
14. Worcestershire Corporation Order Book 2 f 223.
15. Montgomeryshire Collections 1886, Supplement, No. 11.
16. Worcestershire RO 1714/899/192 ff 463–4.
17. ibid. ff 767–8, 771–3.
18. E.45.10.
19. Christ Church MS 164 ff 115–24; Clarendon, *History Of The Rebellion*, 255–6.
20. See p. 101.
21. See p. 31.

22. Birmingham RL 398325–6, 398282.
23. Shropshire RO Box 298.
24. Clarendon, op. cit. IX. 10, 16–17.
25. Brit. L. Add. MS 18982 f 3.
26. Worcestershire RO 1714/899/192 ff 769–70.
27. ibid. ff 776–7.
28. ibid. ff 779–87.
29. Brit. L. Add. MS 18981 f 296.
30. ibid. f 324; NLW Herbert MSS Series 2, 12 f 35.
31. TSANHS 1896, p. 254.
32. Chester RO A/B/2 ff 70–1.
33. NLW Herbert MSS Series 2, 12 f 36.
34. Brit. L. Add. MS 18982 f 36.
35. ibid. f 16.
36. TSANHS 1896, pp. 270–1; Bod. L. Firth MS C6 f 303.
37. ibid. Bod. L. Firth MS C6 f 332.
38. Brit. L. Add. MS 18982 f 33.
39. WSL Salt MS 556.
40. Bod. L. Dugdale MS 19 f 102.
41. TSANHS 1896, pp. 267–8, 272.
42. Worcestershire RO 1714/899/192 f 776.
43. PRO SP 16/506/55.
44. See p. 37.
45. D. Underdown, *Somerset In The Civil War And Interregnum*, pp. 98–117; J.S. Morrill, *The Revolt Of The Provinces*, pp. 97–111; G.J. Lynch, *The Risings Of The Clubmen In The English Civil War*.
46. E.258.6.
47. For example E.23.8.
48. Bod. L. Firth MS C7 f 224.
49. ibid. C6 f 332.
50. ibid. f 303.
51. Somers Tracts, Corbet, p. 367.
52. E.274.2, 274.24
53. Worcestershire RO 1714/899/192 ff 793–6.
54. E.258.36.
55. See pp. 182–3.
56. For example 274.2.
57. See pp. 96–9.
58. See p. 183.
59. See pp. 153–4.
60. For example E.271.17.
61. Brit. L. Add. MS 18982 f 31.
62. Somers Tracts, Corbet, pp. 367–9.
63. Brit. L. Egerton MS 787 f 93.
64. ibid.
65. Brit. L. Add. MS 11043 ff 19–20.
66. Brit. L. Add. MS 18982 f 31.
67. ibid. f 33.
68. Bod. L. Firth MS C6 f 342.
69. Brit. L. Add. MS 11043 f 22.

70. Warburton, op. cit., Vol. 3, pp. 55–6.
71. NLW Wynn MS 1744.
72. Brit. L. Sloane MS 1519 ff 76–7.
73. Warburton, op. cit., Vol. 2, pp. 385–7; Brit. L. Add. MS 18981 f 83 (both misplaced among documents of 1644).
74. Harleian Miscellany, Vol. 7, p. 557.
75. Underdown, *Somerset*, p. 98.
76. Brit. L. Sloane MS 1519 ff 76–7.
77. Staffordshire RO D(W) 1778 I; ff 41, 45.
78. CSPD 1644–5, p. 356.

Chapter 16

1. Bod. L. Carte MS 12 f 519; MS displayed at Chirk Castle.
2. Camden Society, 1859, Symonds, p. 256; Gough, *Human Nature Displayed*, p. 15; Mrs F. Stackhouse–Action, *The Garrisons Of Shropshire During The Civil War*, pp. 72–3.
3. Brit. L. Add. MS 11331 f 48; Bod. L. Tanner MS 60 f 41.
4. E.13.18, 16.3.
5. Somers Tracts Corbet, pp. 361–2; HMC 14th Report, Appendix 2, pp. 130, 134–5; Camden Miscellany 2, pp. 9–10.
6. CSPD 1644–5, pp. 238–9, 267–9.
7. Corbet, pp. 365–7; Bod. L. Firth MS C6 ff 117, 346.
8. D. Lloyd, *Memoirs of Protestant Martyrs*, p. 668.
9. Brit. L. Add. MS 18981 f 338; Bod. L. Fairfax MS 32 ff 89–90, Firth MS C6 ff 306–8.
10. Brit. L. Harl. MS 6802 ff 213–14.
11. See p. 128.
12. Worcestershire RO 1714/899/192 ff 387–9.
13. For example CSPD 1644, pp. 512–13.
14. Brit. L. Add. MS 18981 f 222.
15. ibid. f 326; Brit. L. Egerton MS 785 f 95.
16. Brit. L. Add. MS 18981 f 332, Add. MS 5716 f 11.
17. Hereford RLLC Webb MS 1 ff 129, 167–9.
18. Brit. L. Sloane MS 1519 f 60.
19. Harleian Miscellany, Vol. 7, p. 557.
20. Brit. L. Add. MS 18982 f 27.
21. TSANHS 1896, pp. 266–7.
22. ibid. pp. 268–9.
23. Worcestershire RO 1714/899/192 ff 499–516.
24. ibid. ff 728–9; Brit. L. Add. MS 24023 f 24.
25. Brit. L. Egerton MS 787 f 83; Somers Tracts, Corbet, p. 267.
26. Bod. L. Clarendon MS 28 f 129.
27. ibid; Bod. L. Tanner MS 60 ff 11, 52.
28. NLW Clennenau Letters 551–62, Llanfair-Brynodol MSS 64, 66; *Archaeologia Cambrensis* 1846, p. 38.
29. Bod. L. Carte MS 14 ff 166, 362.
30. Bod. L. Clarendon MS 28 f 129; Burghall's Diary, p. 184; Staffordshire RO D (W) 1778 1 f 42.

31. Brit. L. Egerton MS 787 f 83; CSPD 1644–5, pp. 350–1.
32. E.260.12; Bod. L. Carte MS 14 f 295; Lancashire and Cheshire Record Society, Malbon's Diary, pp. 167–8; Brit. L. Add. MS 11331 f 47.
33. NLW Clennenau Letter 563.
34. Brit. L. Egerton MS 787 f 88.
35. ibid. f 73; E.260.12.
36. NLW Clennenau Letters 554–60.
37. PRO SP 16/507/35.
38. Brit. L. Egerton MS 787 f 83.
39. E.260.4, 8.
40. Brit. L. Add. MS 11043 f 22.
41. Bod. L. Clarendon MS 28 f 129.
42. Brit. L. Egerton MS 787 f 16.
43. E.277.13.
44. Clarendon MS 28 f 129.
45. Staffordshire RO D(W) 177 1 f 44; E.260.27; Somers Tracts, Corbet, p. 369.
46. For example Brit. L. Add. MS 18982 ff 36, 40.
47. G. Ormerod, *History of the County . . . of Chester*, Vol. 2, p. 243.
48. E.260.25.
49. Corbet, pp. 370–1; Worcestershire RO 1714/899/192.
50. Worcestershire RO 1714/899/192 ff 519–20, 531–2.
51. NLW Clennenau Letter 563.
52. WSL Salt MS 502.
53. J.S. Morrill, *The Revolt Of The Provinces*, p. 114.
54. Hereford RL MS 3668 ff 561–73, Webb MS 1 ff 129–91. They were made by the Rev. J. Webb, who refers to them glancingly in his history of Herefordshire, *Memorials Of The Civil War*, Vol. 2, pp. 167–9. A few other extracts appear in Montgomeryshire Collections 1881, pp. 293–330.
55. Their minute-book has survived, as WSL Salt MS 45.
56. Bod. L. Clarendon MS 24 ff 56–127. Clarendon's *History* is totally untrustworthy on these events.
57. WSL Salt MS 45; Clarendon MS 24 ff 107–27.
58. NLW Clennenau Letter 571.
59. E.260.27.
60. E.281.13, E.260.20, 23, 35; Somers Tract, Corbet, pp. 369–71; Bod. L. Clarendon MS 28 f 129.
61. Camden Society 1859, Symonds, pp. 65–6.
62. ibid.; Walker, *Historical Discourses*, p. 126.
63. PRO SP 16/507/35.
64. Symonds, pp. 166, 181; Bod. L. Clarendon MS 28 f 129; Roy, *The Royalist Army*, p. 218.
65. Walker, op. cit., pp. 126–7; Symonds, pp. 166–7.
66. Symonds, p. 181; Bod. L. Clarendon MS 28 f 129.
67. Walker, op. cit., p. 127; Bod. L. Tanner MS 60 f 159.
68. Bod. L. Tanner MS 60 f 154, Carte MS 14 f 609; Brit. L. Add. MS 11331 f 114.
69. Symonds, p. 181; Roy, op. cit., p. 218.
70. Brit. L. Egerton MS 787 f 73.

71. ibid.; *Archaeologia Cambrensis* 1846, p. 39.
72. E.260.13.
73. E.286.17; E.284.20, 23; *Archaeologia Cambrensis* 1915, pp. 7–8.
74. E.286.17; E.288.48.
75. Bod. L. Carte MS 14 f 609; Brit. L. Add. MS 11331 f 130.
76. Bod. L. Clarendon MS 24 f 192.

PART SIX: THE FAILURE OF THE ROYALISTS

Chapter 17

1. Camden Society 1859, Symonds, p. 195.
2. HMC 13th Report, Portland MSS 1, pp. 225–6; CSPD 1644–5, p. 504.
3. Hereford RL 3668 f 573.
4. E.290.11, 292.15; Lancashire and Cheshire Record Society, Malbon's Diary, pp. 176–7.
5. See pp. 56–7.
6. Brit. L. Add. MS 11331 f 139; Bod. L. Carte MS 14 f 609.
7. ibid. Bod. L. Carte MS 14 f 411; PRO SP 16/507/13.
8. Bishop Hacket, *Sounia Reserata*, pp. 218–19.
9. NLW Clennenau Letters, Appendix.
10. UCNW Baron Hill MSS 5375–8.
11. Bod. L. Clarendon MS 24 ff 182–200.
12. G.A. Harrison, *Royalist Organisation In Wiltshire*, pp. 381–435.
13. The most interesting of these are those in J.S. Morrill, *The Revolt Of The Provinces*, pp. 97–111.
14. *Somerset In The Civil War And Interregnum*, pp. 106–7, and 'The Chalk And The Cheese', *Past And Present* 85, 1979, pp. 25–48.
15. Bod. L. Tanner MS 60 ff 163–4; J. Sprigge, *Anglia Rediviva*, pp. 61–90.
16. E.292.33.
17. Bod. L. Clarendon MS 24 f 182.
18. Bod. L. Tanner MS 60 ff 163–4.
19. Bod. L. Clarendon MS 24 ff 182, 188, 196.
20. *Archaeologia* 1857, p. 215.
21. G. Bellet, *Antiquities Of Bridgnorth*, pp. 144–6.
22. Camden Society, Symonds, p. 203.
23. HMC 9th Report, Appendix 2, p. 437; E.292.15.
24. Worcestershire Corporation Order Book 2 f 231; Worcestershire RO 1714/899/192 ff 541–3.
25. E.262.23, 25; E.296.33.
26. Symonds, p. 205; E.292.15, 262.20.
27. Brit. L. Add. MS 11043 f 31.
28. ibid. f 35.
29. Warburton, *Memoirs Of Prince Rupert*, Vol. 3, pp. 119–21.
30. Bod. L. Clarendon MS 28 f 129.
31. Somers Tracts, *Iter Carolinum*.

32. Brit. L. Add. MS 11043 ff 37, 39, Harl. MS 6852 f 279.
33. Brit. L. Hare, MS 6852 ff 101, 103, 113.
34. Symonds, p. 210; Warburton, op. cit., Vol. 3, pp. 145–6; Bod. L. Firth MS C8 f 22.
35. J. and T.W. Webb, *Memorials Of The Civil War*, Vol. 2, p. 37.
36. PRO SP 16/498/8 ff 47–8.
37. Warburton, op. cit., Vol. 3, p. 135.
38. The best description of this campaign is in M.D.E. Wanklyn, *The King's Armies In The West of England*, pp. 234–7.
39. Dugdale's Diary, p. 77; Bod. L. Wood 378 (18).
40. Brit. L. Add. MS 11043 f 43.
41. E.262.34.
42. Brit. L. Harl. MS 6852 f 285.
43. ibid. f 292.
44. ibid. f 302.
45. ibid. ff 305, 308; Symonds, p. 215; Walker, *Historical Discourses*, pp. 116–18.
46. Brit. L. Add. MS 21506 f 38.
47. E.298.15.
48. PRO SP 16/510/78.
49. See pp. 000–0.
50. HMC 13th Report, Portland MSS 1, pp. 255–6; E.297.7, 298.6.
51. Brit. L. Harl. MS 6852 ff 308, 312; Walker, op. cit., pp. 116–18; NLW Add. MS 4849D.
52. Somers Tracts, *Iter Carolinum*; Symonds, pp. 208, 242, 263.
53. WSL Salt MS 109.
54. TSANHS 1896, pp. 285–6; Bod. L. Firth MS C8 f 13.
55. Bod. L. Firth MS C8 ff 14, 16; E.296.24; PRO SP 23/189 f 162, 16/510/78.
56. *Iter Carolinum*; HMC 13th Report Portland MSS 1, pp. 271–3.
57. Symonds, p. 233; Walker, op. cit., p. 129; Brit. L. Add. MS 11043 ff 45, 49.
58. See p. 165.
59. Symonds, pp. 233–9; Walker, op. cit., pp. 129–30.
60. Walker, ibid; Symonds, p. 239.
61. Bod. L. Rawlinson MS B210 f 55, Carte MS 15 f 133, Firth MS C7 f 338; NLW Clennenau Letters 584–93; *Archaeologia Cambrensis* 1846, pp. 40, 333–4.
62. *Iter Carolinum*; E.303.18; Symonds, p. 242; Walker, op. cit., pp. 140–1.
63. Carte, *A Collection Of Original Letters*, p. 99.
64. Bod. L. Clarendon MS 25 ff 122, 149.
65. See my 'Clarendon's "History Of The Rebellion"'.
66. HMC 13th Report, Portland MSS 1, pp. 286–7; Bod. L. Tanner MS 60 f 140.
67. Bod. L. Tanner MS 60 f 140; E.307.14, 308.19.
68. Brit. L. Harl. MS 6852 f 319.
69. PRO SP 16/510/101.
70. E.307.15.
71. PRO SP 23/109 ff 10–12.
72. Symonds, p. 263.
73. E.311.9.

74. HMC 13th Report, Portland MSS 1, p. 315.
75. E.310.6, 309.23.
76. Notably Dr Brian Manning and Mr G.V. Lynch.
77. E.266.24.

Chapter 18

1. For these intrigues, see Harleian Miscellany, Vol 4, pp. 494–9, Vol. 8, pp. 490–505.
2. Bod. L. Dugdale MS 19 f 113, Clarendon MS 26 f 79.
3. Worcestershire RO 1714/899/192 ff 811–7.
4. HMC 13th Report Portland MSS 1, pp. 288–327; NLW Clennenau Letters 598, 616; Burghall's Diary, p. 185; Bod. L. Rawlinson MS B210 ff 57–62.
5. TSANHS 1846, pp. 293–4.
6. Townshend ff 728–9; Worcester Corporation Order Book 2 f 237; E.313.29.
7. WSL Salt MS 545.
8. ibid. 497, 550.
9. Harwood, *History Of . . . Lichfield*, pp. 40–7.
10. CSPD 1645–7, p. 305; Camden Society 1859, Symonds, p. 277; E.315.5. (Misc. Part. Newsp.)
11. E.506.13.
12. PRO SP 16/511/2; E.308.14; Camden Society, 1859, Symonds, pp. 256–8.
13. Symonds, pp. 263, 276; E.314.25; Brit. L. Add. MS 11333 ff 6, 18; HMC 10th Report, Appendix 4, p. 375, 13th Report, Portland MS 1, pp. 324–6.
14. Portland MSS 1, p. 306; E.309.24.
15. Symonds, p. 263.
16. PRO SP 16/510/140.
17. Worcestershire RO 1714/899/192 ff 545–7.
18. HMC 13th Report, Portland MSS 1, p. 264; E.297.4.
19. Worcestershire RO1714/899 192 ff 801–4.
20. Camden Society 1873, pp. 23–30; LJ Vol. 8, pp. 59–60; E.314.12; *Archaeologia Cambrensis* 1871, pp. 298–9.
21. Symonds, p. 277.
22. ibid.
23. Townshend ff 819–26.
24. Brit. L. Add. MS 11333 f 192.
25. HMC 13th Report, Portland MSS 1, p. 339.
26. HMC Hastings MSS 2, p. 137; TSANHS 1896, pp. 295–6; PRO SP 16/513/7, 23.
27. Bod. L. Tanner MS 60 f 386.
28. ibid. f 393; E.320.1; Bod. L. Rawlinson MS B210 ff 62–5.
29. PRO SP 16/511/2.
30. For example Bod. L. Tanner MS 59 f 10; NLW Wynn MS 1763; Brit. L. Lansdowne MS 93 f 171.
31. E.310.5.

32. HMC 13th Report, Portland MSS 1, pp. 348–50; Bod. L. Tanner MS 60 ff 482, 590.
33. Bod. L. Dugdale MS 19 f 113.
34. E.325.8, 313.4; Portland MSS Vol. 1, pp. 320–1.
35. E.322.20; Bod. L. Tanner MS 60 f 440.
36. HMC 13th Report, Portland MSS 1, pp. 348–50.
37. ibid. pp. 351–2; Bod. L. Tanner MS 60 f 484; E.325.17.
38. E.335.3.
39. CSPD 1645–7, pp. 361–2; E.506.12.
40. E.506.10, 322.2, 24.
41. Worcestershire RO 1714/899/192 ff 551–3, 651–6, 679.
42. *Archaeologia Cambrensis* 1846, p. 41.
43. Birmingham RL 347159, 352035.
44. Camden Society 1873, pp. 31–7; E.506.22.
45. Bod. L. Tanner MS 60 ff 444, 461.
46. NLW Wynn MS 1763.
47. NLW Clennenau Letters 608, 610.
48. Bod. L. Carte MS 16 f 517.
49. Bod. L. Tanner MS 60 f 534; E. 333.9.
50. Bod. L. Carte MS 16 f 521.
51. ibid. f 655, MS 17 f 1.
52. ibid. MS 16 f 517.
53. ibid. ff 684–5; NLW Wynn MS 1765; UCNW Baron Hill MS 5380; CSPD 1645–7, pp. 344, 372–3, 382–3.
54. CSPD 1645–7, p. 414; Brit. L. Add. MS 11332 f 113.
55. Bod. L. Carte MS 16 f 682.
56. ibid. ff 684–5.
57. ibid. MS 17 f 166.
58. ibid MS 16 f 521.
59. ibid. MS 17 f 98.
60. CSPD 1645–7, p. 376.
61. Bod. L. Tanner MS 60 f 379; E.340.21.
62. NLW Clennenau Letters 611, 615; *Cambrian Quarterly Magazine* 1829, p. 66.
63. Brit. L. Lansdowne MS 93 f 171.
64. Bod. L. Tanner MS 59 ff 332, 612.
65. NLW Wynn MS 1819, Clennenau Letters 617, 621.
66. Bod. L. Carte MS 17 f 301; E.340.17.
67. NLW Wynn MSS 1789–99, Carreglwyd MS 2/242; HMC 5th Report, Appendix, p. 420; *Archaeologia Cambrensis* 1971, Supplement, pp. 296–8.
68. T.R. Nash, *Collections For The History Of Worcestershire*, Vol. 2, Appendix XCIX; HMC 13th Report, Portland MSS 1, pp. 359, 386; Birmingham RL 595611 ff 172–4; S. Shaw, *The History ... Of Staffordshire*, Vol. 1, p. 48; E.337.35. (Misc. Part. Newsp.)
69. Staffordshire RO D260/M/F/6/1 f 8.
70. Bod. L. Tanner MS 59 ff 10, 28–9.
71. E.335.2.
72. Bod. L. Tanner MS 59 f 319.
73. E.341.6.

74. See Bod. L. Tanner MS 59 f 286; Birmingham RL 595611 ff 248–9.
75. E.349.2.
76. E.345.2.
77. E.342.16, 350.18.
78. Worcestershire RO 1714/899/192 ff 561–631, 686–752.
79. HMC 13th Report, Portland MSS1, p. 389.
80. T. Pennant, *Tours In Wales*, Appendix 8.
81. Brit. L. Lansdowne MS 93 ff 173–5; NLW Clennenau Letters, Appendix.
82. CSPD 1645–7, pp. 514–15.
83. NLW Clennenau Letters, Appendix.

Bibliography: Primary sources

1. MANUSCRIPTS

Public Record Office

SP 16, State Papers.
SP 19, Papers Of The Committee For The Advance Of Money.
SP 23, Papers Of The Committee For Compounding.
WO 55/423, 55/1661, 55/457–9, Papers Of The Royalist Ordnance
  Department.

British Library

Harleian MSS 986, Notebook Of Richard Symonds.
Harleian MSS 2002, 2135, 2107, 2155, 2125, 2158, 2128, 2173, Pa-
  pers Of Alderman Randle Holmes of Chester.
Harleian MSS 6802, 6851, 6804, 6852, Papers Of The Royalist
  Council Of War.
Harleian MSS 6988, Miscellaneous Letters.
Egerton MSS 785–787, Letter Books Of Sir Samuel Luke.
Lansdowne MS 93, Miscellaneous Papers.
Stowe MSS 155, Miscellaneous Letters.
Stowe MSS 190, Letter Book Of Sir Samuel Luke.
Sloane MS 1519, Miscellaneous Letters.
Additional MSS 5716, Miscellaneous Letters.
Additional MSS 11043, Sir Barnabas Scudamore's Papers.
Additional MSS 11331–11333, Letter Books Of Sir William Brere-
  ton.
Additional MSS 11364, History Of Coventry.

Bibliography

Additional MSS 18980–18982, Prince Rupert's Papers.
Additional MSS 21506, Miscellaneous Letters.
Additional MSS 24023, Miscellaneous Letters.
Additional MSS 33374, John Jones's Papers.
Additional MSS 33596, Miscellaneous Letters.
Additional MSS 34253, Miscellaneous Letters.
Additional MSS 34325, Papers Of The Royalist Ordnance Department.
Additional MSS 36913, Sir Thomas Aston's Papers.

See also under 2. Pamphlets.

Bodleian Library

Clarendon MSS 21–28, Sir Edward Hyde's Collections.
Tanner MSS 59–63, The Clerk Of Parliament's Papers.
Tanner MSS 303, Fitzwilliam Coningsby's Defence.
Carte MSS 7–17, The Marquis Of Ormonde's Papers.
Ashmole MSS 830, Papers Of The Cheshire Neutrality Movement.
Ashmole MSS 832, Records Of The Creation Of Peers.
Rawlinson MSS A147, Papers Of Scottish Royalists.
Rawlinson MSS B210, Byron's Account Of The Siege Of Chester.
Rawlinson MSS C125, Copies Of Letters Sent To Western Royalists.
Rawlinson MSS D918, Minutes Of The Worcestershire Committee Of Safety.
Rawlinson MSS D924, Minutes of the Worcestershire Committee of Safety.
Rawlinson MSS D395, Lord Percy's Papers.
Firth MSS C6–C8, Transcripts of some of Prince Rupert's papers apparently made in the 1840's. They include many documents not mentioned in Warburton's published edition of the papers, plus a few original letters. The transcripts are in three different hands. Warburton's may be one, but none were made by Sir Charles Firth, who acquired the volumes and corrected some items.
Dugdale MS 19, Docquet Book Of The Clerks Of Chancery.
Fairfax MS 32, Some Of Prince Rupert's Papers.
MS Eng. Hist. c 53, Letter Book Of Sir Samuel Luke.
MS Eng. Hist. c 309, Letter From King To Worcester Justices.
MS Film 191, Film Of Papers Of Royal Waggonmaster-General.

See also under 2. Pamphlets.

National Library Of Wales

L1/MB/17, Order Book Of The Glamorganshire Committee Of Safety.

Wynn Of Cwydir MSS 1711–1819, Owen Wynn's Papers.

Llanfair-Brynodol MSS 34–69, Griffith Family Papers.

Crosse Of Shawe Hill MSS 1092–1125, John Thelwall's Papers.

Haverfordwest Borough Records 709.

Powys Castle Collection, Correspondence 366, Richard Herbert's Papers.

Herbert MSS, Series 2–Richard Herbert's Papers.

Clennenau Letters And Papers 531–616. And Appendices – Sir John Owen's Papers.

Tredegar MSS, Sir William Morgan's Papers.

Carreglwyd MSS, Documents Concerning Anglesey.

Bettisfield MSS, Hanmer Family Papers.

Llewenny MSS, Sir Thomas Salusbury's Papers.

MS 1546E (iii), Documents Concerning Anglesey And Caernarvonshire.

MS 5390D, Documents Concerning Denbighshire.

Add. MS 320D, Papers Of The High Sheriff Of Flintshire.

Add. MS 4849D, Papers Of The Royalist Council Of War.

Rhual MS 177, Evan Edwards's Papers.

Birmingham Reference Library

347159, Lyttleton Family Papers

351505, Lyttleton Family Papers.

352035, Lyttleton Family Papers.

39827–398331 – Papers Of The High Constable Of Doddingtree Hundred.

595611, Letter Book Of Sir William Brereton.

Cheshire County Record Office

DCH/X/15/14, Sequestration Papers Of Earl Rivers.

DCC/47/42, Miscellaneous Documents.

Chester City Record Office

Cowper MS 2 – History Of Civil War In Cheshire.

CR 63/2/6 – Militia Orders 1625–42.

Bibliography

CR 63/2/19 – William Davenport's Notebook.
ML/2 – Mayor's Letter Book.
A/B/2 – Assembly Books Calendar.
AF – Assembly Files.

Cornwall County Record Office

Bassett MSS – High Sheriff Of Cornwall's Papers.

Devon County Record Office

Seymour Papers 1392, Sir Edward Seymour's Papers.

Gloucester Corporation Archives

Minute Book Of The Common Council 1632–56.

Herefordshire County Record Office

LC Deeds 325 – One Of Prince Rupert's Papers.

Hereford Reference Library

LC Webb MS 1 and 3668 – Transcripts of many different documents, some lost, made by the Rev. John Webb.

John Rylands Library, Manchester

Mainwaring MSS – Roger Whitley's Papers.

House of Lords RO

Hist. Coll. 65 – Papers of the Royalist Council of War.

Lichfield Cathedral Library

'Original Documents Relating to the Siege of the Close, A.D. 1643'.

Northamptonshire County Record Office

Finch-Hatton MS 133 – Transcripts of lists of Commissioners Of Array for several counties.

Christ Church, Oxford, College Library

MS 164 – Original draft of Sir Edward Walker's account of the 1644 royal campaign, published in his *Historical Discourses* (1705), with amendments in the King's own hand.

Shropshire County Record Office

Box 298 – Papers of the Bailiffs of Ludlow.
Boxes 586–91 – Accounts of the Mayors of Shrewsbury.

Somerset County Record Office

Phelips MSS – Sir Robert Phelips's Papers.

Staffordshire County Record Office

QS/R – Quarter Sessions Records.
D593/P/8/1 – Sir Richard Leveson's Papers.
D260/M/F/6 – Persehouse Family Papers.
D260/M/PV/1 – Lewn Book Of Hatherton.
D(W) 1778 1(i) – Will Legge's Papers.

William Salt Library, Stafford

The Salt MSS, Several Of Prince Rupert's Papers-Transcripts of Accounts of Mayors of Stafford. Minute Book Of Council of the West, 1645.

Wiltshire County Record Office

413/444, Prince Rupert's 'Diary'.

Devizes Museum, Wiltshire

Waylen MSS, Transcriptions of local documents.

Worcestershire County Record Office

1714/899/192, Henry Townshend's 'Diary'.
6899/31; 3762/8, Transcripts of Droitwich Corporation Accounts.
705/93; 845/5, Sir Rowland Berkley's Papers.
704/24, Miscellaneous Documents.

Bibliography

Worcestershire Corporation Archives

Corporation Order Book No. 2.

University College of North Wales, Bangor

Baron Hill MSS 5362–5380, Viscount Bulkeley's Papers.
Bangor MS 1921, Viscount Bulkeley's Papers.

Victoria And Albert Museum, London

Forster Bequest, Sir Bevil Grenville's Letters.

Note. Extracts from most of these manuscripts have been published
at some time or another. In particular the editions of the *Letter Books
of Sir Samuel Luke* by I.C. Philip (Oxfordshire Record Society 1950
and 1953) and by H.G. Tibbutt (HMC JP4, 1963), of the various
papers of the Royalist Ordnance Department by I. Roy (Oxfordshire
Record Society 1964 and 1975) and of the Worcester Chamber Order
Book by Shelagh Bond (Worcestershire Historical Society 1974) are
faultless. Likewise the much older Calendar Of State Papers is generally reliable. On the other hand the calendars of the papers of the
committees for Compounding and the Advance Of Money are often
misleading, while the edition of Henry Townshend's *Diary* by J.W.
Willis-Bund (Worcestershire Historical Society 1915–20) is very
dubious, not for its transcription but for the interpretation placed
upon the documents by the editor and the occasional misplacing of
an entry. Hence in general I have returned to the original sources
wherever possible. In each case I have given the reference number to
each document which has obtained me the document itself, or that
by which it has been labelled. Record offices are however prone to
reclassification and I apologise if any reference subsequently proves
obsolete.

2. PAMPHLETS

The British Library

669 f 4 81, *The Petition of the County of Lancaster....*
669 f 5 17, *The Petition of the County of Chester.... 7 May 1642*

669 f 5 65, *The Declaration . . . . by the Grand Jury at Worcester.*

669 f 6 55, *A Declaration of the Inhabitants of Chester . . . .*

669 f 6 58, *The Copy of a Letter from Coventry . . . .*

669 f 6 64, *A Catalogue of the Moneys, Men and Horse subscribed . . . . for His Majesty's Service.*

669 f 6 69, *A Declaration and Protestation . . . . for the County of Salop.*

669 f 6 75, *Remarkable Passages from Nottingham, Lichfield, Leicester . . . .*

669 f 7 1, *A Proclamation by Lord Capel.*

669 f 7 35, *A Report from the Committee of Safety . . . .*

E.42.14, *A True Relation of the success of Captain Swanley . . . .*

E.42.19, *A True Relation of the proceedings of Colonel Laugharne . . . .*

4.45.12, *A True Relation of a Plot against the City of Gloucester . . . .*

E.53.3, *Two Great Victories . . . at Oswestry . . . .*

E.54.16, *A Copy of a Letter sent from Sir Thomas Myddleton . . . .*

E.65.29, *Several Letters . . . by Captain William Smith . . . .*

E.94.37, *The Unfaithfulness of the Cavaliers . . . .*

E.91.19, *The Last Week's Proceedings of the Lord Brooke.*

E.92.18, *England's Loss And Lamentation . . . .*

E.96.22, *A Letter Written from Walsall . . . .*

E.99.18, *The Battle of Hopton Heath.*

E.99.28, *Honour Advanced.*

E.99.30, *A Message with a Letter sent by His Majesty . . . .*

E.100.8, *Prince Rupert's Burning Love for England . . . .*

E.107.32, *Exceeding Good News from Beverley, York, Hull and Newcastle . . . .*

E.109.3, *Some Special Passages from Warwickshire . . . .*

E.109.27, *Two Petitions presented to the King . . . .*

E.110.8, *The Earl of Portland's Charge . . . .*

E.113.6, *A Letter, concerning the Lord Chandos . . . .*

E.114.25, *A True Relation of the first and victorious Skirmish . . . .*

E.115.2, *Several Occurrences that have lately happened at Warwick . . . .*

E.119.3, *A True Relation of His Majesty's coming to Shrewsbury . . . .*

E.119.25, *A True and Exact Relation of the King's Entertainment at Chester . . . .*

E.121.3, *A True and Exact Relation of the proceedings of His Majesty's Army . . . .*

E.122.14, *A Loving and Loyal Speech spoken unto our Noble Prince. . . .*

E.127.2, *True News out of Herefordshire . . . .*

E.128.4, *A Most Blessed Victory obtained against the Marquis of Hertford . . . .*

Bibliography

E.130.22, *Wiltshire's Resolution* . . . .

E.146.1, *Five Remarkable Passages between His Majesty and Parliament* . . . .

E.146.16, *Two petitions . . . from the County of Hereford . . . the Town of Ludlow* . . . .

E.146.20, *The Declaration of Parliament concerning the Magazine at Hull* . . . .

E.147.5, *The Answer of Parliament presented to His Majesty at York* . . . .

E.147.17, *A Relation of Proceedings between the King's Majesty and his subjects* . . . .

E.149.15, *Horrible News from Lancashire.*

E.149.25, *Strange News from Staffordshire.*

E.149.30, *The Resolution of the Protestants of Cheshire* . . . .

E.150.28, *A Collection of Petitions presented to the King's Majesty* . . . .

E.150.29, *His Majesty's Answer to a Book* . . . .

E.152.2, *His Majesty's Answer To the Petition of the Parliament* . . . .

E.200.61, *His Majesty's Speech to the Inhabitants of Denbigh* . . . .

E.271.2, *A True and Full Relation of the Taking of Shrewsbury* . . . .

E.290.11, *Intelligence from Shropshire of Three Great Victories* . . . .

E.292.27, *The King's Cabinet Opened.*

E.293.33, *. . . . the Proceedings of the Army under Sir Thomas Fairfax 11–19 July* . . . .

E.298.6, *A True Relation of the late Success . . . in Pembrokeshire* . . . .

E.303.18, *The King's Forces totally routed . . . on Rowton Heath* . . . .

E.307.14, *Two Letters from Colonel Morgan* . . . .

E.307.15, *Major-General Laugharne's Letter* . . . .

E.308.14, *A True Relation of a Great Victory . . . near Denbigh.*

E.308.19, *A Full Relation of the Desperate Design . . . for the Betraying of Monmouth.*

E.311.9, *A Declaration of the County of Brecknock.*

E.314.12, *A New Trick To Take Towns.*

E.320.1, *Articles for the Surrender of Chester* . . . .

E.325.8, *A Great Overthrow . . . by Lieutenant-General Laugharne, Colonel Morgan and Sir Trevor Williams* . . . .

E.340.17, *The Taking of Caernarvon by Major-General Mytton* . . . .

E.340.21, *A Bloody Fight at Blackwater in Ireland* . . . .

E.341.6, *Letters between Sir William Brereton and Sir Thomas Tyldesley* . . . .

E.342.16, *A Letter . . . concerning . . . the Siege before Raglan Castle* . . . .

E.345.2, *Articles for the Delivering Up of Lichfield Close* . . . .

E.349.2, *The Strong Castle of Goodrich taken by Colonel Birch* . . . .

248

E.350.18, *An Exact Relation . . . of Raglan Castle, touching the Surrender thereof.*

E.436.7, *A Declaration of Divers Gentlemen of Wales . . . .*

Mercurius Aulicus

E.4.12 (29th week, 1644)

E.14.12 (40th week, 1644)

E.16.3 (41st week, 1644)

E.32.17 (4th week, 1644)

E.33.20 (5th week, 1644)

E.37.1 (8th week, 1644)

E.39.3 (10th week, 1644)

E.42.26 (13th week, 1644)

E.43.18 (14th week, 1644)

E.44.6 (15th week 1644)

E.45.10 (16th week 1644)

E.51.7 (21st week, 1644)

E.59.8 (25th week, 1643)

E67.7 (35th week, 1643)

E.75.13 (43rd week, 1643)

E.77.33 (47th week, 1643)

E.81.19 (52nd week, 1643)

E.86.22 (2nd week, 1643)

E.86.41 (9th week, 1643)

E.99.22 (15th week, 1643)

E.103.10 (19th week, 1643)

E.246.16 (4th week, 1643)

E.247.20 (12th week, 1643)

E.269.5 (12–19 Jan. 1645)

E.281.13 (13–20 Apr. 1645)

E.284.20 (20–27 Apr. 1645)

E.286.17 (27 Apr.–4 May 1645)

E.288.48 (25 May–8 June 1645)

E.296.33 (13–20 July 1645)

Kingdom's Weekly Intelligencer

E.6.12 (6–4 Aug. 1644)

E13.19 (18–25 Sept. 1644)

E.46.19 (7–14 May 1644)

E.77.10 (21–28 Nov. 1643)

E.77.27 (28 Nov.–5 Dec. 1643)

E.90.11 (14–21 Feb. 1643)

E.103.8 (16–23 May 1643)

E.105.8 (30 May–6 June 1643)

E.274.2 (11–18 Mar. 1645)

E.274.24 (18–25 Mar. 1645)

E.284.23 (13–20 May 1645)

E.292.15 (25 June–2 July 1645)

E.314.25 (18–25 Dec. 1645)

A Perfect Diurnall

E.242 (4 issues, 31 Oct.–24 Nov. 1642)

E.246 (4 issues, 31 Jan.–27 Feb. 1643)

E.249.3 (8 May 1643)

E.252 (2 issues, 25 Dec. 1643 and 2 Apr. 1644)

E.254 (2 issues, 19 Aug. and 26 Aug. 1644)

E.256.2 (9 Sept. 1644)

E.258.22 (10 Feb. 1645)

Bibliography

E.258.25 (17 Feb. 1645)
E.262.23 (7 July 1645)
E.262.25 (14 July 1645)
E.506.10 (16 Feb. 1646)
E.506.13 (23 Feb. 1646)

Perfect Occurrences

E.256.44 (6 Dec. 1644)
E.258.6 (20 Dec. 1644)
E.260.4 (26 Mar. 1645)
E.260.13 (11 Apr. 1645)

E.260.27 (25 Apr. 1645)
E.262.20 (4 July 1645)
E.266.24 (21 Nov. 1645)
E.506.22 (27 Mar. 1646)

Perfect Passages

E.258.34 (5 Mar. 1645)
E.260.8 (2 Apr. 1645)
E.260.12 (9 Apr. 1645)
E.260.20 (16 Apr. 1645)
E.16.8 (6 Nov. 1644)
E.25.17 (21 Jan. 1645)

E.260.25 (23 Apr. 1645)
E.260.36 (7 May 1645)
E.262.34 (23 July 1645)
E.270.33 (26 Feb. 1645)
E.26.9 (27 Jan. 1645)

The Scottish Dove

E.71.16 (27 Oct.–2 Nov. 1643)

E.309.24 (12–19 Nov. 1645)

Mercurius Civicus
E.313.4 (11–18 Dec. 1645)
E.322.20 (5–12 Feb. 1646)

E.335.3 (16–23 Apr. 1646)

Mercurius Academicus

E.322.2 (9th week 1646)

A Perfect Declaration

E.260.23 (26 Apr. 1645)

Parliament Scout

E.71.1 (21–28 Oct. 1643)

A Diary

E.271.17 (21–28 Feb. 1645)

Miscellaneous Parliamentarian Newspapers

1642

E.118.10	E.121.34	E.126.23	E.240.9
E.118.28	E.121.36	E.127.3	E.242.27
E.121.9	E.124.14	E.240.2	

1643

E.30.7	E.77.2	E.99.15	E.247.25
E.55.4	E.89.17	E.101.2	E.247.26
E.56.2	E.90.11	E.103.10	E.250.5
E.60.17	E.91.5	E.104.16	
E.71.1	E.91.8	E.246.37	
E.71.16	E.94.11	E.247.20	

1644

E.6.23	E.13.18	E.23.8	E.46.10
E.9.4	E.14.6	E.33.33	E.46.25
E.12.8	E.21.26	E.42.13	E.46.28

1645

E.258.36	E.297.4	E.309.23	E.313.29
E.277.13	E.297.7	E.310.5	
E.296.24	E.298.15	E.310.6	

1646

E.315.5	E.333.9	E.337.35
E.322.24	E.335.2	E.506.12

Bodleian Library

The Wentworth Proclamations.

Ashmole H.23.25, *Declaration . . . of the County of Hereford.*

Z1.17.16, *Declaration . . . of Tenby . . . .*

Wood 376 (51), *The Association . . . of the Counties of Cornwall and Devon.*

Wood 378 (18), *A True Relation of the Proceedings of the Scotch Army.*

Wood 378 (21), *A Letter . . . from Sir Barnabas Scudamore . . . .*

Bibliography

Corpus Christi College Library, Oxford

Complete set of *Mercurius Aulicus*

Exeter City Library

A Declaration Made By The Hon. The Earl of Bath . . . .

Published Collections

The Harleian Miscellany. London, 1810.

Somers Tracts. 2nd edition by Walter Scott, London, 1811, Vol. 5;
Iter Carolinum (A journal of the King's marches), pp. 263–75.

John Corbet, *A History Of The Military Government Of Gloucester*,
pp. 296–375. (Although not trustworthy in its general reflections
upon the nature of the war, the factual information provided in
this narrative is corroborated by every other source.)

Short Memorials Of Thomas Lord Fairfax, Written By Himself,
pp. 375–98.

George Ormerod (ed.), *Tracts Relating To Military Proceedings In Lancashire During The Great Civil War*. Chetham Society, 1844.

Rev. James Augustus Atkinson (ed.), *Tracts Relating To The Civil War In Cheshire*. Chetham Society, 1909.

Falconer Madan (ed.), *Oxford Books*. Oxford, 1912, Vol. 2, summarises many Royalists pamphlets.

Most of the partisan tracts listed above are exceptionally dangerous
sources to employ. Each generation of historians discovers more
information within them to be misreported, deliberately distorted or
completely fallacious. This book contributes its own quota to these
categories. Hence I have observed the following general rule when
admitting information from them: to accept only those assertions
which are corroborated by a hostile or neutral source or which can
contribute no benefit to the teller. I relax this rule in the case of
official despatches which are printed in full giving the name of the
author, the date and the location, and for Parliamentarian newspapers after December 1645, when the obvious defeat of the
Royalists made misrepresentation unnecessary and I can detect no
cases of it.

3. REPORTS OF THE HISTORICAL MANUSCRIPTS COMMISSION

Second Report, Appendix

pp. 46–8, Wrottesley Family Papers.
p. 36, Lyttleton Family Papers.
pp. 62–3, 67, Papers of Denbighshire Commissioners of Array.
p. 86, Sir John Owen's Papers.

Third Report, Appendix

p. 259, Dod Family Papers.
p. 420, Marquis of Worcester's Papers.

Fourth Report, Appendix

pp. 15–44, House of Lords Papers.
pp. 141–5, 175, Sir Richard Leveson's Papers.
pp. 344–7, Cholmondeley Collection.
pp. 414, 420, Papers Relating To Anglesey.

Sixth Report, Appendix

p. 472, Papers Relating to Cheshire and Montgomeryshire.

Seventh Report, Appendix

p. 689, Papers Relating to Herefordshire and Monmouthshire.

Ninth Report

Appendix 2, pp. 434–7, Morison Collection.

Tenth Report

Appendix 4, pp. 65–72, Colonel Moore's Papers.
Appendix 4, p. 373, Lord Kilmurrey's Papers.
Appendix 4, p. 375, Leighton Collection.
Appendix 4, pp. 394, 399, Richard Herbert's Papers.
Appendix 4, pp. 403–4, Corporation of Bishop's Castle's Papers.
Appendix 4, pp. 430–6, Corporation of Bridgnorth's Papers.
Appendix 6, pp. 86, 95, Bouverie Collection.

Bibliography

Twelfth Report

Appendix 2, p. 320, Sir John Coke's Papers.
Appendix 9, pp. 12–14, Marquis Of Worcester's Papers.

Thirteenth Report

Appendix 1, 'Portland MSS, Volume 1', The Clerk of the Parliament's Papers.

Fourteenth Report

Appendix 2, pp. 86–141, Harley Family Papers.
Appendix 4, p. 62, Kenyon Collection.
Appendix 8, p. 203, Worcester Cathedral Chapter's Papers.

Fifteenth Report

Appendix 2, pp. 99–106, Papers of the Royalist Council of War.
Appendix 7, pp. 65–86, Sir Edward Seymour's Papers.
Earl Cowper MSS, Miscellaneous Letters.
Hastings MSS, Vol. 2, Henry Hastings's Papers.
Marquis of Bath MSS, Vol. 1, Harley Family Papers.
Earl of Denbigh MSS, Vol. 1.

4. BOOKS

Atkyns, Richard, *A Vindication* (ed. by Peter Young). London, 1967.
Bamfield, Joseph, *An Apologie*. The Hague, 1685.
Baxter, Richard, *Reliquiae Baxterianae* (ed. by Matthew Sylvester). London, 1696.
Bulstrode, Sir Richard, *Memoirs And Reflections Upon The Reign And Government Of Charles I and II*. London, 1721.
Burghall, Edward, The Diary Of, printed in T. Worthington Barlow, *Cheshire: Its Historical And Literary Associations*. Manchester and London 1855.
Clarendon, Edward Hyde, Earl of, *The History Of The Rebellion And Civil War In England* (ed. by W. Dunn Macray). Oxford, 1888.
— *The Life Of Edward, Earl Of Clarendon*. Oxford, 1827.
Dugdale, Sir William, The Diary Of (ed. by William Hamper). London, 1821.

Gough, Richard, *Human Nature Displayed In The History Of Myddle*. London, 1834.

Hacket, John, Bishop of Lichfield, *Socrinia Reserata* (A Life of Archbishop Williams). London, 1692.

Lloyd, David, *Memoirs Of Protestant Martyrs*. London, 1668.

— *State Worthies*. London, 1766.

Newcastle, Margaret, Duchess of, *The Life Of William Cavendish, Duke Of Newcastle* (ed. by Sir Charles Firth). London, 1886.

Sprigge, Joshua, *Anglia Rediviva*. London, 1647; reprinted Oxford, 1854.

Vicars, John, *God's Ark*. London, 1644.

Walker, Sir Edward, *Historical Discourses Upon Several Occasions*. London, 1705.

5. EDITIONS OF DOCUMENTS

Calendar Of State Papers, Domestic Series, edited by W.D. Hamilton. London, 1887.

Carte, Thomas (ed.), *A Collection Of Original Letters And Papers . . . Found Among The Duke Of Ormonde's Papers*. London, 1739. (Some of the Marquis of Ormonde's papers.)

Collins, Arthur (ed.), *Letters And Memorials Of State*. London, 1746. (Sydney Family Papers.)

Day, W.A. (ed.), *The Pythouse Papers*. London, 1879. (Some more of Prince Rupert's papers. Some are mis-dated and placed out of context by the editor.)

Dillwyn, L.W., *Contributions Towards A History Of Swansea*. Swansea, 1840.

Journals Of The House Of Commons, Volumes 2–4.

Journals Of The House Of Lords, Volumes 4–8.

Rushworth, John (ed.), *Historical Collections*. London, 1659–1701. (A great range of official documents.)

Warburton, Eliot (ed.), *Memoirs Of Prince Rupert And The Cavaliers*. London, 1849, 3 volumes. (Transcripts and abstracts of the original huge collection of Prince Rupert's papers. The transcripts are accurate, but the abstracts suffer both from Warburton's lack of a really thorough knowledge of the period and from a certain amount of carelessness. This is particularly distressing as many of these documents are now lost. Warburton himself is to be easily forgiven for these blemishes, however, for he was an amateur historian working in a great hurry, and under these circumstances his achievement is impressive.)

Worth, R.N. (ed.), *The Buller Papers.* Plymouth, 1895.

6. DOCUMENTS EDITED BY HISTORICAL SOCIETIES AND JOURNALS

Archaeologia

1801 (No. 14), pp. 119–31, Edmund Turnor (ed.), 'Remarks On The Military History Of Bristol In The Seventeenth Century, With A Sketch Of The Outworks'.

1857 (No. 37), pp. 189–223, Rev. John Webb (ed.), 'The Account Book Of Mrs Joyce Jeffries'.

Archaeologia Cambrensis

1846 (No. 1), pp. 33–42, Robert Williams (ed.), 'The Notebook Of William Maurice'.

Ibid. pp. 326–33, 'Papers of Viscout Bulkeley'.

1917 (Series 6, No. 17), Supplement, pp. 275–306, John Fisher (ed.), 'An Account of the Civil War in Anglesey'.

Camden Society

1853 Thomas Taylor Lewis (ed.), 'Letters Of The Lady Brilliana Harley'.

Camden Miscellany 2, William Durrant Cooper (ed.), 'The Trelawney Papers'.

1859 C.E. Long (ed.), 'The Diary Of The Marches Of The Royal Army During The Great Civil War Kept By Richard Symonds'.

1872 Sir W.C. and Sir C.E. Trevelyan (eds), 'The Trevelyan Papers', Part 111.

1873 T.W. Webb (ed.), 'A Military Memoir Of Colonel John Birch Written By Roe His Secretary'.

1889 George F. Warner (ed.), 'The Nicholas Papers', Vol. 1.

Cambrian Quarterly Magazine

1829 (No. 1), pp. 60–74, 'A Diary from Penrith'.

Chester and North Wales Historical and Archaeological Society

1914 (New Series 20), pp. 148–52, James Hall (ed.), Beverley Family Papers.

Reports and Transactions of The Devonshire Association

1913 (No. 45), pp. 220–7, Edward Windeatt, 'Totnes And The Civil War'.

1928 (No. 60), pp. 291–8, E.H. Young, 'Okehampton During The Civil War'.

Lancashire and Cheshire Record Society

1889 (No. 19), James Hall (ed.), Thomas Malbon's Diary.

Montgomeryshire Collections

1886 (No. 12), Supplement, M.C. Jones (ed.), Papers of Richard Herbert.

Shropshire Archaeological and Natural History Society

1894–6 (2nd Series, Nos. 6–8), William Phillips (ed.) Sir Francis Ottley's Papers.

1898 (2nd Series, No. 10), pp. 157–72, William Phillips (ed.), Shrewsbury Corporation Records.

1905 (3rd Series, No. 5), pp. 303–48, Rev. John Burton (ed.), Humphrey Walcot's Papers.

Somerset Archaeological and Natural History Society

1919 (No. 65), pp. 48–75, Henry Symonds (ed.), 'A By-Path Of The Civil War'.

Somerset Record Society

1902 (N.18), C.E.H. Chadwyck-Healey (ed.), *'Bellum Civile'*.

Worcestershire Historical Society

1915–20, J.W. Willis-Bund (ed.), Henry Townshend's 'Diary'. (I have expressed my reservations about this edition earlier, but the work remains valuable not merely for the accuracy of the transcription but also because in the introduction are reprinted papers of Sir William Russell, now lost.)

Note: Valuable records are also reprinted in the works of 'RWB', Bayley, Bellet, Burton, Christie, Coate, Dircks, Dore, Duncumb, Earwaker, Fox, Harwood, Mahler, Nash, Ormerod, Owen and Blakeway, Pennant, J. Phillips, J.R. Phillips, Stebbing Shaw, Stackhouse-Action and the Webbs, in the secondary sources which follow.

Bibliography: Secondary sources

Andriette, Eugene A., *Devon And Exeter In The Civil War*. Newton Abbot, 1971.

'RWB', 'The Taking Of Hereford By Colonel Birch, 18 December 1645', *Archaeologia Cambrensis*, 4th series Vol. 2, pp. 287–300.

Bayley, A.R., *The Great Civil War In Dorset 1642–1660*. Taunton, 1910.

Bellet, Rev. G., *The Antiquities Of Bridgnorth*. Bridgnorth, 1856.

Burton, J.R., *A History Of Bewdley*. London, 1883.

Christie, W.D., *A Life Of Anthony Ashley Cooper,* London, 1871, Vol. 1.

Coate, Mary, *Cornwall In The Great Civil War And Interregnum. A Social And Political Study*. Oxford, 1933.

Cockayne, G.B., *The Complete Peerage*. London, 1910, 13 volumes; *The Complete Baronetage*. London, 1900, 5 volumes.

Court, W.H.E., *The Rise Of The Midland Industries 1600–1838*. Oxford and London, 1938.

Davies, D.J., *The Economic History Of South Wales Prior To 1800*. Cardiff, 1933.

Dictionary Of National Biography, Oxford University Press.

Dictionary Of Welsh Biography. (Honourable Society of Cymmrodorion 1959)

Dircks, Henry, *The Life, Times And Scientific Labours Of The Second Marquis Of Worcester*. London, 1865.

Dodd, A.H., 'Wales In The Parliaments Of Charles 1', THSC, 1945, pp. 16–49; and 1946–7, pp. 59–96.

Dodd, A.H., 'The Pattern Of Politics In Stuart Wales', THSC, 1948, pp. 8–91.

Dodd, A.H., *Studies In Stuart Wales*. Cardiff, 1952.

Bibliography

Dodd, A.H., 'Anglesey In The Civil War', *Trans. of the Anglesey Antiquarian Society and Field Club*, 1952, pp. 1–33.

Dodd, A.H., 'Caernarvonshire In The Civil War', *Trans. of the Caernarvonshire Historical Society*, **14**, 1953, pp. 1–34.

Dore, R.N., 'Sir William Brereton's Siege Of Chester And The Campaign Of Naseby', *Trans. of the Lancashire and Cheshire Antiquarian Society*, **67**, 1957, pp. 17–44.

Dore, R.N., 'Sir Thomas Myddleton's Attempted Conquest Of Powys', *Montgomeryshire Collections*, **57**, 1961–2, pp. 91–118.

Dore, R.N., *The Civil Wars In Cheshire*. Chester, 1966.

Dugdale, Sir William, *The Baronage Of England*. London, 1676, 2 volumes.

Dugdale, Sir William, *The Antiquities Of Warwickshire*. London, 1730, 2 volumes.

Duncumb, John, *Collections Towards The History And Antiquities Of The County Of Hereford*. Hereford and London, 1804.

Earwaker, J.P., *East Cheshire: Past and Present*. London, 1888, 2 volumes.

Engberg, Jens, 'Royalist Finances During The English Civil War 1642–1646; *Scandinavian Economic History Review*, **14.2,** 1966, pp. 73–96.

Everitt, Alan, *The Community Of Kent And The Great Rebellion*. Leicester, 1966.

Everitt, Alan, *The Local Community And The Great Rebellion*. Historical Association Pamphlet G.70, 1969.

Firth, Sir Charles, *Cromwell's Army*. London, 1902.

Fletcher, Anthony, *A County Community In Peace And War: Sussex 1600–1660*. London, 1975.

Fox, Levi, *The Borough Town Of Stratford-Upon-Avon*. Stratford, 1953.

Harrison, George Anthony, *Royalist Organisation In Wiltshire 1642–1646*. London, Ph.D. thesis, 1963.

Harwood, Rev. T., *History Of The Church And City Of Lichfield*. Lichfield, 1806.

Holmes, Clive, *The Eastern Association In The English Civil War*. Cambridge, 1975.

Howell, Roger, *Newcastle-Upon-Tyne And The Puritan Revolution*. Oxford, 1967.

Hutton, Ronald, 'The Worcestershire Clubmen In The English Civil War', *Midland History*, **5** (1979–80), pp. 40–49.

Hutton, Ronald, 'The Failure Of The Lancashire Cavaliers', *Trans. of the Lancashire and Cheshire Historical Society*. **129** (1980), pp. 47–69.

Hutton, Ronald, 'The Structure Of The Royalist Party 1642–1646', forth-coming in the *Historical Journal*.

Hutton, Ronald, 'Clarendon's "History Of The Rebellion"', forthcoming in the *English Historical Review*.

Johnson, A.M., 'Politics In Chester During The Civil War And Interregnum', in Peter Clark and Paul Slack (eds) *Crisis And Order In English Towns 1500–1700*. London, 1972, pp. 204–36.

Keeler, M.R., *The Long Parliament 1640–1641. A Biographical Study Of Its Members*. Philadelphia, 1954.

Leach, Arthur Leonard, *The History Of The Civil War (1642–1649) In Pembrokeshire And On Its Borders*. London, 1937.

Lindley, K.J., *The Part Played By Catholics In The Civil War In Lancashire And Monmouthshire*. Manchester M.A. thesis, 1965.

Lloyd, Howell A., *The Century Of South-West Wales 1540–1640*. University of Wales, 1968.

Lowe, John, 'The Campaign Of The Irish Royalist Army In Cheshire, November 1643–January 1644', *Trans. of the Lancashire and Cheshire Historical Society*, **cxi**, 1959, pp. 49–76.

Lowe, John and Dore, R.N., 'The Battle of Nantwich, 25 January 1644' *Trans. of the Lancashire and Cheshire Historical Society*, **cxiii**, 1961, pp. 97–124.

Lynch, G.J., *The Risings Of The Clubmen In The English Civil War*. Manchester MA thesis, 1973.

Mahler, Margaret, *A History Of Chirk Castle And Chirkland*. London, 1912.

Malcolm, Joyce L., *The English People And The Crown's Cause 1642–1646*. Brandeis Ph.D. thesis, 1977.

Malcolm, Joyce L., A King In Search Of Soldiers: Charles 1 In 1642' *Historical Journal*, **21**, 1978, pp. 251–74.

Mander, G.P. *A History of Wolverhampton* (ed. N.W. Tildesley) Wolverhampton; 1960.

Manning, Brian, *Neutrals And Neutralism In The English Civil War*. Oxford D.Phil. thesis, 1957.

Manning, Brian, *The English People And The English Revolution 1640–1649*. London, 1976.

Morrill, J.S., *Cheshire 1630–60: County Government And Society During The English Revolution*. Oxford, 1974.

Morrill, J.A., *The Cheshire Grand Jury*. Leicester, 1976.

Morrill, J.S., *The Revolt Of The Provinces: Conservatives And Radicals In The English Civil War 1630–1650*. Oxford, 1976.

Morrill, J.S., 'Provincial Squires And "Middling Sorts" In The Great Rebellion', *Historical Journal*, **20**, 1977, pp. 229–36.

Morrill, J.S., 'The Northern Gentry And The Great Rebellion', *Northern History*, **xv**, 1979, pp. 66–87.

Nash, Treadway Russell, *Collections For The History Of Worcestershire*. London, 1783, 2 volumes.

Newman, P.R., *The Royalist Armies In Northern England 1642–1645*, York D.Phil. thesis, 1978.

Newman, P.R., 'Catholic Royalist Activists In The North 1642–6', *Recusant History*, **14.1**, 1977, pp. 26–38.

Newman, P.R., 'Catholic Royalists Of Northern England 1642–1645', *Northern History*, **xv**, 1979, pp. 88–95.

Ormerod, George, *The History Of The County Palatine And City Of Chester*. London, 1882, 2 volumes.

Owen, H., and Blakeway, J.B., *A History Of Shrewsbury*. London, 1825, Vol. 1.

Pennant, Thomas, *Tours In Wales*, London, 1810, 3 volumes.

Pennington, Donald, 'County And Country: Staffordshire In Civil War Politics, 1640–44', *North Staffordshire Journal Of Field Studies*, **6**, 1966, pp. 12–24.

Pennington, Donald and Roots, Ivan, Introduction to *The Committee At Stafford 1643–1645. The Order Book Of The Staffordshire County Committee*. Manchester, 1957.

Phillips, C.B., 'County Committees And Local Government In Cumberland and Westmoreland 1642–1660, *Northern History*, **v**, 1970, pp. 37–56.

Phillips, C.B., 'The Royalist North: The Cumberland and Westmoreland Gentry, 1642–1660', *Northern History*, **xiv**, 1978, pp. 170–89.

Phillips, James, 'Haverfordwest In The Civil War', *Archaeologia Cambrensis*, 6th series vol. 15, 1915, pp. 1–16.

Phillips, John Rowland, *Memoirs Of The Civil War In Wales And The Marches 1642–1649*. London, 1874, 2 volumes.

Pickles, J.T., *Studies In Royalism In The English Civil War 1642–1646. With Special Reference To Staffordshire*. Manchester M.A. thesis, 1968.

Prestwich, Menna, *Cranfield. Politics And Profits Under The Early Stuarts*. Oxford, 1960.

Ralph, Philip L., *Sir Humphrey Mildmay: Royalist Gentleman*. New Brunswick, 1947.

Roberts, B. Dew, 'Cheadles Against Bulkeleys', *Trans. Anglesey Antiq. Soc. and Field Club*, 1945, pp. 25–37.

Roy, Ian, 'The Royalist Council Of War 1642–6', *Bulletin of the Institute of Historical Research*, **35**, 1962, pp. 150–68.

Roy, Ian, *The Royalist Army In The First Civil War,* Oxford D. Phil. thesis, 1963.

Roy, Ian, Introduction to 'The Royalist Ordnance Papers', *Oxfordshire Record Society*, 43, 1964.

Roy, Ian, 'England Turned Germany? The Aftermath Of The Civil War In Its European Context', TRHS 5th series 28, 1978, pp. 127–44.

Shaw, Rev. Stebbing, *The History And Antiquities Of Staffordshire.* London, 1798 and 1801.

Shaw, W.A., *The Knights Of England.* London, 1906, 2 volumes.

Sherwood, R.E., *Civil Strife In The Midlands 1642–1651.* London and Chichester, 1974.

Silcock, R.H., *County Government In Worcestershire 1603–1660.* London D.Phil. thesis, 1974.

Stackhouse-Action, Mrs F., *The Garrisons Of Shropshire During The Civil War.* Shrewsbury, 1867.

Styles, Philip, 'The Royalist Government Of Worcestershire During The Civil War 1642–6', *Trans. Worcestershire Archaeological Society*, 3rd Series no. 5, 1976, pp. 23–40.

Taylor, John K.G., 'The Civil Government Of Gloucester 1640–6', *Trans. Bristol and Gloucestershire Archaeological Society*, **67**, 1948, pp. 59–118.

Thomas, C.M., *The First Civil War In Glamorgan 1642–46,* University Of Wales M.A. thesis, 1963.

Tucker, Norman, *Royalist Officers Of North Wales 1642–1660.* Denbigh, 1961.

Tucker, Norman, *Denbighshire Officers In The Civil War.* Denbigh, 1964.

Underdown, David, *Somerset In The Civil War And Interregnum.* Newton Abbot, 1973.

Underdown, David, 'The Chalk And The Cheese: Contrasts Among The English Clubmen', *Past and Present*, **85**, 1979, pp. 25–48.

Victoria County History Of Shropshire, edited by A.T. Gaydon. Oxford, 1968, Vol. 8.

Victoria County History Of Worcestershire, edited by J.W. Willis-Bund. London, 1901–24, Vols 2–4.

Wanklyn, M.D.E., *The King's Armies In The West Of England.* Manchester M.A. thesis, 1966.

Waylen, James, *A History . . . Of Marlborough.* London, 1854.

Webb, Rev. John and Rev. T.W., *Memorials Of The Civil War . . . As It Affected Herefordshire And The Adjacent Counties.* London, 1879, 2 volumes.

Bibliography

Wedgwood, Dame C.V., *The King's War*. London, 1958.

Wood, A.C., *Nottinghamshire In The Civil War*. London, 1937.

Young, Brigadier Peter, *Edgehill 1642. The Campaign And The Battle*. Kineton, 1967.

Young, Brigadier Peter, *Marston Moor 1644. The Campaign And The Battle*. Kineton, 1970.

Young, Brigadier Peter and Toynbee, Margaret, *Cropredy Bridge 1644. The Campaign And The Battle*. Kineton, 1970.

Young, Brigadier Peter and Toynbee, Margaret, *Strangers In Oxford*. London and Chichester, 1973.

Index

Index

Index